Christian Understandings of Creation

Christian Understandings of Creation

The Historical Trajectory

DENIS EDWARDS

FORTRESS PRESS
MINNEAPOLIS

CHRISTIAN UNDERSTANDINGS OF CREATION
The Historical Trajectory

Cover image: Abstract Painting/ntonEvmeshkin/©iStock/Thinkstock
Cover design: Laurie Ingram

Print ISBN: 978-1-4514-8287-4
eBook ISBN: 978-1-5064-3835-1

The paper used in this publication meets the minimum requirements of American National Standard for Information Sciences — Permanence of Paper for Printed Library Materials, ANSI Z329.48-1984.

Manufactured in the U.S.A.

Contents

Introduction

This book attempts to explore a trajectory of the Christian theology of creation that begins with the Scriptures, and runs through the work of theologians from the second to the twenty-first centuries. There is a sense in which this broad theological tradition constitutes a trajectory, in the singular. But there is a rich diversity of creation theologies in this tradition, beginning with the diversity of the biblical texts themselves. So I see the project undertaken here as a study of trajectories, in the plural, that make up the broad and rich trajectory, in the singular, of the Christian theologies of creation through the centuries.

This exploration of these historical trajectories begins from the perspective of the twenty-first century, a very particular moment in the history of life on our planet. We live in a time that scientists have begun to call the Anthropocene, a period when the human impact on the life systems of the planet and on other species has reached a new, critical, level. It is a time when human actions are contributing to dangerous climate change, extreme pollution of the land, rivers, and seas, the loss of habitats, the consequent extinction of species, and rapid diminishment of the biodiversity of the planet.

At the same time, our knowledge of the natural world has

gone through an extraordinary expansion because of developments in sciences such as astronomy and cosmology, evolutionary biology, and neuroscience. The sciences offer us a radically new worldview, in which we are part of an expanding universe of perhaps two trillion galaxies, and in which we, with all other species, are the products of the evolution of life on our planet that began with the emergence of the first microbrial forms of life 3.7 billion years ago. We are still at the beginning of bringing these sciences into creative interrelationship with Christian theology. Both this new worldview and the extreme crisis of life on our planet demand a new theology of the natural world for the twenty-first century. I am conscious that many theologians are already collaborating on this fundamental task. It is this task that constitutes the hermeneutical lens for the historical approach to the Christian theology of creation that I undertake in this volume.

My methodological approach might be described as a hermeneutics of critical retrieval, an attempt to reclaim trajectories from the history of theology that can assist in the envisioning of a renewed theology of the natural world. The intention, then, is to seek to discover what Paul Santmire calls the "hidden ecological and cosmic riches" of the theological tradition, so that they might prove to be resources for a renewed theology of nature.[1] He says of those who take up this approach: "We have wanted not to abandon or defend the classical theological tradition, but to reclaim it, and then to reenvision it, for the purpose of serving the worship, the teaching, and the public witness of the church in our own time of global environmental and existential crisis."[2]

The approach I take to the theologies of the past, then, will be one of critical appreciation. It will be critical in the sense that I will begin from what I think is well-established, that failures in Christian theology have contributed to the present situation. In *The Travail of Nature*, for example, Paul Santmire identifies two trends in the history of the Christian theology of creation.[3] One of these, which he calls the *spiritual* motif, is represented in theologies which advocate leaving the world of matter and flesh behind, in the quest for the ascent to a higher spiritual plane. The other tendency, which Santmire calls the *ecological* motif, finds God in the natural world, and envisages Christian life as a down-to-earth engagement with the world of nature and of humanity. Because these two tendencies exist in the Christian tradition, Santmire's subtitle speaks of the "ambiguous ecological promise" of Christian theology.

At a broader level, I will also take as read the widespread analysis in ecological theology that, for most of the last millennium, Christianity has been largely concerned with individual human salvation. The focus has been on the human person before God. In the Bible, and for the theologians of the first millennium, by contrast, human life tended to be understood as involving three relationships, with God, with other humans, and with the natural world. But since before the Reformation, and certainly after it, Western Churches have tended to ignore the relationship with nature. Thankfully there are exceptions to this, in great theologians and spiritual writers such as John of the Cross, and in some teachings of the great Reformers, Luther and Calvin, which will be taken up in this book.

Two further negative trajectories appear in the history of theology. One is that there have been times when influential thinkers, such as Francis Bacon (1561–1626), have interpreted the dominion text from Genesis as a God-given license for humanity to control and exploit the natural world. A second is a legacy from the great medieval theologians. Although Aquinas also makes many positive contributions to a theology of the natural world, his comments on plants and animals as being for human use had an anthropocentric impact on the Christian tradition, and both he and Bonaventure found no place for animals or plants in the final fulfilment of all things in Christ.

Granted a critical awareness of these negative trajectories, my intention is to read *appreciatively* the theologians whose work I have selected for this volume. While recognizing that there have been Christian theologies, or aspects of these theologies, that have been other-worldly, and even at times disparaging and deprecating of the natural world, I will attempt to approach major theologians of the Christian tradition with the assumption that they may have something to offer as we seek a renewed theology of the natural world. I will highlight trajectories in their theology that may inspire Christian thought and practice in this radically new moment. So in each instance I will provide an empathetic reading of a theologian's work, and conclude with a list of trajectories. Because it seems only fair to readers to indicate a little of where I stand, I will write a few brief words, before the trajectories section, pointing to what I see as critical issues or to where I take a different approach.

There will be unevenness in the scope of what is discussed in the work of individual theologians. With some, it seems that an overview of their thought will be useful, even if it be necessarily partial and limited. With other prolific figures in theology, like Augustine and Aquinas, I will be able to take up only particular aspects of the whole picture.

After the opening chapter, which briefly sketches eight biblical trajectories on creation, there are thirteen chapters on individual theologians. Three come from the early Christian period, Irenaeus, Athanasius, and Augustine. There are three medieval theologians represented, Hildegard of Bingen, Bonaventure, and Aquinas. These are followed by two chapters on the Reformers—Luther and Calvin. Then I discuss five theologians from the twentieth and twenty-first centuries, Teilhard de Chardin, Karl Rahner, Jürgen Moltmann, Sallie McFague, and Elizabeth Johnson.

I am painfully aware of theologians I am leaving out because of restrictions on the size of the books in this series. Of course, these omissions are also the result of my own choice to deal with individual theologians in some detail. Among the early church theologians, I would love to have offered a chapter on Basil of Caesarea. And among more recent theologians, it was my firm intention to include Orthodox scholars, convinced as I am that they have an enormous contribution to make to a renewed theology of the natural world as God's good creation. I am also well aware that in this kind of volume I have not been able to deal with the work of many good colleagues and friends in the emerging fields of ecological theology and the theology-science dialogue, whose work I greatly respect and value. I hope this book will complement their work, and prove useful to them and to their students.

It was a great joy, while I was hard at work on the manuscript for this book, to read Pope Francis's *Laudato Si'*.[4] It is a revolutionary document, calling us to a new appreciation of the natural world as possessing its own intrinsic value, as speaking words of God to us, and as constituting, with us, a splendid universal communion of creation in God. Pope Francis speaks explicitly of building on the long-standing leadership of Ecumenical Patriarch Bartholomew of the Orthodox Church. Other church leaders, along with the World Council of Churches, have long been calling the Christian community to ecological awareness, commitment, and practice. All of this is part of a new time of the Spirit, a time of profound ecological conversion not only of individuals but also of our Christian churches, in cooperation with other religious traditions and with all people who care about the well-being of our planet. It is all the more important, in this moment, to dig deep into the resources of the Christian tradition, to find there the theological trajectories that can inspire us and lead us to profound respect for God's creation and to act for its protection and flourishing.

I am particularly grateful to two theological colleagues from Adelaide—James McEvoy and Patricia Fox RSM—who have generously read these chapters and offered thoughtful and insightful comments on them. I am grateful, too, that I was able to present and discuss several of these chapters at annual conferences of the Australian Catholic Theological Association. I offer my sincere thanks to Professor Denis Janz for his generous, committed, insightful and patient leadership in this project, and to all at Fortress Press for their professional work on this book. Biblical quotations are from the New Revised Standard Version Bible.

Notes

1. H. Paul Santmire, *Nature Reborn: The Ecological and Cosmic Promise of Christian Theology* (Minneapolis: Fortress Press, 2000), 9.
2. Ibid.
3. H. Paul Santmire, *TheTravail of Nature: The Ambiguous Ecological Promise of Christian Theology* (Minneapolis: Fortress Press, 1985).
4. Pope Francis, *Laudato Si'* (Vatican City: Libreria Editrice Vaticana, 2015).

1.

Key Biblical Trajectories

The Biblical theology of creation is often associated simply with the magnificent six-day account of creation in the opening chapter of Genesis, and the Garden of Eden narrative found in the second and third chapters. The result is that the biblical trajectories on creation that are considered are limited to those found in the first three chapters of the Bible, and other key creation texts are ignored. In this chapter, by contrast, I will outline a wide range of trajectories on creation from various parts of the biblical tradition: God, Creation and Humanity (Gen 1:1–3:24); Putting Humans in their Place (Job 38:1–41:34); The Community of Creation (Psalms 104; 148); Creation through Wisdom (Prov 8:22–9:6); New Creation (Isa 65:17–25); Creation and Incarnation (John 1:1–18); Creation and Redemption (Rom 8:18–25); and the Cosmic Christ (Col 1:15–20). This brief sketch will remain an incomplete account of creation in the Bible, and I will offer only a few comments on each individual text.[1] My hope is simply that such a sketch might provide a useful overview or map of key biblical trajectories on creation.

GOD, CREATION, AND HUMANITY (GENESIS 1:1–3:24)

There are two accounts of creation in the opening chapters of Genesis. The first I refer to as the Seven-Day account (1:1–2:4), and the second as the Garden of Eden account (2:4–3:24). Many biblical scholars consider the Garden of Eden to be the oldest account, possibly going back to the ninth century BCE. It is a hands-on and down-to-earth narrative with God shaping the human from the dust and breathing into the first human's nostril the breath of life. The Seven-Day account is thought of as part of the Priestly tradition, possibly from the time of the Babylonian Exile (597–539 BCE). It has a vast cosmic scope, and it flows in an ordered and rhythmic way.

In the interpretation of these texts it is important to recognize that the first eleven chapters of Genesis have a mythic character which is different from other parts of the Bible. "Mythic" here describes the literary form of these narratives, and is meant to indicate that they point to a primeval time, long before the time of Israel, with characters and stories that are larger-than-life. To say that these stories have a mythic character is not to suggest that they are untrue. Mythic stories can communicate profound *religious* truth. But it would be a big mistake to look to these stories for an accurate historical account of the origins of the universe, or of life on our planet, or to see them as providing some kind of reliable science.

What these texts offer us are profound theological truths.[2] I will take up just three of these theological insights here. The most important is a claim about God. The God of Genesis is the one and only Creator of absolutely everything. This is a Creator who is radically beyond every creature. Whereas other cultures could see the Sun, the Moon, animals, plants, the fertility of the natural world, emperors, or kings, as divine, for Genesis all of these are God's creatures. The God of Genesis transcends every aspect of the human and natural world we see around us. Yet this God is also portrayed as fully present and engaged with the world of creatures (Gen 2:4–9). Genesis implies, and the rest of the Bible confirms, that God is not only the original Creator, but also the continuous Creator. God not only creates things in the beginning, but is their constant source of existence and fruitfulness. God is constantly creating each entity, enabling it to exist and act at every moment and sustaining it within the community of creation.

A second fundamental theological truth communicated in these texts concerns the goodness of the whole creation. The wonderful diversity and abundance of creatures comes from God, who delights in each of them. In the Seven-Day account, we find the constant refrain: "And God saw that it was good" (Gen 1:10); and at the end of the sixth day the words: "God saw everything that he had made, and indeed, it was very good" (Gen 1:31). Unlike views, ancient and modern, that see matter, flesh, or the natural world, as something to be despised, the biblical view strongly claims their goodness before God. The fruitfulness of creation is a gift of God and stands under the divine blessing (Gen 1:22). For human beings the wider creation is a gift of the ever-bountiful God (Gen 2:8–9).

A third theological truth found in these texts concerns humanity. God creates humankind in the image of God: "in the image of God he made them; male and female he created them" (Gen 1:27). Male and female are equally in the divine image. The fundamental equality of male and female, and their inter-relationship, is also communicated in the Eden account with the woman created from a rib of the first human. Genesis 2–3 also describes a pull to evil in the human, and the narratives that follow, Cain and Abel, Noah and the Flood, and Babel, describe the alienation from one another, from the natural world, from oneself, that springs from rejection of God. But there is hope because the God who creates is the God who saves: "Salvation is embedded by God in God's act of creation, and the redemption of a particular people is universalized to encompass humankind (Gen 12:3)."[3]

There can be no doubt that the divine command to "subdue" the earth and to have "dominion" (Gen 1:28) has been interpreted by some as justifying ruthless exploitation. Norman Habel points out that in itself the word "subdue" (*kabash*) is very harsh language.[4] I think it is important to recognize it as dangerous and time-conditioned language. It was written for its own time, perhaps as an encouragement to relatively powerless human beings to take their place in a natural world that could appear as intimidating, dangerous, and the place of powerful spirits. It is not to be read in our time as an endorsement of the massive and ruthless exploitation and destruction of the natural world. Pope Francis comments: "Although it is true that we Christians have at times incorrectly interpreted the Scriptures nowadays we must forcefully reject the notion that our being created in God's image and given dominion over the earth justifies absolute domination over other creatures. The biblical texts are to be read in their context, with an appropriate hermeneutic, recognizing that they tell us to 'till and keep' the garden of the world (cf. Gen 2:15)."[5] The ideas of tilling and keeping, he says, involve protecting and imply "a relationship of mutual responsibility between human beings and nature."[6] The text of Genesis 1:28, then, is to be interpreted in light of the broader theology of Genesis and the whole Bible, where creation is seen as God's good creation, God delights in creation, the whole creation is under God's blessing, and human beings are called to act towards other creatures in ways that reflect God's care for them.[7]

The religious insights I have described, concerning God, the goodness of creation, and the human as in the divine image, are not at all in conflict with the findings of scientific cosmology and evolutionary biology. They provide theological insights that can offer new meaning in a contemporary scientific context. There is every reason for a Christian today to embrace *both* the discoveries of contemporary science and the theological truths found in Genesis.

At the end of the Seven-Day account, we are told that Sabbath rest is a sign and promise of the fulfillment of creation, of God's *Shalom*. It is an invitation to take time for rest, for celebration, for joy in family, for friends and community life, for receiving the blessings of creation. It is a time to give thanks for flowers and trees, birds and animals, rain and sunshine, food and drink, and to offer praise to God with the whole creation.

CREATION THROUGH WISDOM (PROVERBS 8:22–9:6)

The Wisdom literature of the Bible is very much a creation theology. The wisdom seekers find the wisdom of God expressed and revealed in the natural world around them. They personify the presence, revelation, and action of God in creation as a female figure, the Wisdom of God. It is not only that the word *wisdom* is feminine in Hebrew (*Hokmah*) and Greek (*Sophia*). Wisdom is personified in a highly developed way as the Wisdom Woman, who is God's companion in the creating and sustaining all things (Prov 8:22–31; Sir 24:3–7; Wis 8:1–4). In the eighth chapter of Proverbs, for example, we find the Wisdom Woman speaking in her own voice:

> The Lord created me at the beginning of his work,
> the first of his acts of long ago.

> Ages ago I was set up,
> at the first, before the beginning of the earth...
> When he established the heavens, I was there,
> when he drew a circle on the face of the deep,
> when he made firm the skies above,
> when he established the fountains of the deep,
> when he assigned to the sea its limit,
> so that the waters might not transgress his command,
> when he marked out the foundations of the earth,
> then I was beside him, like a master worker;
> and I was daily his delight, rejoicing before him always, rejoicing in his inhabited world
> and delighting in the human race. (Prov 8:22–31)

Wisdom is a cosmic figure. She is present with God in the creation of earth, sky, and seas, and shares God's delight in the creatures of the world, including the human ones.

Wisdom is before all things and all things are created through her. But Wisdom is not simply a distant cosmic figure. She comes to make her home with us: "Wisdom has built her house. . . . She has set her table" (Prov 9:1–2; Sir 24:8–22; Wis 8:16–21). Wisdom, the one through whom God sustains and orders the creation, comes to dwell with us, and invites us to her table. Jewish thinkers could see Wisdom come to us as Torah (Sir 24:23). Early Christians could see Jesus as the preexisting Wisdom or Word, through whom all things are created, and who comes to us in flesh (John 1:1–14), and invites us to his table (John 6:1–14).[8]

PUTTING HUMANS IN THEIR PLACE (JOB 38:1–41:34)

While the first chapter of Genesis presents the human as uniquely made in the divine image, the book of Job highlights a different aspect of the human in relation to the wider creation. It challenges human arrogance, putting humans in their place before God and before the rest of the creation.[9] Although the book of Job is not always recognized as a creation text, God's response to Job contains the longest passage in the Bible about non-human creation.

God's answer to Job's questions comes only after an intense dialogue between Job and his three friends (3:1–31:40) reveals the complete inadequacy of standard responses to the problem of the suffering of the innocent, and after Elihu's speeches (32:1–37:24) remind Job of the transcendent greatness of the Creator. Then God answers Job out of the whirlwind in two speeches (38:1–40:2; 40:6–41:26). God's response is not an explanation, but a series of questions that are put to Job. Job is cross-examined about God's creative action throughout the universe, and on God's continuous provision for all the animals, birds and sea-creatures. As Richard Bauckham writes: "What God does is to invite Job into a vast panorama of the cosmos, taking Job on a sort of imaginative tour of his creation, all the time buffeting Job with questions."[10] God's questions challenge Job's worldview and call him into a new way of seeing everything. The first question immediately puts Job in his place and sets the tone for what follows:

> Where were you when I laid the foundation of the earth?
> Tell me if you have understanding.
> Who determined its measurements – surely you know!
> Or who stretched the line upon it?
> On what were its bases sunk, or who laid its cornerstone
> when the morning stars sang together
> and all the heavenly beings shouted for joy? (Job 38:4–7)

God demands that Job observe the physical universe in its immensity and mystery, and asks Job who he thinks he is in relation to this vast creation, and particularly in relation to the God who creates it all. Job is called to ponder the Creator of the land, the oceans, the dawn, the underworld, the light and darkness, the weather, and the constellations of stars: "Can you bind the chains of the Pleiades, or loose the cords of Orion?" (38:31). God then invites Job to consider the animals and birds. Does he have any idea how God sustains them?

> Who provides for the raven its prey,
> when its young ones cry to God,
> and wander about for lack of food?
> Do you know when the mountain goats give birth?
> Do you observe the calving of the deer? (38:39–41)

In this text, God points to ten animals and birds, describing them in detail, in species-specific ways. Each has its own integrity and stands in relationship to God its Creator in its own right, independently of humans. Job is called both to cosmic humility and to share in God's delight in creatures. Bauckham says of these passages: "Surely they express God's sheer joy in his creatures, their variety and idiosyncrasies, the freedom of the wild ass and the massive strength of the wild ox and the horse, the soaring flight of the hawk and even the apparent stupidity of the sand grouse."[11]

THE COMMUNITY OF CREATION (PSALMS 104; 148)

Alongside the biblical paradigms of humans as made in the divine image (Genesis 1), and as called to cosmic humility (Job), there is a third biblical paradigm: human beings and other creatures can be seen as united in a community of creation before God.[12] I will focus on this theme as it finds expression is Psalms 104 and 148. Psalm 104 is the greatest biblical song of creation, celebrating God's original creation and ongoing providential care for creatures. It begins with God's creative work in the physical universe, and then turns to God's care for living creatures:

> You make springs gush forth in the valleys;
> they flow between the hills,
> giving drink to every wild animal;
> the wild asses quench their thirst.
> By the streams the birds of the air have their habitation;
> they sing among the branches. (Ps 104:10–12)

This Psalm is a glorious hymn of praise to God for the abundance of life and the diversity of creatures—"O Lord, how manifold are your works! In wisdom you have made them all" (Ps 104:24). It is God who breathes life into all these creatures (Ps 104:30), and enables their ongoing existence and provides for them. They are represented not as dependent on humans, but as provided for directly by the Creator. Humans are understood as fellow creatures in the midst of this world of God's creatures (Ps 104:14–15). The Psalmist prays that the glory of the Lord might endure forever and that God's creatures might bring God joy (Ps 104:31).

Psalm 148 is much shorter, a wonderful hymn of praise, where the Psalmist joins with the whole creation in praising God:

> Praise him, sun and moon;
> praise him, all you shining stars!
> Praise him, you highest heavens,
> and you waters above the heavens!
> Mountains and all hills,
> fruit trees and all cedars!
> Wild animals and all cattle,
> creeping things and flying birds! (Ps 148:3–4; 9–10)

More than thirty categories of creatures are addressed in this Psalm.[13] Each is thought of as praising God in its own unique way, and humans are again seen as fellow creatures before God, this time within a community of creatures united in praise of their Creator. Bauckham suggests that Jesus's invitation to radical trust in God in the Sermon on the Mount, and his references to God's provident care for the lilies of the field and the birds of the air, reflect something of the place of the Psalms in his spirituality: "Jesus has very much made his own the Psalmist's understanding of creation as a common home for living creatures, in which God provides for all their needs."[14]

THE NEW CREATION (ISAIAH 65:17–18)

A striking expression of eschatological hope is found at the end of Isaiah, in what scholars think is a later addition to the original text, which is often called Third Isaiah:

> For I am about to create new heavens and a new earth;
> The former things shall not be remembered or come to mind.
> But be glad and rejoice forever in what I am creating;
> for I am about to create Jerusalem as a joy, and its people as a delight.
> (Isa 65:17–18)

The text goes on to quote Isaiah 11:6: "The wolf and the lamb shall feed together. . . . They shall not hurt or destroy on all my holy mountain" (Isa 67:25). The idea of a new creation articulates the hope of Israel that the promises of God would be fulfilled. It is taken up by the Christian community in the light of Christ. Paul describes the radically new existence of those who are in Christ: "So if anyone is in Christ, there is a new creation; everything old has passed away; see, everything has become new!" (2 Cor 5:17). He resists those who would demand circumcision by insisting on the new creation already begun in Christ: "For neither circumcision nor uncircumcision is anything; but a new creation is everything" (Gal 6:15).

The theme of the new heavens and new earth is taken up in 2 Peter, in the context of the coming of day of the Lord, when heavens will be set ablaze and elements will melt with fire: "But in accordance with his promise, we wait for new heavens and a new earth, where righteousness is at home" (2 Pet 3:13). In Revelation we find: "Then I saw a new heaven and a new earth; for the first heaven and the first earth had passed away and the sea was no more" (Rev 21:1). A new Jerusalem comes down from heaven, God dwells among mortals and wipes away all tears, death is no more, and the one seated on the throne says: "See, I am making all things new" (Rev 21:5).

Does this trajectory of new creation involve the destruction of the original creation, or its fulfillment? Is it a matter of discontinuity or continuity? These questions were discussed in the early church, and, as Brian Daley notes, the enduring trend in Christian interpretation from the second century saw continuity between the old creation and the new.[15] Paul Blowers comments on the responses of early Christian theologians: "the ultimately prevailing conviction of East and West was that, whatever the constitution of this new cosmic order, the original creation was not to be rendered null and void."[16] He points out that for Irenaeus, Origen, John Chrysostom, and Augustine, among others, the dictum of Paul was decisive: "For the present form of this world is passing away" (1 Cor 7:31). He notes Augustine's influential comment on this text in *The City of God*, "it is the form (*figura*) of the world that passes away, not its very nature (*natura*)."[17] The original creation is not to be annihilated but wonderfully transfigured in the new creation.

CREATION AND INCARNATION (JOHN 1:1–18)

In their encounters with Jesus as risen from the dead, the disciples began to see Jesus in a new way. Looking back from the resurrection experiences, they saw him as God-with-us

(Matt 1:23) from the very beginning. They needed ways to express something of his meaning for them and for the wider creation. In the biblical literature, they found the figure of the Wisdom of God, a trajectory that proved illuminating and fruitful. As has been noted above, Wisdom is God's companion in creating and sustaining all things. She also comes to make her home among us, inviting us to her table to share the food and drink she provides. In the light of the resurrection, the early Christian community saw Jesus as the Wisdom of God.

Paul tells us that Christ crucified is the true Wisdom of God (1 Cor 1:24). In John, we find Jesus-Wisdom as the living bread that has come down from heaven to give life to the world (John 6:51). In the period in which the Christian Scriptures were written, the trajectory of *Wisdom of God* language was closely related to that of *Word of God* language. The Jewish contemporary of Jesus and Paul, Philo of Alexandria (c. 25 BCE–50 CE) used both *Wisdom* and *Word* language, almost interchangeably, to speak of God's creating and revealing presence. In the Prologue to the Gospel of John, Jesus is celebrated as the eternal Word of God, in ways that consistently echo and build on the biblical texts that speak of the Wisdom of God.[18] For John, Jesus is the Word of God, the one through whom all things are created, the one who is made flesh in the midst of the creation:

> In the beginning was the Word, and the Word was with God,
> and the Word was God.
> He was in the beginning with God.
> All things came into being through him, and without him
> not one thing came into being . . .
> He was in the world, and the world came into being through
> him;
> yet the world did not know him . . .
> And the Word became flesh and lived among us,
> and we have seen his glory, the glory of the father's only son,

full of grace and truth. (John 1:1–14)

Francis Moloney points to the parallel with the opening of Genesis: "The first words of the Prologue, 'In the beginning (*en arche*) was the Word,' establish a parallel between the opening of the Gospel and the biblical account of the beginnings of the human story in Gen 1:1."[19] Before time and space, in the beginning, the Word already "was" (*ēn*). This pre-existing Word was "turned towards God" (*pros to theon*).[20] It is from this intimacy of being with God, turned towards God, that the Word will be spoken into a world of creatures.

From the Prologue we learn that all things (*panta*) came into being (*egeneto*) through the Word, and nothing occurs without the Word. This means that the creatures that human beings encounter can be understood as expressions of the eternal Word of God. But humans fail to recognize creation as God's gift: "yet the world did not know him." So God does something far more radical for the world. The Word enters into the flesh of the world. The Word became flesh (*sarx egeneto*) and dwells (*eskēnōsen*) among us. The Prologue seems to reflect what is said of Wisdom pitching her tent in Israel: "My Creator chose the place for my tent. He said, 'Make your dwelling (*kataskēnōson*) in Jacob'" (Sir 24:8). And the Word dwelling with us brings to mind the glory (*kabod*) of God dwelling in the tabernacle (Exod 25:8; 40:35).[21]

It would be hard to exaggerate the importance of the trajectory of this text in Christian theology. For someone like Athanasius, discussed later in this book, it is radically foundational for his whole theological vision that the Word through whom all things are made is the very Word made flesh. The Word of creation is made flesh that humans might become God's daughters and sons, and creation be brought to fulfillment. The Word of creation is the Word on the cross, the

Word of risen life. In this Christian trajectory, creation and salvation are inextricably united.

Today we might say that the emergence of our observable universe in what has been called the Big Bang 13.7 billion years ago is the expression of this creative Word of God. The evolutionary abundance of life, of frogs, rainbow lorikeets, wallabies and human beings, occurs through the Word. All these manifestations of life speak a word of the Word to us. But in the staggering event of incarnation, this dynamic creative Word has now become part of what we are—vulnerable creatures of flesh and blood in a healing and transforming act of love for human beings, and the world of creatures which will never be revoked.

CREATION AND REDEMPTION (ROMANS 8:18–25)

In his letter to the Romans, Paul sees the whole creation as waiting in eager longing for its liberation. He speaks of it groaning as though it were undergoing the pains of childbirth (8:22), and of the Christian community groaning as it awaits the fullness of redemption (8:23). The Spirit, too, groans along with the Christian community, and perhaps we might say with the wider creation, in prayer that is too deep for words (8:26). Paul says of the creation:

> For the creation waits with eager longing for the revealing of the children of God; for the creation was subjected to futility, not of its own will but by the will of the one who subjected it, in hope that the creation itself will be set free from its bondage to decay and will obtain the freedom of the glory of the children of God. We know that the whole creation has been groaning in labor pains until now, and not only the creation, but we ourselves who have the first fruits of the Spirit, groan inwardly while we wait for adoption, the redemption of our bodies. (Rom 8:18–25).

This text is fundamental for a theological understanding of the natural world because of its insistence that God's other creatures will participate in salvation with human beings. What is distinctive about this text, writes biblical scholar Brendan Byrne, is the way it "includes the whole of non-human creation within the sweep of salvation alongside human beings."[22] He notes that Paul is building on a widespread biblical understanding that human beings and the rest of creation are closely linked in their destiny.[23]

Paul sees non-human creation as sharing with human beings in the liberation and renewal of all things in Christ. In First Corinthians, taking up the image of a great cosmic victory, he speaks of the risen Christ as one who conquers death and all negative forces so that "all things" are subject to him, and who then "hands over the kingdom to God the Father" (1 Cor 15:24). Whether using the image of creation giving birth, or the image of cosmic victory, Paul is well aware that we have no clear sight of the final transformation of all things in Christ. What we possess in Christ is not sight, but promise and hope: "For in hope we were saved. Now hope that is seen is not hope. For who hopes for what is seen? But if we hope for what we do not see, we wait for it in patience" (Rom 8:24–25). The trajectory offered in these Pauline texts is not one of clear vision, but one of promise given in the resurrection of Jesus Christ, and one of hope that we human beings and with us the wider creation will come to liberation in the risen Christ.

THE COSMIC CHRIST (COLOSSIANS 1:15-20)

It seems that the Christians of Colossae were in danger of being led astray by astrological cults, centered on cosmic forces, which were angelic-like spirits that were thought of as powerfully at work in the universe. These cults encouraged practices that were thought to bring about release from bodily limitations and enable participation in the higher spiritual realm. Colossians counters the attraction of these cosmic cults with its theology of the cosmic salvific role of Jesus Christ, expressed in its great hymn:

> He is the image of the invisible God, the firstborn of all creation;
> for in him all things in heaven and on earth were created,
> things visible and invisible,
> whether thrones or dominions or rulers or powers—
> all things have been created through him and for him.
> He himself is before all things, and in him all things hold together.
> He is the head of the body, the church;
> he is the beginning, the firstborn from the dead,
> so that he might come to have first place in everything.
> For in him all the fullness of God was pleased to dwell,
> and through him God was pleased to reconcile to himself all things,
> whether on earth or in heaven,
> by making peace through the blood of his cross. (Col 1:15–20)

Jesus Christ is the true image of the unseen God, the firstborn of all creation. As biblical hymns sing of God creating all things through Wisdom, this hymn sings of all things as created "through" Christ and "in" Christ. It also speaks of all things as created "for" Christ, as directed towards his fulfillment of the whole creation. The hymn repeats the words "all things" (*ta panta*) over and over again. It further reinforces the universal cosmic reach of Christ's mission by specifying that it involves everything on earth and in heaven, whether visible or invisible, and that it includes all cosmic powers. The whole universe is sustained and held together in Christ (See Wis 8:1; Heb 1:3). Christ is the first-born from the dead, the beginning of resurrection life for all things, the one through whom God reconciles the whole creation to God's self.

Creation and cosmic reconciliation are closely interlinked in this theology. Dianne Bergant sums up the christological theology of this hymn:

> The entire universe was brought into existence through Christ, has been sustained by him, and has been reconciled to God through his death and resurrection. . . . Nothing is excluded here, nothing lacks importance of worth. The repetition of the phrase "all things" makes this quite clear. This very rich poem depicts Christ, image of God and firstborn of all creation, as embracing the entire community of Earth reconciling all of creation to God. This is a glorious picture.[24]

A similar cosmic theology appears in Ephesians: "With all wisdom and insight he has make known to us the mystery of his will, according to his good pleasure that he set forth in Christ, as a plan for the fullness of time, to gather up all things in him, things in heaven and things on earth" (Eph 1:9–10). Later in the text we find that God has "put all things under his feet and has made him the head over all things for the church, which his body, the fullness of him who fills all things" (Eph 1:22). While Colossians speaks of God reconciling all things in Christ, Ephesians speaks of all things being "gathered up" or recapitulated in him. The cosmic theology of Christ found in these letters becomes a major inspiration and trajectory for theologians from Irenaeus, whom I will take up in the next chapter, to Teilhard de Chardin and Jürgen Moltmann, who appear later in this book.

This chapter is far from a complete picture of the Bible on creation, but it is meant to make clear that there are multiple creation texts in the Scriptures, and that in their diversity these texts provide a range of different aspects that can contribute to a renewed theology of creation. It will become evident that they constitute trajectories through the various theologies explored in the rest of this book, and that they are foundational for these theologies.

Notes

1. For an example of the many other biblical insights and trajectories that might be taken up, see Francis Moloney's work on the theme of the lamb that was slain "before the foundation of the world" (Rev 13:8), in his "The Gospel of Creation: A Biblical Response to *Laudato Si',*" *Salesianum Studia* 78 (2016): 583–605.
2. The Second Vatican Council points to the fundamental importance of salvific truth: "we must acknowledge that that the books of scripture teach firmly, faithfully, and without error such truth as God, for the sake of our salvation, wished the biblical text to contain" (*Dogmatic Constitution on Divine Revelation,* par. 11, trans. Norman P. Tanner, *Decrees of the Ecumenical Councils* [Washington: Georgetown University Press, 1990], 2:976).
3. Peter C. Bouteneff, *Beginnings: Ancient Christian Readings of the Biblical Creation Narratives* (Grand Rapids, MI: Baker Academic, 2008), 8.
4. Norman Habel, "Geophany: The Earth Story in Genesis 1," in *The Earth Story in Genesis*, ed. Norman Habel (Sheffield, UK, Sheffield Academic, 2000), 47.
5. Pope Francis, *Laudato Si'* (Vatican City: Libreria Editrice Vaticana, 2015), 60, par. 67.
6. Ibid.
7. See Richard Clifford, "Hebrew Scriptures and the Theology of Creation," *Theological Studies* 46 (1985): 507–23.
8. Wisdom seems to stand behind other texts which speak of the universe as created through the Word (Heb 1:1–4), and of all things as created and reconciled in Christ (Col 1:15–20).
9. See Richard Bauckham, *The Bible and Ecology: Rediscovering the Community of Creation* (London: Darton, Longman & Todd, 2010).
10. Ibid., 39.

11. Ibid., 51.
12. Ibid., 64–102.
13. Ibid., 77.
14. Ibid., 73.
15. Brian Daley, *The Hope of the Early Church: A Handbook of Patristic Eschatology* (Cambridge: Cambridge University Press, 1991), 54.
16. Paul Blowers, *Drama of the Divine Economy: Creator and Creation in Early Christian Theology and Piety* (Oxford: Oxford University Press, 2012), 239.
17. Ibid., 240.
18. For analysis of Wisdom texts that are evoked in the prologue see Raymond E. Brown, *The Anchor Bible: The Gospel According to John (i-xii)* (Garden City, NY: Doubleday, 1966), cxxii–cxxv.
19. Francis J. Maloney, *The Gospel of John*, *Sacra Pagina* Series, Volume 4 (Collegeville, MN: Liturgical, 1998), 35.
20. Maloney, *The Gospel of John*, 35.
21. Ibid., 38–39.
22. Brendan Byrne, *Romans*, *Sacra Pagina* Series, Volume 6 (Collegeville, MN: Liturgical Press, 1996), 255.
23. Ibid., 256.
24. Dianne Bergant, *A New Heaven and a New Earth: The Bible and Catholicity* (Maryknoll, NY: Orbis Books, 2016), 158–59.

2.

Irenaeus of Lyons (c. 130–198)

Life and Context: In the first half of the second century, the Christian community in Rome was made up of diverse house churches, with many members being recent immigrants. Some of these communities were led by extraordinary teachers from the East, including Valentinus, Marcion, and Justin Martyr. Justin opposed the theologies of Valentinus and Marcion, both of whom eventually separated themselves from the wider Christian community. Irenaeus seems to have come to Rome from Smyrna in Asia Minor (Izmir, in today's Turkey). He tells of being profoundly influenced in his early life by Polycarp, who had known John, the disciple of Jesus, and of Polycarp's visit to Rome (c. 154–55) that convinced many Christians to turn away from the teachings of Valentinus and Marcion. Irenaeus moved from Rome to Gaul where he became a leading figure in the churches of Lyons and Vienne. In 177, these churches suffered fierce persecution, and during this time sent letters to the churches of Asia and Phrygia, with remarkable descriptions of their own church of martyrs, particularly of the heroism of the slave girl Blandina. They also sent Irenaeus to Eleutherus, bishop of Rome (c. 174–89), with a letter of peace that introduces Irenaeus as a presbyter. Irenaeus was able to contribute to peace between Eleutherus and communities in Rome made up of immigrants from Asia and Phrygia influenced by the enthusiasm of the Montanist movement. Irenaeus

> intervened again in Rome in the time of the next bishop, Victor (c. 189–98), to bring peace in the dispute over the date of Easter. Irenaeus's great work, *Against Heresies*, was written in instalments during the period of Eleutherus and Victor.[1] Within this period he also wrote a shorter work, *The Demonstration of the Apostolic Preaching*.[2]

Irenaeus wrote *Against Heresies* in opposition to views that he regarded as dangerous distortions of Christian faith. While describing and combating these views, he articulates the first fully developed theology of the Christian tradition. My focus is on his positive contribution, but an appreciation of his theology requires some attention to the views he opposed. Chief among the opponents he discusses are Valentinus and his disciples, commonly called Gnostics, although scholars today are cautious about including diverse second century views under this term. There is new information about some of these groups and their writings, including texts Irenaeus had before him, from the recently discovered Coptic texts of Nag Hammadi, Egypt. Before turning to Irenaeus's own theology, I will outline briefly his view of the teaching he was opposing, that of Valentinus and his disciples, and then of Marcion.

VALENTINUS AND HIS DISCIPLES

Valentinus came from the Nile delta and was educated in Christian, Middle Platonic, and ancient Egyptian philosophies in Alexandria, where he emerged as a charismatic teacher. He moved to Rome about 136 CE, and became prominent in the church, but eventually fell out with the wider Christian community, moving to Cyprus where he taught until his death about 161 CE. One of his disciples was Ptolemaius, and Irenaeus devotes the first eight chapters of *Against Heresies* to a detailed description of Ptolemaius's thought.[3] Irenaeus says that he writes this description "after chancing upon the commentaries of the disciples of Valentinus—as they style themselves—and after conversing with some of them and becoming acquainted with their doctrine."[4]

In this school of thought, the divinity includes different ways of being, called Aeons, and thirty Aeons together make up the fullness of the divinity, the Pleroma. Each male and female pair of Aeons brings forth further pairs in a descending hierarchy of being. At the top of the hierarchy is the divine principle, the Father, called Depth (*Bythos*), with his consort who has three names, Purposive Thought, Silence, and Grace. This pair gives rise to a second, Mind and Truth, and the process continues all the way down to the projection of "Wisdom" (*Sophia*) at the bottom of the hierarchy of divine being.

The material world, along with evil, arises from instability and failure within the divine Pleroma. It begins from Mind failing in an attempt to communicate to the other Aeons the knowledge of the transcendent Father, which is meant for him alone. The other Aeons develop an unfulfilled desire to contemplate the Father, and this desire becomes extreme in *Sophia*, who rejects her own consort, Desired, and experiences such passion and suffering in her need to comprehend the Father that she is in danger of destroying herself. The other Aeons manage to save her and keep her in the divine Pleroma. However, she is separated from her Desire, which is cast out beyond the Pleroma.

This Desire, now called Achamoth, cut off from the divine realm, is left with an unfulfilled longing for the world it does not possess. Meanwhile, Christ and the Spirit are produced to bring harmony to the Pleroma and from this harmony Jesus Savior comes forth. Outside the Pleroma, Achamoth produces the Demiurge,[5] who creates the material world from Achamoth's suffering and passion: "material substance took its beginning from ignorance and grief, fear and bewilderment."[6] The Savior comes to save those who are ensouled in the world, and is clothed with a body of 'ensouled substance.' This Savior's body is carefully prepared so as to be visible and tangible, but it is not really a body of matter and flesh, "since material substance is incapable of receiving salvation."[7] The fact that matter and flesh arise as the side-effect of unhappy events within the divine *Pleroma* explains why evil is to be found in the natural world, and why it is a place of sorrows: "All the distress we suffer is simply part of the cosmic rubbish left behind by the primordial near-catastrophe within the divine realm."[8]

Humans are divided into three classes. On the one hand, there are the spirituals—those in whom there is the divine spark put into the creation by Achamoth. These spirituals possess salvific knowledge, the knowledge that, in their highest selves, they are divine, and that they will eventually be freed from matter and return to the divine realm. On the other hand, there are those who are nothing but matter, whose only future is corruption (the "*hylics*"). In between are the "*psychics*" who, although they do not have the divine spark, have souls and free will. Since they do not possess salvific knowledge, they cannot attain the salvation of the spirituals, but can have faith and may reach a garden of rest after death. Most ordinary Christians belong to this category.

MARCION

For Marcion, the key issue is the contradiction he sees between the loving and merciful Father revealed in Jesus Christ and the God of justice and vengeance he finds in the (First Testament) Scriptures.[9] Marcion takes literally the text "no one knows the Father except the Son" (Luke 10:22), and claims that the Father is not known before the revelation of

Jesus Christ. The God of the First Testament, then, is not the God of Jesus. The Creator of Genesis is not the true God. Jesus Christ liberates us from the Creator and from material creation. Because Marcion thinks that only Paul understands the message of Jesus, he accepts as Scripture only his own edited versions of the main letters of Paul, and a much revised Gospel of Luke, whom he sees as connected to Paul.

Both Marcion, and the followers of Valentinus, then, see the Creator God of the First Testament as an inferior deity. Both despise the world of created material entities. The followers of Valentinus go much further, seeing the creation as the unplanned and accidental by-product of discord and failure in the deity. They have no respect for matter or the body, reject the idea that the Word of God is really made flesh, and reject the bodily nature of resurrection life. All of this seems a dangerous and demeaning distortion of Christian faith to Irenaeus. He opposes it with a theology of the Creator as the very God of Jesus Christ, who creates out of love, and whose good creation is directed to Christ and recapitulated in him.

ALL THINGS RECAPITULATED IN CHRIST

As a Christian of the second century, Irenaeus reads the Scriptures in a way that differs from contemporary historical approaches. For him, Christ crucified and risen is both the beginning and the end of Scripture. He sees the cross of Christ as the key to the interpretation of Scripture. In opposing the Valentinians, he gives expression to his own approach to biblical hermeneutics with the image of the mosaic of the king:

> By way of illustration, suppose someone would take the beautiful image of a king, carefully made out of precious stones by a skillful artist, and would destroy the features of the man on it and change around and rearrange the jewels, and make the

> form of a dog, or of a fox, out of them, and that a rather bad piece of work. Suppose he would then say with determination that this is the beautiful image of the king that the skillful artist had made, at the same time pointing to the jewels that had been beautifully fitted together by the first artist into the image of the king, but which had been badly changed by the second into the form of a dog.[10]

For Irenaeus the biblical writings form such a beautiful mosaic, a brilliant portrait of the crucified and risen Jesus. Every stone plays its part in the whole. What prevents the stones being jumbled up and the portrait distorted, is the apostolic witness to Christ, the gospel that has come down to us from the apostles. This gospel is expressed in writing (the New Testament), and witnessed to in the life of the Christian community, particularly though it presbyter-bishops.[11] It is the gospel in the singular, expounded by the Apostles, held in the church, and cast in biblical terms, that enables us read the mosaic and see its truth and beauty.

Irenaeus offers a second image for his approach to biblical interpretation, building on the parable of the treasure hidden in a field. He says that "Christ is the treasure that was hid in the field, that is in this world."[12] Christ is the Word who was at work in hidden ways in creation from the very beginning. But in a more explicit way, Christ is the treasure that is hidden in the Scriptures: "the treasure hid in the Scriptures is Christ, since he was pointed out by means of types and parables."[13]

All the patriarchal and prophetic writings prefigure and prepare the way for Christ. When the law is read "with attention" by Christians, it is a treasure that is "brought to light by the cross of Christ."[14] For Irenaeus, then, Scripture is a storehouse of abundant riches: "he sees Scripture as being, as it were, a compendium, or 'thesaurus,' that is, a 'treasury' of images, words, and reports, which gives flesh to the Christ proclaimed by the apostles, who in turn reveals the work of God deployed throughout the whole economy described in Scripture."[15] In the light cast from the cross, Scripture shows forth the wisdom of God, making known the economy of God.

The words *economy* and *recapitulation* are both central to Irenaeus's theological vision. Both words were used in the Greek schools of rhetoric.[16] Both can also be found in the Pauline writings. The word *economy* (*oikonomia*) comes from the ordering of a household (*oikos*), but it had been used in classical Greek from the time of Plato to speak of an arrangement, a plan, or the management of affairs.[17] In the New Testament it is used of God's plan and accomplishment of salvation in Jesus Christ (Eph 1:10; 3:2). Irenaeus can speak in the plural of the economies of God, but he characteristically uses it in the singular, in a comprehensive sense, to bring together all the aspects of God's plan, embracing both creation and salvation in Christ.

This economy is known from reading the Scriptures in the light of the gospel preached by the apostles: "we received the knowledge of the economy of our salvation through no others than those through whom the gospel has come down to us. This gospel they first preached orally, but later by God's will they handed it on [*tradiderunt*] to us in the Scriptures, so that it would be *the foundation and pillar of our faith*."[18] For Irenaeus, then, there is an identity between the Scriptures and the Gospel. While the Scriptures speak of the economy of God in Christ at length, the gospel proclaims this same economy in summary form. The economy of God is recapitulated in the Gospel of Jesus Christ.

In the Greek rhetorical schools the *recapitulation* was the restatement of the whole argument, the summing up, the epitome or résumé, which brings all the details of the presentation into a unified and complete picture. In the New

Testament, Paul speaks of the various commandments of the Law as being recapitulated in the word of Jesus: "Love your neighbor as yourself" (Rom 13:9). In Ephesians we hear that God's economy, the plan of creation and redemption, is that the whole creation would be recapitulated in Christ: God's will is revealed as "a plan (economy) for the fullness of times, to sum up (recapitulate) all things in Christ, in heaven and on earth" (Eph 1:10). God's purpose in creation and salvation is to bring all things under Christ as head (Eph 1:22).[19] Irenaeus sees all the various words of Scripture as recapitulated in the Word made flesh, who is the "concise Word" of God, in and for the world.[20]

For Irenaeus, the Word is present in the whole creation, which is the handiwork of the Word. He says that the Word reveals the Creator through the means of creation itself.[21] This same Word was engaged with Abraham, Moses, and all the economies recounted in the Scriptures. All of this culminates in the Word made flesh, who "suffered for us and rose for out sakes, and will come again in glory to raise up all flesh."[22] In his death and resurrection, the incarnate Word recapitulates, saves and brings to fulfilment, all things:

> There is therefore as we have shown, one God the Father and one Christ Jesus our Lord, who comes through every economy and *recapitulates in himself all things*. Now humanity, too, God's handiwork, is contained in this "all." So he also recapitulated in himself humanity; the invisible becoming visible; the incomprehensible, comprehensible, the impassible, passible; the Word, human. Thus *he recapitulated in himself all things*, so that just as the Word of God is the sovereign ruler over supercelestial, spiritual and invisible beings, so he might possess sovereign rule over visible and corporeal things; and thus, by taking to himself the primacy, and constituting himself head of the church, he might draw all things to himself in the proper time.[23]

Against Valentinus and Marcion, and their view of the inferior nature of the Creator God, Irenaeus insists that there is one God who is both the Creator and Father of Jesus. This God's creative and saving acts are united in the one saving purpose, the one overarching economy, of the one God and the one Christ, in whom the whole is recapitulated and brought to its fulfillment. And, Irenaeus insists, this transforming recapitulation involves not just spiritual reality, but "visible and corporeal things." He resists all disembodied theologies. What happens in Christ involves "all things"—the whole visible, material, biological and human world. Irenaeus has a clear focus on the human, but as the above quotation makes clear, the human is part of the wider "all things," that are recapitulated in Christ.

CREATION OF ALL THINGS *EX NIHILO*

Against both the Valentinians and Marcion, then, Irenaeus intends to establish, above all, that there is one God, who is both Father of Jesus Christ and "the Creator God who made heaven and earth and all things in them."[24] He seeks to convince his readers, concerning this one Creator God, that "there is nothing either above him or after him, and that he was influenced by no one but, rather, made all things by his own counsel and free will, since he alone is God, and he alone is Lord, and he alone is Creator, and he alone is Father, and he alone contains all things, and he himself gives existence to all things."[25]

Several of Irenaeus's key ideas appear in the above quotation, along with his central claim that there is only one God of creation and of Jesus Christ. One of these key ideas is that creation springs from the "counsel and free will" of this one God alone. This is closely connected to the concept addressed below, that God creates out of nothing (*ex nihilo*), as an act that springs wholly from God's freedom. A further key idea is that God *alone* creates. Irenaeus argues at length that God has absolutely no need of intermediaries—God has no need of angels to create and it was not angels who made humans in the image of God.[26] Only God creates, and God creates immediately. An important implication of this position is that there is a direct relationship between each creature and the living God.

Another key idea is that God contains all things and is contained by none—several times Irenaeus adopts this phrase, a quotation from the Shepherd of Hermas.[27] For Irenaeus it expresses the radical ontological difference between the one Creator and the whole world of creatures. In the above quotation he says of the Creator that "he himself gives existence to all things."[28] Every entity in the universe exists as coming into being from God's conferral of existence upon it. Irenaeus, then, totally opposes the Valentinian idea of a continuous chain of being that links all things, whether divine or creaturely. For him there is absolutely no continuity between creatures and their one Creator. Denis Minns writes:

> Rather God is the only reality, the only thing that really *is*, and over against God, called into existence out of nothingness by God, and held in being, poised over nothingness by God, is everything that God creates. There is no substance or essence or being common to all created things, much less common to all created things and God. The only "substance" of created things, all that underpins them, is the will of God.[29]

This very emphasis on the radical transcendence of God means that Irenaeus can have a far more profound sense of the closeness of God to creatures than his opponents who hold to the descending chain of being. Irenaeus explicitly invokes the concept of creation from nothing when he writes: "God made those things that were made in order that all things might exist *out of things that did not exist*, just as he willed, making use of matter by his own will and power."[30] Later, he says: "First of all believe that there is one God, who has established all things, and completed them, and having caused that from what had no being, all things should come into existence."[31]

While Justin Martyr holds that God created out of unformed matter, and Irenaeus's contemporary, Theophilus of Antioch, insists that God is the Creator of this unformed matter, Irenaeus directly opposes the Greek philosophical idea that "the Creator made the world out of existing matter."[32] God creates out of nothing. Irenaeus's constant emphasis is that all the entities of the universe owe their whole existence to God's creative act—"For God to create out of nothing is for him to create the actual, individualized entities of the cosmos from a state of non-existence."[33] This strong concept of creation *ex nihilo*, however, coexists with a view of God as enabling creation to develop: "he alone is truly God and Father, who both made this world and fashioned humanity, and endowed his creation with the [the power of] developing and gave the call (of rising) from his lesser (stages) to greater ones that are within himself."[34] Irenaeus goes on to give examples of development: the infant in the womb that comes into the light of day as a new-born child; the wheat on the stem that ends up as food in the granary. All such developments of the natural world are the work of the one and only Creator.

The motive for creation is the divine goodness. Irenaeus says that compared to the Valentinians, and their view that the creation springs from ignorance and error, Plato shows himself to be "more religious," since he sees "the Creator and Maker of this world to be good;" there is no jealousy towards creatures in this divine goodness.[35] In Plato, divine goodness is "the beginning and cause" of the creation of the world.[36]

Irenaeus, of course, goes far beyond Plato in his understanding of this goodness. For him, it is fully revealed and reaches its culmination only in Christ. Creation seen in the light of Christ is a radical act of love.

Michael Slusser proposes that the very heart of Irenaeus theology in this divine love. He points to the contrast Irenaeus sets up between the greatness (*magnitudo*) of the transcendent God and the love (*dilectio*) of God, and the way he makes clear that God's transcendence is not an obstacle to God's relationship with creatures, because God's love is able to overcome all such apparent obstacles. It is God's initiative in love that "overrides the insuperable metaphysical obstacle constituted by God's incomprehensibility and *magnitudo*."[37] The divine initiative enables us to know God in love, and this knowledge "in and according to love is, for Irenaeus, the true knowledge of God, the true Gnosis, and it is the church people who know about it and live by it."[38]

THE TWO HANDS OF THE CREATOR

Although Irenaeus never uses the word "Trinity," the structure of his creation theology is fully Trinitarian.[39] In many instances he simply attributes creation to God, or to God as Father, above all when he seeking to make it clear that there is only one God who is both the Creator and the Father of Jesus Christ. He often describes the Word of God as the Creator and maker of all things—constantly referring to John 1:3, which says of the Word: "All things came into being through him, and without him not one thing came into being." At one point he also speaks directly of the Holy Spirit as the Creator: "The Spirit of God by whom all things were made."[40] Particularly from book 3 of *Against Heresies*, Irenaeus presents the Spirit as Creator, involved with the Father and the Word in creating all things, creatively anointing Jesus's humanity in the incarnation, and bringing Christians fully alive.[41] The theology of the Spirit as Creator would be lost sight of in the theologies of Origen and Tertullian in the next century.

While Irenaeus could attribute creation to each of the Three, Father, Son and Spirit, his structure of thought is that they are all involved together in the one act of creation, yet each in a distinct way. In his *Demonstration of the Apostolic Preaching*, he writes:

> In this way, then, it is demonstrated [that there is] one God, [the] Father, uncreated, invisible, Creator of all, above whom there is no other God, and after whom there is no other God. And as God is verbal [*logikos*] therefore he made created things by the Word; and as God is Spirit, so he adorned all things by the Spirit, as the prophet also says, "By the Word of the Lord were the heavens established, and all their power by his Spirit" (Ps 32:6). Thus, since the Word "establishes," that is works bodily and confers existence, while the Spirit arranges and forms the various "powers," so rightly is the Son called Word and the Spirit the Wisdom of God.[42]

Irenaeus sees the Father as Creator, the Word as the means of creation, and the Spirit as the "arranger," the "adorner," of creation. Each has a particular role in the one work: creation comes from the Father, "through" the Word and "in" the Spirit.[43] Along with Theophilus of Antioch, Irenaeus identifies the Spirit as the Wisdom of God.[44] So he understands God, the invisible one, the Father, as creating through Word and Wisdom—"There is therefore one God, who by the Word and Wisdom created and arranged all things."[45]

Irenaeus often expresses this Trinitarian structure in the image of God creating through God's two hands, the hand of the Word and the hand of the Spirit, above all when he discusses God moulding the human from mud.[46] In language that is typical, he writes in his preface to book 4 of *Against*

Heresies that the human being is "formed after the likeness of God, and moulded by his two hands, that is by the Son and the Holy Spirit."[47] This central idea is taken up in the next section.

MADE FROM MUD

For Irenaeus, the divine intention in creating humans is expressed in Genesis 1:26: "Let us make humankind in our image, according to our likeness." He interprets the plural here as a reference to the Father, Word and Spirit. The divine intention is carried out in Genesis 1:27: "God created humankind in his own image, in the image of God he created them, male and female he created them." Irenaeus sees this creative act as explained in more detail in the second chapter of Genesis: "Then the Lord formed man from the dust of the ground, and breathed into his nostrils the breath of life" (Gen 2:7). As Irenaeus sees it, it is precisely the earth creature made from mud who is the image of the eternal Word. There is a direct connection with Jesus Christ the truly living human being, the true image: "what is sketched out in Adam, clay animated by a breath of life, is brought to perfection by Christ vivified by Holy Spirit, the Hands of God through whom God himself has been at work throughout the whole economy."[48]

The word *plasma* in both Greek and Latin refers to something that is moulded or fashioned. Irenaeus makes constant use of this word to refer to human beings as creatures moulded from Earth by God. They are, then, God's handiwork—suggesting both the "earthy character" of the human being, and the "hands-on immediacy" of God's creative work, fashioning humans from mud as a potter moulds clay.[49] Irenaeus's embrace of earthiness is a direct contrast to the earth-denying theology of his opponents. The bodily flesh, he insists, is moulded in the image of God. Christ, then, is true flesh, and so recapitulates and saves God's original handiwork.[50] We certainly are creatures of soul as well as flesh, but we are not human without the flesh that is moulded in the divine image.[51] Irenaeus sees the Spirit as bestowed in two ways, first in the breath of life given in creation and, then, in the transformation by which we are made fully alive as adopted children of God. It is only in this transformation that we can grow fully, body and soul, into the likeness of God. But in Irenaeus's view we always possess the flesh molded by the two hands in the image of God.[52]

The newly created Adam and Eve are, according to Irenaeus, very young and inexperienced, but are already formed in the divine image, and are intended to grow into the perfect likeness of God through a gradual process of development.[53] But in their immaturity they are seduced by the power of evil and give way to temptation. In the divine economy Christ recapitulates this defeat, himself defeating sin and the tyranny of death. Christ is the true and full image of God, the true human being. Even though Adam and Eve were created in the image, the true image had not yet appeared. They suffered the disadvantage that the true image was not yet visible in our history. While the Father is invisible and incomprehensible, "the Son is the visible of the Father," as "the Father is the invisible of the Son."[54] When the Word of God became flesh, he not only showed forth the image truly, he also re-established the likeness in a sure manner by assimilating the human person to the Father by means of the visible Word.[55] By Christ recapitulating in himself the whole economy, including all the ages of the human, humanity comes to share fully in divine life through the Spirit.[56]

Irenaeus Steenberg points out that Irenaeus's theology, as opposed to his description of his opponents, is little referenced in the early church. He argues that the reason for this is simply that it was received as the church's theology: "Irenaeus's theology was the church's theology."[57] For Irenaeus, the Word becomes flesh that humans may partake of the Word and have communion in God.[58] The Word of God becomes a human in order that humans might be adopted as God's sons and daughters.[59] This theology will later be taken up by Athanasius in an explicit theology of deification. In a well-known expression, Irenaeus expresses the meaning of incarnation and the work of the Spirit in terms of the fully alive human being who is the glory of God—"For the glory of God is a living human being; and the life of the human consists in beholding God."[60]

CREATION'S TRANSFORMATION

Irenaeus was among those in the second century, like Papias, who awaited a kingdom of God that would involve the renewal of earth, the raising of the dead and the coming of the risen Christ to dwell on earth for a thousand years.[61] For some theologians of the next century, under the influence of Platonism, this vision of an earthly kingdom was replaced by a far more spiritual interpretation. Some tended to be embarrassed by the body—Origen would see it as joined to the soul as a punishment for a previous rebellion against God. But as Minns says, "so much of Irenaeus's own fight had been in favour of the positive value of the material creation, and especially of the human body, that he could not countenance so spiritualizing an interpretation."[62] With his understanding of the economy as centering on the body made from mud, Irenaeus completely rejects the idea that the promise of the resurrection can be explained away in an allegorical or spiritual interpretation.[63]

In Irenaeus's view, those who have toiled and suffered in this creation will rise in this very same creation that will itself be renewed.[64] Inspired by the apocalyptic books of the Bible, Irenaeus sees the Antichrist as establishing a kingdom in Jerusalem for three and a half years. But Christ will come to overthrow the Antichrist, and the just will rise from the dead to dwell in the Kingdom of the Son in a renewed Jerusalem. At the end of this period, the Son will hand the Kingdom over to the Father, there will be a new heaven and a new earth, and the heavenly Jerusalem will come down to the new earth.[65] Some of the just will enter the new heaven, others the garden of paradise and others the holy city, but all will see God and grow in their capacity to know and love God.

The Kingdom will be the fulfillment of the promise of the land that was long ago made to Abraham and his descendants. In that land, "the creation, having been renovated and set free, shall fructify with an abundance of all kinds of food, from the dew of heaven, and from the fertility of the earth."[66] Irenaeus offers a detailed picture of a marvelously fruitful earth:

> The days will come, in which vines shall grow, each having ten thousand branches, and each branch ten thousand twigs, and in each true twig then thousand shoots, and in each one of the shoots ten thousand clusters, and on every one of the clusters ten thousand grapes, and every grape when pressed will give five and twenty metretes of wine . . . [the Lord declared] that a grain of wheat would produce ten thousand ears, and that every ear should have ten thousand grains, and every grain should yield ten pounds of clear, pure, fine flour; and that all other fruit-bearing trees, and seeds and grass, would produce in similar proportions; and that all animals feeding [only] on the production of the earth, should [in those days] become peaceful and harmonious among each other, and be in perfect subjection to the human.[67]

Irenaeus understands this picture of the fruitful land as fulfilling the promises of Isaiah 11:6–9 that the wolf will live with the lamb and the lion will eat straw like the ox.[68] He says that he is well aware that some people see this promise as referring to violent human beings of different nations coming to peace. Nevertheless, he insists, in the resurrection of the just, these words will apply to the animals.

Irenaeus points out that the promise of a new heaven and a new earth (Isa 65:17; Rev 21:1) does not mean the annihilation of the present earth: "for neither is the substance nor the essence of the creation annihilated."[69] He appeals to Paul's words "the fashion of this world shall pass away" (1 Cor 7:31), to argue that is only the "fashion" or current form of the world that will pass away. There will be "progress" or transformation of the world that exists.[70] When the fashion of this world passes away, when the human being has been renewed and flourishes in incorruptibility, then "there shall be the new heaven and the new earth, in which the new human shall remain [continually], always holding fresh converse with God."[71]

TRAJECTORIES

While most contemporary theologians would not read apocalyptic predictions of the coming reign of Christ as literally as Irenaeus, I believe that his theology has much to offer a contemporary theology of creation. I will conclude by highlighting aspects of Irenaeus's creation theology that can have fresh meaning in today's world:

1. Creation and saving incarnation are inseparably embraced in the one intention and economy of God. The Creator God is identical with the one Jesus calls *Abba.* The whole creation is recapitulated in Christ.
2. God creates through the Two Hands of the Word and the Spirit. Creation is one undivided act of the Three,

from the Father, through the Word, and in the Spirit. Creation is an act of love, an expression of divine goodness.

3. God creates *ex nihilo*. There is a radical ontological difference between the world of creatures and their Creator. But this ontological gap is overcome by God's love. The Creator is immediately present holding every individual entity in being, conferring existence on all things.
4. Irenaeus's vision is a developmental one. God enables all the developments found in the natural world. He sees the human as developing from the youthful naivety of Adam and Eve to maturity in Christ, and from possessing the breath of life to becoming fully alive in the Spirit. While very different to contemporary views of the emergence of the universe and the evolution of life, there are points of connection to be explored.
5. In Irenaeus's theological vision, human beings have a central place. They are molded from mud by the Two Hands, in the image of Word made flesh, and destined in the Spirit to grow into the likeness of God and become fully alive, and so to be the glory of God.
6. While his focus on the human means that his theology does not constitute the ecological theology of the whole creation needed for today, key aspects of Irenaeus's thought can contribute to such a theology: his strong resistance to all the disembodied theologies of his day; his insistence on the earthiness and physicality of the creation, with the human molded from mud; his idea of the immediacy of the Creator to each creature; his insistence on the goodness of creation, of matter, of flesh; his concept that it is our bodies that we are made in the divine image; his defense of the bodily reality of the incarnation

and of the human death of Jesus; his position that not just humanity but all things are recapitulated in Christ.

7. Irenaeus's eschatology involves animals and plants and the land. What happens in Christ involves the transformation of "all things"—the whole visible, material, biological and human world. As Hans Urs von Balthasar says: "In his eschatology Irenaeus produces an important counterweight to the flight from the world and the failure to take seriously the resurrection of the flesh which marks the Platonizing Christian eschatologies of a later period and indeed the average Christian consciousness."[72]

Notes

1. The text of the five books of *Against Heresies* (AH) can be found in the *Source chétiennes* series, 263–64, 293–94, 210–11, 100, 152–53, published in Paris by *Les éditions du Cerf* between 1952 and 1982. The English translation of the first three books is from the Ancient Christian Writers series (New York, NY: Newman): book 1, vol. 55 (1992), and book 2, vol. 64 (2012), both trans. Dominic J. Unger, revised John J. Dillon; book 3, vol. 65 (2012), trans. Dominic J. Unger, revised Irenaeus M.C. Steenberg. The English translation of books 4 and 5 is from the *Anti-Nicene Fathers* series, vol. 1 (Edinburgh, 1887, reprinted Grand Rapids: Eerdmans, 2012), trans. A. Roberts and W. J. Rambaut. I will modify the translation, substituting "the human" or "human being" for the generic "man," and reducing some upper case letters to lower case.
2. This text can be found in *Source chétiennes* 406 (Paris: *Les éditions du Cerf*, 1995), ed. A. Rousseau. English translation (*Demonstration*) is from John Behr, *St Irenaeus of Lyons. On the Apostolic Preaching* (Crestwood, NY: St. Vladimir's Seminary Press, 1997).
3. AH 1. Preface. 2.
4. Ibid.

5. This word originally meant an artisan or maker, and in Greek philosophy and in early Christian writings it comes to mean "creator."
6. AH 1.2.3.
7. AH 1.6.1.
8. See Denis Minns, *Irenaeus: An Introduction* (London: T&T Clark, 2010), 25.
9. In the middle of the second century, "the Scriptures" refer to the Septuagint, the Greek translation of the First Testament. While the gospels and the letters of Paul are resources for the Christian community, and also seen as Scriptures, there is nothing like a single book of the Christian Bible, and no settled canon. The canon of Scripture is largely settled in the works of Irenaeus and Theophilus later in the second century. See Minns, *Irenaeus*, 26.
10. AH 1.8.1.
11. AH 3.1–4.
12. AH 4.26.1.
13. Ibid.
14. Ibid.
15. John Behr, *Irenaeus of Lyons: Identifying Christianity* (Oxford: Oxford University Press, 2013), 128.
16. See Robert Grant, *Irenaeus of Lyons* (New York: Routledge, 1997), 46–53, for discussion of Irenaeus's debt to rhetoric for the terms *economy* and *recapitulation*, as well as *hypothesis*.
17. In the Latin text of Irenaeus, two words are used: *dispensatio* and *dispositio*.
18. AH 3.1.1. Behr thus writes of an "identity" between Scripture and tradition in Irenaeus, in *Asceticism and Anthropology in Irenaeus and Clement* (Oxford: Oxford University Press, 2000), 31. See also Behr, *Irenaeus of Lyons*, 139.
19. See also Eph 4:15; Col 1:18; 2:10.
20. *Demonstration*, 87. See Behr, *Irenaeus of Lyons*, 124–44.
21. AH 4.6.6.
22. AH 3.16.6.
23. Ibid.

24. AH 2.1.1.
25. AH 2.1.1.
26. AH 4.20.1.
27. AH 2.30.9; 4.20.2. This phrase had earlier been used by the Jewish philosopher Philo, and has its origins in the wider Greek philosophical tradition.
28. AH 2.1.1.
29. Minns, *Irenaeus*, 42.
30. AH 2.10.2 (italics added).
31. AH 4.20.2.
32. AH 2.14.4.
33. M. C. Steenberg, *Irenaeus on Creation: The Cosmic Christ and the Saga of Redemption* (Leiden, Boston: Brill, 2008), 48.
34. AH 2.28.1.
35. AH 3.25.5.
36. Ibid.
37. Michael Slusser, "The Heart of Irenaeus's Theology," in *Irenaeus: Life, Scripture, Legacy*, ed. Paul Foster and Sarah Parvis (Minneapolis: Fortress Press, 2012), 133–40, at 135.
38. Ibid., 138.
39. The first known use of the Greek word "*Trias*" for God is found in Theophilus of Antioch.
40. AH 4.31.2.
41. See Anthony Briggman, *Irenaeus of Lyons and the Theology of the Holy Spirit* (Oxford: Oxford University Press, 2012).
42. *Demonstration*, 5.
43. Ibid.
44. Most of the later tradition will see Christ as Wisdom and Word of God.
45. AH 4.20.4.
46. While scholars such as Steenberg (*Irenaeus on Creation*, 104n11) think that the two hand image applies to the whole creation, Briggman (*Irenaeus of Lyons*, 114n41) sees it as limited to the creation of

the human.

47. AH 4. Preface, 4.

48. Behr, *Irenaeus of Lyons*, 123.

49. Behr, *Irenaeus of Lyons*, 165; *Asceticism and Anthropology*, 38.

50. AH 5.16.2.

51. AH 5.6.1. See Behr, *Irenaeus of Lyons*, 157.

52. Ibid.

53. See Minns, *Irenaeus*, 75.

54. AH 4.6.6.

55. AH 5.16.2.

56. AH 2.22.4.

57. Irenaeus Steenberg, "Tracing the Irenaean Legacy," in *Irenaeus*, eds., Foster and Parvis, 199–211, at 210.

58. AH 3.18.7.

59. AH 3.19.1.

60. AH 4.20.7.

61. AH 5.33.4.

62. Minns, *Irenaeus*, 142.

63. AH 5.35.1–2.

64. AH 5.32.1–2.

65. AH 5.35.2.

66. AH 5.33.3.

67. AH 5.33.3.

68. Irenaeus points out that this picture of the wonderfully fruitful earth is "borne witness to in writing, by Papias, the hearer of John, and a companion of Polycarp" (AH 5.33.4).

69. AH 5.36.1.

70. Ibid.

71. Ibid.

72. Hans Urs von Balthasar, *The Glory of the Lord: A Theological Aesthetics, II. Studies in Theological Style: Clerical Styles* (Edinburgh: T&T Clark, 1984), 93.

3.

Athanasius of Alexandria (c. 297–373)

Life and Context: Athanasius grew up in Alexandria, a great trading city and centre of learning, with an important Christian catechetical school. As a young man, he was educated in Greek rhetoric and philosophy and gained a deep knowledge of the Bible. He was mentored by Bishop Alexander, became his secretary, and was ordained a deacon in 319. About this time a conflict erupted between Alexander and Arius, an influential local priest. Arius defended a subordinationist view of the Word of God—denying the eternity and divinity of the Word. Many others shared Arius's views, including powerful bishops like Eusebius of Nicomedia. When the conflict escalated, the Emperor Constantine called the Council of Nicaea in 325. Athanasius attended the council with Alexander. Arius was condemned and the Word was declared to be fully and eternally divine, of one being or substance (*homoousios*) with the Father. Athanasius succeeded Alexander as bishop in 328. He would be in continual conflict with Arius and others who held non-Nicene views of the Word. Athanasius was patriarch of Alexandria for forty-five years, but he spent seventeen of these years in five exiles, in Trier (Germany), Rome, the monasteries of the Egyptian desert (twice), and close to Alexandria. He found supporters in the West, among the monks of Egypt, and the Christian community in Alexandria. Facing strong opposition from anti-Nicene emperors and bishops, Athanasius remained a

> powerful advocate of Nicene theology, insisting on the full and eternal divinity of the Word and, later, of the Holy Spirit. By the end of his life the church in the East was coming to a new consensus on pro-Nicene theology, and Athanasius's life's work was carried forward by younger bishops like the three Cappadocians, Basil, Gregory of Nazianzus, and Gregory of Nyssa. The Council of Constantinople of 381 reaffirmed Nicaea and taught the full divinity of the Holy Spirit.

Athanasius's theology is a biblical, narrative theology of God's action in creation and salvation through the Word and in the Spirit. At its center is the incarnation of the Word, the life, death and resurrection of Christ that overcomes death and transforms creaturely existence. What Athanasius defends is the realism of this story, the conviction that Jesus is the eternal, divine Word and Wisdom of God, and that the Spirit who unites creatures to this eternal Word is not a creature but the uncreated gift, the Holy Spirit of God.

Athanasius discusses creation from the perspective of the cross of Jesus.[1] When he treats the creation of the world in his double work *Against the Greeks-On the Incarnation*,[2] his starting point is the scandal of the cross. His response to those who mock the idea of a crucified savior is to show that the one on the cross is the eternal Word who enters into death to bring salvation to the whole creation. Those who mock the cross, he says, fail to understand that the crucified Christ is "the Savior of the universe and that the cross was not the ruin but the salvation of creation."[3] The Word of the Cross is the Word of creation. So John Behr writes: "It is the Word of the Cross, or the Word on the Cross, that Athanasius expounds by describing how all things have come into being by and for him."[4]

GOD CREATES THROUGH THE WORD IN THE SPIRIT

Athanasius always sees creation in the light of Christ.[5] What John 1:3 says of the Word of God is foundational for his theology: "All things came into being through him, and without him not one thing came into being." Athanasius interprets biblical references to the Word and the Wisdom of God in an intertextual way. So when Paul calls Christ "the Wisdom of God" (1 Cor 1:24, 30), Athanasius understands this in relation to Wisdom's description of her cosmic role in creation in Proverbs: "When he marked out the foundations of the earth, then I was beside him, like a master worker" (8:29). God creates through God's Wisdom and it is this Wisdom that we encounter in the cross of Christ. Athanasius refers often to Christ as the *Wisdom of God*, the *Radiance of God*, and the *Image of God*, as well as the *Word of God* and the *Son of God*.

Athanasius sees God as radically beyond creaturely limits and as beyond comprehension, but precisely as such, as boundlessly generous to creatures and as intimately present to them. There is, then, in Athanasius, a "simultaneous contrast and interplay" between God's radical beyondness and God's "goodness and loving kindness (*philanthopia*)."[6] Creation is the relationship whereby the God beyond comprehension becomes the generous source of existence for finite created beings. In Athanasius's view, generosity characterizes God's relations with creatures from the beginning.

His strong concept of creation *ex nihilo* means that Athanasius sees creatures, in themselves, as having no reason for their own existence. They exist out of nothing at every point. Of themselves they are inherently unstable and insecure in their existence. They continue to exist and flourish only because of the divine benevolence by which God continually creates each entity through the Word. Creation, then, concerns not only the original existence of things, but their continued existence and flourishing. Creatures exist and continue in existence because they participate in the Word of God:

> After making everything by his own eternal Word and bringing creation into existence, he did not abandon it to be carried away and suffer through its own nature, lest it run the risk of returning to nothing. But being good, he governs and establishes the whole world through his Word who is himself God, in order that creation, illuminated by the leadership, providence and ordering of the Word, may be able to remain firm, since it *participates* in the Word who is truly from the Father and is aided by him to exist, and lest it suffer what would happen, I mean a relapse into nonexistence, if it were not protected by the Word.[7]

From the creaturely side, creation is an ongoing relation of participation, by which creatures exist securely because they partake of the Word of God. In the above text, Athanasius speaks of the Word of God as "bringing into existence," "governing," "establishing," "leading," "providing for," and "ordering" creation. He goes on to say that the Word is "present in all things" and "gives life and protection to everything, everywhere, to each individually and to all together."[8]

The Wisdom/Word brings all the diverse creatures of the natural world and all the elements of nature into balance and harmony. Athanasius offers a musical image for the integrating work of divine Wisdom: "The Wisdom of God, holding the universe like a lyre," draws together the variety of created things, "thus producing in beauty and harmony a single world and a single order within it."[9] Because of the Word all the elements of creation work together in a kind of kinship:

> Through him and his power fire does not fight with cold, nor the moist with the dry, but things which of themselves are opposites come together like friends and kin, animating the

> visible world, and becoming the principles of existence of bodies. By obedience to the Word of God things on earth receive life and things in heaven subsist. Through him all the sea and the great ocean limit their movements to their proper boundaries, and all the dry land is covered with all kinds of different plants, as I said above. And so that I do not have to prolong my discourse by naming each visible thing, there is nothing existing or created which did not come into being and subsist in him and through him, as the theologian says: "In the beginning was the Word and the Word was with God and the Word was God. All things were made by him and without him nothing was made" (John 1:1–3).[10]

If it is through the Word that all things exist and are brought into productive relationship with one another, what is the role of the Holy Spirit in the act of creation? In fact, in Athanasius's earlier work, *Against the Greeks–On the Incarnation*, his whole focus is on the divinity of the Word, and he has little to say about the Spirit. But in his *Orations against the Arians*[11] and particularly in his *Letters to Serapion*,[12] he articulates a rich theology of the Holy Spirit. In defending the full divinity of the Spirit he insists on the Spirit's role in creation with the Father and the Word. Athanasius does not limit the Spirit's role to sanctification, like Origen, but finds the Spirit at work in every aspect of God's action towards creatures. In the second of his *Letters to Serapion*, he quotes Psalm 104:30, "When you send forth your Spirit they are created," and then comments:

> Seeing that this has been written, it is clear that the Spirit is not a creature but is involved in the act of creating. The Father creates all things through the Word in the Spirit. For where the Word is, there also is the Spirit, and the things created through the Word have their strength to exist through the Spirit from the Word. Thus it is written in Psalm 32: *By the Word of the Lord the heavens were made, and by the Spirit of his mouth all their power* [Ps 32:6].[13]

Here we find a classical statement of a fully Trinitarian theology of creation: The Father creates all things through the Word in the Spirit. It is typical of Athanasius to insist that where the Word is, there also is the Spirit. In his view, the Spirit is not apart from the Word either in creation or in salvation, but is always in the Word: "The Spirit cannot be divided from the Son. . . . For the Spirit is not external to the Word, but is in the Word, and through the Word is in God."[14] Athanasius speaks of the Holy Spirit as "that which joins creatures to the Word."[15] For him the indwelling Spirit is the fully divine bond that unites creatures to the Word and, through the Word, to the Father. He sees the Spirit as actualizing all that is done by the Father through the Son: "For there is nothing which is not brought into being and actualized through the Word in the Spirit."[16] In the divine act of continuous creation, the Spirit enables each creature to be open to, and to receive, the creative Word.

Creation, then, is a fully Trinitarian act by which the world of creatures partakes of the Word in the Spirit. It is only through this participation that individual creatures exist and interact in the community of creation. Not only creation, but also new creation, occurs through this structure of participation of the Word in the Spirit: "the Father creates and renews all things through the Word in the Holy Spirit."[17] The consistent use of the two propositions—*through* and *in*—points to Athanasius's view of the distinction of roles within the one action of the Trinity in creation and new creation. Athanasius sums up his view of the Christian tradition on the Trinity in act:

> So, the Trinity is holy and perfect, confessed in Father and Son and Holy Spirit. It has nothing foreign or external mixed with it, nor is it composed of Creator and creatures, but is entirely given to creating and making. It is self-consistent and indivisible in nature, and has one activity. The Father does all things

> through the Word in the Holy Spirit. In this way is the unity of the Holy Trinity preserved, and in this way is the one God preached in the Church, *who is above all and through all and in all* (Eph 4:6)—*above all* as Father, as beginning, as source; *through all*, through the Word; *in all*, through the Holy Spirit. It is not a Trinity in name alone and in linguistic expression, but in truth and actual existence.[18]

In this text, Athanasius expresses his radical commitment to the unity and indivisibility of the Holy Trinity, and the ontological distinction between the divine Three and the world of creatures. The indivisible Trinity is united in action (*energeia*). Yet immediately Athanasius expresses the proper distinctions in this one act: "For the Father does all things through the Word and in the Holy Spirit," and reinforces this distinction with his quotation from Ephesians, going on to insist on the reality of the Three in "truth," and in "actual existence."[19]

CREATION SPRINGS FROM THE GENERATIVITY OF TRINITARIAN LIFE

Athanasius sees the divine life of the Trinity as wonderfully dynamic and fruitful. This becomes apparent in his delight in bringing together the various biblical names or titles that can be applied to Jesus Christ, such as *Radiance*, *Wisdom*, *Life*, *River*, along with *Word*, *Image*, *Power*, and following Irenaeus, *Hand*, as well as *Son*.[20] He calls them symbols (*paradeigmata*) and sees them as revealing partial insight into divine being: "Since human nature is not capable of comprehension of God, Scripture has placed before us such symbols (*paradeigmata*) and such images (*eikonas*), so that we may understand from them however slightly and obscurely, as much as is accessible to us."[21] These symbols have a dynamic and correlational character.[22] The Father cannot be Father without the Son. There is no Light without its Radiance. There is no Fountain without its flowing River. The symbols point to the dynamic generativity that is at the heart of Trinitarian life.

Athanasius shows how these symbols apply not only to the Father and the Word, but also the Spirit. God is a Fountain, ever pouring forth a River from which we drink in the Spirit. God is a Light with its eternal Radiance that enlightens us in the Spirit. God is the Father, eternally begetting the Son in whom we participate by adoption as God's children in the Spirit. God is the Fountain of Wisdom, bringing forth the Wisdom of God, which we receive through the Spirit of Wisdom. God is the Source of Life, Life, and the Life-Giving Spirit.[23] As Anatolios points out, "in each case the Father is the source, the Son is the outgoing manifestation and imaged content of the source, and the Spirit is the outward actualization of that content in and towards creation."[24]

In his argument against opponents who claim the Word had a beginning, Athanasius insists that the wonderful fruitfulness of God's creation clearly must point back to its source in the *eternal* generativity of divine life. The fecundity of creation can only be grounded in the eternal dynamic generativity of divine life. If, as his opponents suppose, the creative Word/Wisdom of God were a creature who had a beginning, then this would completely undermine what Athanasius calls the eternal "generative nature" of God.[25] If the divine Word is a creature who had a beginning, then God would not be eternally generative. The divine being would then be like a fountain that is dry, a light that does not shine. Athanasius finds a perverse emptiness in such a view of God:

> In accord with them, let not God be of a generative nature, so that there may be no Word nor Wisdom nor any Image at all of his own essence. For if he is not Son, then neither is he Image. But if there is no Son, how then do you say that God is Creator, if indeed it is through the Word and in Wisdom

> that everything that is made comes to be and without which nothing comes to be, and yet, according to you, God does not possess that in which and through which he makes all things (cf. Wis 9:2; Jn 1:3; Ps 104:20, 24). But if, according to them, the divine essence itself is not fruitful but barren, like a light that does not shine and a fountain that is dry, how are they not ashamed to say that God has creative energy?[26]

For Athanasius, by contrast, God is a Light with its everlasting Radiance that enlightens us in the Spirit, a Fountain always pouring forth a River of living water from which we creatures drink in the Spirit. The full divinity of the Word and the Spirit is absolutely essential to the dynamic life of God that is the source of the creation for a world of creatures. The Trinitarian God that he defends is a God of endless life, a God who is fruitful by nature. The stars of the night sky, rain forests with their uncounted life forms, this bird I can see in a tree, this human being near me, all spring from God's eternally dynamic, wonderfully fruitful, and unthinkably relational being.

THE IMMEDIACY OF THE PRESENCE OF GOD TO EACH CREATURE

Athanasius has a particularly strong conviction of the immediacy of the triune God to all creatures. Such a position can have important consequences for an ecological theology and for ecological ethics. Athanasius's reasons, of course, are not ecological ones; his priority, as always, is to articulate and defend the full divinity of the Word and Spirit.

Athanasius opposes a dominant assumption of the worldview of his time, an assumption made by various forms of Platonic philosophy and shared by many Christian theologians and bishops, that a created intermediary is needed between the entities of the world around us and the holy, transcendent God. The created intermediary might be the Demiurge, the Logos, the Soul or simply the whole world of ideas. In this view, creatures participate in the intermediary, while the intermediary participates in God, but is not God.

For Athanasius's Christian opponents, the transcendent otherness of God seems to rule out a direct relationship between God and created entities as unthinkable. A direct connection would be unworthy of God and would compromise the absolute transcendence of God. To Arius, and many others, this seems a proper assumption to make if one holds a high view of God's otherness. And from a creaturely perspective, finite creatures would not be able to bear the blazing touch of the infinite all-holy God. For these reasons, the opponents argue, the good God creates the Word as a mediator to carry out God's purposes. In Peter Leithart's summary of their view, the Word of God "serves as a buffer between God and creation."[27]

Athanasius completely rejects the notion of any such buffer. In his view there is absolutely no intermediary between God and God's creatures. He certainly shares with his opponents a conviction of the radical otherness of the Creator, and he insists on the poverty of being of all creatures—they exist not from themselves but from God. Athanasius's theology of creation *ex nihilo* means that there is an infinite difference, an ontological gulf, between creatures and their Creator. How, then, does Athanasius see this gulf as being bridged? Not, for him, by any created intermediaries but only by God. He certainly agrees with his opponents that God creates through the Word. But for Athanasius, this Word is no created intermediary but the very presence of God to creatures in self-giving and humble love. The Word of God is truly God, who "condescends" to engage with creatures in a way that lovingly respects their being and their limits. Commenting on the Colossians text that speaks of Christ as "the firstborn of creation" (1:15), Athanasius says:

> For it is clear to all that he was called the "firstborn" of creation not as being of himself a creature nor because of any kinship of essence with all creation, but because the Word condescended (*sunkatabebēke*) to the things coming into being when he was creating them at the beginning so that they be enabled to come into being. For they would not have withstood his nature, being that of the unmitigated splendor of the Father, if he had not condescended (*sunkatabas*) by the Father's love for humanity and supported, strengthened, and carried them into being.[28]

The word *condescension*, in Athanasius's usage, does not suggest a patronizing attitude, as it can in contemporary usage. It simply has its literal meaning: In both creation and incarnation the Word of God "comes down" to be with creatures and is immediately present to them in their finitude out of generous, compassionate love. So while Athanasius's model of participation in God is broadly Platonic, it is developed by him in a distinctively Christian way. Khaled Anatolios points out that what Athanasius does is radically to transform the idea of divine transcendence by means of the biblical categories of divine mercy and loving kindness. Because of these divine attributes, Anatolios comments, God can transcend God's own transcendence.[29] Because of the divine mercy and love, no creaturely mediation is needed. For Athanasius, then, the character of God in creating accords with the kenotic character of God revealed in the incarnation.[30] In both creation and incarnation, the Word of God is a self-humbling God, who descends to be with creatures, for the sake of their creation and deification.[31]

The radical ontological distinction between God and all creatures is bridged not by a created intermediary, but solely from God's side, in a loving generosity that is itself fully divine. Because Word and Spirit are one with the Father in essence, their creative presence to creatures means that the Father, the Source of All, is also immediately present to each creature.[32] As Athanasius puts it, using again a favorite image, the one who experiences the Radiance is enlightened by the Sun itself and not by any intermediary.[33]

In Athanasius, then, we find a theology of the immediate presence of the triune God to all creatures. In the act of creation, the Word can be certainly be thought of as a mediator, but only as a fully divine mediator of Trinitarian presence. Only a Trinitarian theology of God as Creator enables us to glimpse the immediacy of the relationship between God and God's creatures. Every creature on Earth, every whale, every sparrow, exists by participation in the Source of All through the Word in the Spirit—"not one of them is forgotten in God's sight" (Luke 12:6).

DEIFICATION OF HUMAN BEINGS AND WITH THEM THE WIDER NATURAL WORLD

In a particularly rich passage in his *Orations against the Arians*, Athanasius reflects on the Wisdom of God as the Creator of all things, and on the whole creation as bearing the created imprint of Wisdom. It is this created imprint of Wisdom that enables creatures to be and to flourish:

> But in order that creatures may not only be but also thrive in well-being, it pleased God to have his own Wisdom condescend to creatures. Therefore he placed in each and every creature and in the totality of creation a certain imprint (*typon*) and reflection of the Image of Wisdom, so that the things that come into being may prove to be works that are wise and worthy of God.[34]

All the creatures around us, in his view, bear the imprint and reflection of the Image of Wisdom. This can only mean that, for Athanasius, all creatures are in some way created in the image of God. In human beings, he say, "the wisdom that comes to be within us is an image of his Wisdom."[35] Because our human wisdom is an image of divine Wisdom, we have the capacity to recognize the imprint of Wisdom in other creatures—"Thus did the imprint of Wisdom come to be in created things, so that the world, as I have said, may come to know its Creator and Word, and through him, the Father."[36]

Athanasius points to Sirach where Wisdom is said to be "poured forth" (Sir 1:18) upon all God's works. He argues that this refers not to Wisdom's divine being, but to Wisdom's image that is poured out in all creatures.[37] He thus distinguishes between divine Wisdom and her created image in creatures: "For while Wisdom herself is Creator and Maker, her imprint is created in the works and is [made] according to the image of the Image."[38] Athanasius notes, with Paul, that in spite of God's attributes being evident in the creation since the beginning, human beings have over and over failed to recognize God and have instead worshipped false gods (Rom 1:19–21). Nevertheless, God does not abandon humanity, but out of extravagant divine generosity, sends divine Wisdom to be with us in the flesh:

> For God willed to make himself known no longer as in previous times through the image and shadow of wisdom, which is in creatures, but has made the true Wisdom herself take flesh and become a mortal human being and endure the death of the cross, so that henceforth all those who put their faith in him may be saved. But it is the same Wisdom of God, who previously manifested herself, and her Father through herself, by means of her image in creatures—and thus is said to be "created"—but which later on, being Word, became flesh (John 1:14) as John said.[39]

The Word and Wisdom of God becomes flesh, first, in order to overcome death and, second, so that in in our knowing of the Word "in the body" we might know the Father.[40] Athanasius sees humans being given, at their creation, a special grace of participating in the Word, and in this way made according to the Image and sharers in eternal life. But they reject God and lose the gift of eternal life. God's response is unthinkably generous: the Word in whom all things are created comes in the flesh to bring forgiveness of sin and to enter into death and overcome it in the power of resurrection. The Word who is the Image of the Father comes to humanity to renew this image in us, to seek out the lost, bring forgiveness of sins, and abolish our debt to death.

Athanasius makes use of a range of biblical images for the death and resurrection of Christ which he finds in Paul and in Hebrews, and also offers an overarching vision of what God does for us in Christwith his theology of deification. This theology appears in the well-known passage of his *On the Incarnation*: "For he became human that we might become divine."[41] But he uses deification language, the verb *theopoiéō*, and the noun he coins, *theopoiēsis*, much more often in his later anti-Arian writing, to defend the real divinity of the Word, who is made flesh that we might be made divine: "So he was not a human being and later became God. But, being God, he later became a human being in order that we may be divinized."[42]

Athanasius builds on Irenaeus and others, but he uses deification language more often than his predecessors, clarifies its meaning, pairing it with the synonyms: adoption, renewal, salvation, sanctification, grace, transcendence, illumination, and vivification.[43] Because the Word is eternal and the source of deification, he insists against his opponents that the Word of God is not deified. Importantly, however, he holds that the bodily humanity of Jesus *is* deified by its union with the Word, and it is this that enables the deification of humanity.[44]

This process embraces more than humanity. Athanasius

sees an ontological transformation in creaturely reality occurring through the incarnation, a transformation that is already at work not only in human beings but also in the wider creation. Athanasius's focus is on humanity, but he seems naturally to include the wider creation. In the following example he refers explicitly to Romans 8:19–23 and Colossians 1:15–20, and clearly includes the whole creation in the liberation that comes through Christ's resurrection:

> The truth that refutes them is that he is called "firstborn among many brothers" (Rom 8:29) because of the kinship of the flesh, and "firstborn from the dead" (Col 1:18) because the resurrection of the dead comes from him and after him, and "firstborn of all creation" (Col 1:15) because of the Father's love for humanity, on account of which he not only gave consistence to all things in his Word but brought it about that the creation itself, of which the apostle says that it "awaits the revelation of the children of God," will at a certain point be delivered "from the bondage of corruption into the glorious freedom of the children of God" (Rom 8:19, 21).[45]

In another example, this time defending the full divinity of the Spirit, he insists that both Word and Spirit are at work in the bodily incarnation of the Word, for the sake of uniting and reconciling the whole creation with the Father:

> Thus also when the Word visited the holy Virgin Mary, the Spirit came to her with him, and the Word in the Spirit formed the body and accommodated it to himself, out of a desire to join and present the created order to the Father through himself, and *to reconcile all things in himself, making peace between the things that are in heaven and the things that are on earth* (Col 1:20).[46]

In other places, Athanasius speaks more generally of creation being deified, often in the context of the divine adoption of human beings: "In him [the Spirit] the Word divinizes all that has come into existence. And the one in whom creatures are divinized cannot himself be external to the divinity of the Father."[47] It may be that Athanasius's focus in on the human, but it is clear that he is not interested in making sharp distinctions between humanity and the rest of creation. From the texts mentioned earlier, which refer directly to the wider natural world, it is clear that Athanasius's view is inclusive. The Word is made flesh that human beings might be forgiven, deified, and adopted as beloved sons and daughters and that the rest of creation might be transformed in Christ in its own proper way. Late in his life Athanasius writes of Christ as "the Liberator of all flesh and of all creation (cf. Rom 8.21)," and as "the Creator and Maker coming to be in a creature so that, by granting freedom to all in himself, he may present the world to the Father and give peace to all, in heaven and on earth."[48]

TRAJECTORIES

Key aspects of Athanasius's theology of creation that can have new meaning in today's world include the following:

1. Creation and deifying incarnation are understood as intrinsically interconnected—the Word of creation is the Word made flesh for the sake of creatures.
2. Creation is an ongoing relation of participation, by which creatures exist because they partake of the Word of God in the Spirit.
3. Athanasius offers us a variety of biblical symbols for the Trinity that point to the dynamic life and beauty of the God beyond all language: Light, Radiance, Enlightening Spirit; Fountain, Stream of Living Water, Spirit of whom we drink; Font of Wisdom, Wisdom herself, Spirit of Wisdom; and Father, Son, Adopting Spirit.
4. God's action towards creation is always the action of the

Trinity: It is radically one, but the Three act in distinct ways within the one act: "the Father creates and renews all things through the Word in the Holy Spirit."[49]

5. The actions of the Trinity spring from the eternal dynamic generativity of divine life where the Light always Radiates, the Spring always produces its flowing Stream, the Father eternally generates the Son.
6. God is immediately present through the Word and in the Spirit to all creatures enabling their existence and their flourishing. The natural world is the place of divine indwelling.
7. Each creature bears the imprint of the Image of the Wisdom of God.
8. Athanasius's theology of deification and final fulfillment involves not just human beings, but with them, in their own proper ways, all creatures. Along with human beings the natural world will be transfigured and fulfilled through Christ in the Spirit.

Notes

1. See Khaled Anatolios, *Athanasius: The Coherence of His Thought* (London: Routledge, 1998), 28.
2. Greek text with English translation of *Against the Greeks* and *On the Incarnation* (= *Incarnation*) can be found in *Athanasius: Contra Gentes and De Incarnatione*, trans. Robert Thomson (Oxford, UK: Clarendon, 1971).
3. Athanasius, *Against the Greeks*, 5.
4. John Behr, *The Nicene Faith: Part 1: True God of True God*, The Formation of Christian Theology, vol. 2 (Crestwood, NY: St. Vladimir's Seminary Press, 2004), 181.

5. This chapter builds on my *Partaking of God: Trinity, Evolution and Ecology* (Collegeville, MN: Liturgical, 2014), and "Athanasius's Letters to Serapion: Resource for a Twenty-First Century Theology of God the Trinity," *Phronema* 29:2 (2014), 41–64.
6. Anatolios, *Athanasius* (London and New York: Routledge, 2004), 40.
7. Athanasius, *Against the Greeks*, 41. I have modified the translation, replacing *shares* with the stronger word *participates* as translation of Athanasius's *metalambánousa.*
8. Ibid.
9. Ibid., 42.
10. Ibid.
11. Athanasius wrote the first two of his *Orations against the Arians* (=*Arians*) about 339 during his second exile in Rome. They can be found in K. Metzler and K. Savvidis, *Athanasius Werke* 1:1 (Berlin and New York: Walter de Gruyter, 1998–2000). I will make use of the partial translation in Anatolios, *Athanasius*, 87–175.
12. There is a new critical edition of the *Letters to Serapion on the Holy Spirit* (=*Serapion*), eds., D. Wyrwa and S. Kyriakos, *Athanasius Werke I:I. Die Dogmatischen Schriften. 4. Lieferung. Epistulae I–IV ad Serapionem* (Berlin and New York: Walter de Gruyter, 2010). I will use the new translation from this edition by M. Del Cogliano, A. Radde-Gallwitz and L. Ayres, in *Works on the Spirit: Athanasius and Didymus: Athanasius's Letters to Serapion on the Holy Spirit and Didymus's On the Holy Spirit* (New York: St. Vladimir's Seminary Press, 2011), 51-137.
13. Athanasius, *Serapion* 2.13.4.
14. Ibid., 2.14.2–4.
15. Ibid., 1.25.5.
16. Ibid., 1.31.2.
17. Ibid., 1.24.6.
18. Ibid., 1.28.2.
19. Athanasius continues with a strong statement that each of the Three—the Father, Word, and Spirit—truly exists, and explicitly rules out Sabellian modalism as well as Greek polytheism (*Serapion*

1.28.2–3).

20. On these symbols see Khaled Anatolios, *Retrieving Nicaea: The Development and Meaning of Trinitarian Doctrine* (Grand Rapids, MI: Baker Academic, 2011), 141–43; Peter J. Leithart, *Athanasius* (Grand Rapids, MI: Baker Academic, 2011), 41–53.
21. Athanasius, *Arians* 2.32.
22. Ibid., 2.31–32.
23. See Athanasius, *Serapion* 1.19.1–9, where he offers biblical texts to support each of these references to the Father, Son, and Spirit.
24. Anatolios, *Retrieving Nicaea*, 142–43.
25. Athanasius, *Arians* 2.2.
26. Ibid.
27. Leithart, *Athanasius*, 91.
28. Athanasius, *Arians* 2.64.
29. Anatolios, *Retrieving Nicaea*, 104.
30. Ibid.
31. Athanasius, *Arians* 1.39; 3.52.
32. Anatolios, *Athanasius: The Coherence of His Thought*, 113.
33. Athanasius, *Arians* 3.14.
34. Ibid., 2.78.
35. Ibid.
36. Ibid.
37. Ibid., 2.79.
38. Ibid., 2.80.
39. Ibid., 2.81.
40. Athanasius, *Incarnation* 10, 14.
41. Ibid., 54.
42. Athanasius, *Arians* 1.39.
43. See N. Russell, *The Doctrine of Deification in the Greek Patristic Tradition* (Oxford: Oxford University Press, 2004), 177–78.
44. Athanasius, *Arians* 1.42.

45. Ibid., 2.63.

46. Athanasius, *Serapion* 1.31.12.

47. Ibid., 1.25.5.

48. Athanasius, *To Adelphius* 4 (in Anatolios, *Athanasius*, 238, 242).

49. Athanasius, *Serapion* 1.24.6.

4.

Augustine of Hippo (354–430)

Life and Context: Augustine was born at Thagaste in Numidia (now Algeria), a small Roman town about forty miles from the African coast. His mother Monica was a baptized Christian, while his father Patricius became a Christian late in life and was baptized on his death bed. Augustine, well-educated at Madaura and Carthage, and a brilliant student, became a teacher of rhetoric in Carthage. In his search for wisdom he came under the influence of the Manichee movement, but his engagement with Neo-Platonic philosophy led him to abandon the materialism and dualism of Manichaeism. He left Carthage for Rome, and soon found a teaching position in Milan. Attracted at first by the rhetoric of Ambrose, bishop of Milan, and then by his theology, and influenced by Monica, Augustine embraced Christianity and was baptized by Ambrose at Easter in 387. He abandoned his relationship with an unnamed woman whom he clearly loved, and with whom he had a beloved son, Adeodatus. After a mystical experience with Monica at Ostia, and her death soon afterwards, Augustine returned to Thagaste intending to lead a monastic life. But in 391 Valerius, bishop of Hippo, insisted that he be ordained a priest. In 396, he became the bishop of Hippo, and remained in this role until he died at the age of seventy-six, as the Vandals besieged his city. As a North African bishop he was much involved in theological controversies, particularly the Donatist controversy over the holiness of the church, and the Pelagian controversy over grace. Augustine's writings, his hundred and thirteen books, eight hundred sermons, and two hundred and fifty letters, have had an enormous influence on Western Christianity. Among his best-known works are his *Confessions*, a personal account of his spiritual journey, *The City of God*, a Christian approach to history written after the sack of Rome by the Visigoths in 410, and his theological masterpiece, *On the Trinity*.

Near the end of *The City of God*, Augustine reflects on the gifts that the Creator has poured out on humanity. In spite of human sin, he finds the goodness of God abundantly evident in the creation of the human. He goes on to ask how he might tell of the beauty of the rest of creation:

> Shall I speak of the manifold and various loveliness of sky, and earth, and sea; of the plentiful supply and wonderful qualities of the light; of sun, moon, and stars; of the shade of trees; of the colors and perfume of flowers; of the multitude of birds, all differing in plumage and in song; of the variety of animals, of which the smallest in size are often the most wonderful—the works of ants and bees astonishing us more than the huge bodies of whales? Shall I speak of the sea, which itself is so grand a spectacle, when it arrays itself as it were in vestures of various colors, now running through every shade of green, and again becoming purple or blue?[1]

Augustine seems to have been a keen observer of the natural world, and to have been open to receive it as the gift of a bountiful and generous Creator. Among the many possible approaches to Augustine's theology of creation, I will limit my focus to his interpretations of the creation accounts in Genesis. Throughout his life Augustine was preoccupied with these texts. The Manichees rejected the Old Testament as irrational and ridiculed the first chapters of Genesis, interpreting them extremely literally, and then pointing to absurdities they found in such a literal interpretation of the text. With their dualistic understanding of both good and evil as originating principles, they flatly opposed Genesis's theology of the one Creator and its teaching of the goodness of creation. As a former auditor of the Manicheans, Augustine felt a life-long responsibility to defend the reliability of the Bible, and the one God who makes all things from nothing and declares them to be good. He explores the opening chapters of Genesis in three commentaries, as well focusing on them in the last three books of his *Confessions* (397–400) and in the eleventh book of *The City of God* (413–27).

His first attempt at a commentary, written as a layman in the monastic community of Thagaste soon after his return to Africa, is his *On Genesis: A Refutation of the Manichees* (388–89),[2] in which he very often resorts to figurative interpretation. After his ordination as a priest, he tried again, convinced that he should attempt to offer a more literal interpretation, but was unable to finish the work: his *Unfinished Literal Commentary on Genesis* (393–94). Finally, as a bishop, Augustine gathered all his resources in a final commentary written over a fifteen year period, his *The Literal Meaning of Genesis* (c. 401–16). This work, which represents his mature thought and is by far his longest commentary, will be the focus of this chapter.

The Literal Meaning of Genesis is concerned with the two accounts of creation found in the opening three chapters of Genesis. Books 1–4 deal with the Seven-Day account of creation. Book 5 discusses the meaning of the fact that there are two biblical accounts. Books 6–12 then take up the second account of creation, discussing in detail such matters as Adam's body and soul, the garden of paradise, the creation of Eve, the origins of human souls, the fall, the expulsion from paradise, and the nature of visions. My focus will not be on

Augustine's theological anthropology, but on his idea of a literal interpretation of Genesis, his understanding of the role of scientific knowledge in this act of interpretation, and his understanding of creation as possessing a two-fold structure, as both simultaneous and unfolding in time.

LITERAL INTERPRETATION

Augustine begins his book by explaining his approach to biblical interpretation. He sees Scripture as possessing both figurative and literal meanings. He has no doubt that Genesis can be interpreted in a figurative sense, that is, in the light of Christ. After all Paul says of the earlier Scriptures that such things "happened among them in figure" (1 Cor 10:11).[3] So Augustine's question is whether the events of Genesis have only a figurative sense or whether they also have a literal sense. He tells us immediately what he means by this literal sense—it is the interpretation of events "as a faithful account of what actually happened."[4]

Augustine recognizes that some things in the Bible are purely figurative, such as the parables of Jesus.[5] He points to the figurative character of the Song of Songs and notes that it has a different character from the books of Samuel and Kings.[6] In his view, Genesis is not to be interpreted like the Song of Songs, but is to be understood as pointing to what God really did in the creation of the world. At the heart of Augustine's idea of a literal interpretation is his conviction that Genesis describes events that truly happened, the creation of the universe of creatures and of human beings. Edmund Hill says that, for him, this act of creation is "the happening" par excellence. It is, however, a "completely unique and incomparable event that does not take place within history, but is instead the basis of time and history."[7] As Augustine tells his readers, "time begins from the creation rather than the creation from time."[8]

It is important to note that Augustine's idea of a literal interpretation involves a critical recognition of the limited nature of the anthropomorphic God-language of Genesis. And it involves the further recognition that there are two accounts of creation (Gen 1:1–2:4 and 2:4b–3:24), with the first having God rest on the seventh day at the completion of all God's work, and with the second having God begin to create again. Furthermore, in the two accounts, there are quite different descriptions of the creation of vegetation and of human beings. Augustine's commitment to the idea that the text is to be interpreted as telling what really happened means that he has to labor to make sense of these inconsistencies. In the last section, I will describe how he does this by interpreting the Seven-Day narrative in a way that bears no relation to human experience of solar days—he sees it as pointing to a single primordial act of God. This is clearly far from what many today think of a literal interpretation. Augustine then goes on to treat the second account as historical, with a really existing garden, and a real tree of knowledge of good and evil, and with the creation of the first humans and their first sin as real events in time.

A further aspect of Augustine's interpretive method is its questioning and searching nature. It resists easy answers and short cuts. The reader of the opening pages of this book is confronted with an extraordinary series of questions, some of which will later find answers, while others will not. In his *Revisions*, Augustine says of this book: "It is a work in which more questions were asked than answers found; and of those that were found only a few were assured, while the rest were so stated as still to require further investigation."[9] It seems clear that this questioning approach to creation is an integral aspect of Augustine's life-long search into the mystery of God. At one point, he names three criteria for interpreting difficult texts, the intention of the author, the scriptural context, and "sound faith."[10] Augustine applies these, along with other criteria, such as accordance with right reason, diligently but still finds many instances where different explanations are possible, and where no one answer can be proposed with certainty.

He often expresses his views humbly and tentatively. He is clearly open to revising his opinions. In exploring the origin of the human soul, for instance he writes: "So with God's help let us undertake the more thorough examination of this question; and even if we do not end up with a limpid judgment, let us see if we cannot perhaps come to a conclusion of such general acceptability that it would not be absurd for us to hold it until something more certain emerges."[11] He goes on to express the hope that, if others are more certain of the right opinion, they will instruct him in it. However, he adds, if their view is based not on the word of God, nor on clear reasoning, but on their own assumption of certainty, he hopes they will not disdain to share his doubts. Augustine's commitment to a literal interpretation, to what really happened in creation, means that he is also committed to bring into the discussion the best available information from the secular studies of his day that bear on the nature and origin of the world.[12]

BIBLICAL INTERPRETATION AND THE SCIENCE OF THE DAY

In his *The Literal Meaning of Genesis*, Augustine shows evidence of having read widely in all the available fields of learning of the classical world, not only in philosophy but also in mathematics, physics, astronomy, geography, anatomy, medicine, and psychology.[13] He constantly brings this range of learning to bear on his interpretation of the biblical text. At times his discussion of ancient theories can be tedious for a contemporary reader. At other times his insights are strikingly current. What is highly relevant today is his view of the place of science and reason in the theological interpretation of the biblical text.

Augustine was convinced that the truth of faith found in the Scriptures and the truth about the natural world discovered by reason cannot ultimately be in opposition, because they spring from the one truth of God. Where there is an apparent conflict, he sees the work of the interpreter as a twofold task: "So we should show that whatever they have been able to demonstrate from reliable sources about the world of nature is not contrary to our literature, while whatever they may have produced from any of their volumes that is contrary to this literature that is ours, that is, to the Catholic faith, we must either show with some ease, or else believe without any hesitation, to be entirely false."[14] On the one hand, if there is well-based scientific evidence for a position, then the interpreter has the task of showing how this might be compatible with biblical faith. On the other hand, if a clear teaching of the Christian faith is contradicted by a scientific claim, then the interpreter, if he or she can, must show the inadequacy of the scientific account, or if this is not possible at least hold to the truth of faith.

Augustine rejects the two extremes, that of a rationalism that leaves no place for faith, and that of a religion that opposes the evidence of scientific reason: "we are neither seduced by the chatter of false philosophy, nor frightened our of our wits by the superstitions of false religion."[15] He was convinced of the importance, for Christians and nonbelievers alike, of showing that Christian faith does not mean abandoning reason or empirical observation of the natural world. He is particularly severe in his criticism of Christians who stubbornly appeal to their interpretation of the Bible in order to challenge truths well-established by reason and empirical experience. I will include here a long but important quotation from him that will be broken up into four sections. He begins by outlining the kind of well-established knowledge of the natural world he has in mind:

> There is knowledge to be had, after all, about the earth, about the sky, about the other elements of this world, about the movements and revolutions or even the magnitude and distances of the constellations, about the predictable eclipses of moon and sun, about the cycles of years and seasons, about the nature of animals, fruits, stones and everything else of this kind. And it frequently happens that even non-Christians will have knowledge of this sort in a way that they can substantiate with scientific arguments (*certissima ratio*) or experiments (*experientia*).[16]

Augustine could be dealing with the contemporary discussion of science and religion when he brings to the discussion of Genesis knowledge of the empirical world that has been well-established "with scientific arguments or experiments." He clearly has a deep interest in and respect for the integrity of both reason and experimental knowledge, as able to lead to true conclusions about the natural world. As a consequence he is highly critical of unthinking Christians who fail to respect the place of reason and scientific evidence in the interpretation of biblical faith:

> Now it is quite disgraceful and disastrous, something to be on one's guard against at all costs, that they should ever hear Christians spouting what they claim our Christian literature has to say on these topics and talking such nonsense that they can scarcely contain their laughter when they see them to be *toto caelo*, as the saying goes, wide of the mark. And what is so vexing is not that misguided people should be laughed at, as that

> our authors should be assumed by outsiders to have held such views and, to the great detriment of those about whose salvation we are so concerned, should be written off and consigned to the waste paper basket as so many ignoramuses.[17]

When non-Christians see members of the faith community stubbornly hold to views that the nonbelievers know to be absurd or wrong, this becomes an impediment to nonbelievers being prepared to receive the good news of Christ and his resurrection:

> Whenever, you see, they catch out some members of the Christian community making mistakes on a subject which they know inside out, and defending their hollow opinions on the authority of our books, on what grounds are they going to trust those books on the resurrection of the dead and the hope of eternal life and the kingdom of heaven, when they suppose they include any number of mistakes and fallacies on matters which they themselves have been able to master either by experiment or the surest of calculations?[18]

Augustine's deep respect for reason and empirical evidence is evident in his reference to "experiment and the surest of calculations." Just before the passage quoted here, he seems to recognize that some empirical findings can be proved with "absolute certainty."[19] If such an established truth appeared to be in conflict with the Scriptures, he thinks that the problem will likely be with the interpretation: "this is not what divine scripture contained, but what human ignorance had opined."[20] Augustine continues his criticism of Christians who create a stumbling-block for those inside and outside the faith by their intransigent rejection of experience and reason:

> It is impossible to say what trouble and grief such rash self-assured know-alls cause the more cautious and experienced brothers and sisters. Whenever they find themselves challenged and taken to task for some shaky and false theory of theirs by people who do not recognize the authority of our books, they

> try to defend what they have aired with the most frivolous temerity and patent falsehood by bringing forward these same books to justify it. Or they even quote from memory many things said in them which they imagine will provide them with valid evidence, *not understanding either what they are saying, or the matters on which they are asserting themselves* (1 Tim 1:7).[21]

Later in *The Literal Meaning of Genesis*, Augustine offers an important example of his approach to interpretation in his comments on the disputed question of the shape and form of the sky. Is it like a sphere enclosing Earth that is suspended in the middle of the universe, or is it more like a disk (the firmament)? In his response to this question, Augustine notes that some people simply do not understand "the style of the divine utterances."[22] The result of not respecting the style of the text is that when they find something in the text that seems to contradict what they think they know about the natural world, they then have no confidence in the Scriptures when it speaks of more important things. With regard to the shape of the sky, Augustine concludes that there is a need to recognize in interpreting the Scriptures that "the Spirit of God who was speaking through them did not wish to teach people about such things which would contribute nothing to their salvation."[23] The Scriptures are concerned not with the shape of the sky, but with the truths of salvation.

In this passage, Augustine anticipates principles of contemporary theological interpretation of the Bible, respecting the nature of the literary form in question and approaching the text in search of its theological and salvific meaning rather than its scientific presuppositions.[24] He goes on, in the next paragraph, to offer a third: the interpreter is bound to demonstrate that his or her interpretation is not opposed to what is clearly demonstrated by reason and experience about the natural world, including the shape of the sky. Proper interpretation, he says, cannot be opposed "to those explanations, should they happen to be shown by rational arguments to be true, which inform us that they sky has the shape of a hollow globe all around us—provided, once again, it can be proved."[25] Augustine's stance before this controversy of his day might suggest, I think, that were he alive today, he would not be among those who would oppose biological evolution on the basis of Genesis.

GOD'S CREATIVE ACT: SIMULTANEOUS AND DEVELOPING IN TIME

Three things are characteristic of the theology of creation found in *The Literal Meaning of Genesis* and throughout Augustine's other works. The first is that Augustine completely embraces the concept of *creatio ex nihilo*, and opposes all emanationist views, above all those of his Manichean past. All things are created from nothing both in their origin and in their present existence. If God's creative and providential act were to be withdrawn from creatures they would simply cease to exist.[26]

The second characteristic is that for Augustine creation is a fully Trinitarian act. All things are created through the Word, who Augustine sees as the "beginning" of Genesis 1:1. For Augustine, everything that comes to be in creation has its reason (*ratio*), its form and exemplar, in the eternal Word and Wisdom of God.[27] He sees the Holy Spirit, stirring over the waters of creation, as divine goodness and love, creating the goodness of creation. Through the love of the Spirit, creatures are not only brought into existence, but also enabled to abide in their existence.[28] Like Basil before him, Augustine sees the action of the Spirit as brooding over the water "in the way birds brood over their eggs, where that warmth of the mother's body in some way also supports the forming of chicks through a kind of influence of her own kind of love."[29]

A third characteristic, closely connected to the second, is that God's Spirit-given good creation reflects the beauty of its Maker, pointing beyond itself to divine Wisdom. This seems to be the rationale for Augustine's adding three chapters on Genesis to his *Confessions;* after tracing and confessing the loving presence of God in his own life, he then goes on to confess and praise God at work in the whole universe.[30] For Augustine the beauty of creatures gives rise to joy that should lead the recipient to be mindful of the source of beauty.[31] Augustine is aware that sensible beauty of creatures can be ambivalent, and he consistently points to the far greater beauty of their maker, but scholars like Carol Harrison have shown that he also deeply appreciates the beauty of creatures in themselves.[32]

In developing his theology of creation, Augustine recognizes many of the difficulties that modern interpreters find with the book of Genesis. As I have noted, he is critically aware of the limits of anthropomorphic language about God, commenting, for example, on the text that God formed the human from the dust of the ground (Gen 2:7), that the idea "that God molded the man from mud with actual material hands is an excessively childish notion."[33] The transcendent God does not have body parts, does not breathe, does not walk, and does not speak—except through created realities. I have already mentioned, as well, that Augustine was fully conscious that in Genesis there are two accounts of creation, with major problems in sequence between them. Without the benefit of contemporary biblical scholarship, which understands the two accounts as springing from different sources and times, Augustine developed his own interpretation of the two narratives, and used them as a structure on which to build his theology of creation.

His idea of the structure of creation is twofold. First, referring to the Seven-Day account, he sees God's work as a primordial act, involving "those invisible days in which he created all things simultaneously." Second, referring to the second account, he sees God as enabling creation to unfold in ordinary days, "these visible ones in which he is working every day at whatever is being as it were unwrapped in time from those primordial wrappings."[34] The seven days of Genesis (1:1–2:4a) are understood as a description of the original simultaneous creation of all things either actually, or in the case of living creatures, in their potential for existence.[35] Augustine takes with utmost seriousness the idea of simultaneous creation that he finds in his Old Latin version of Sirach 18:1: "He who lives forever created the whole universe simultaneously."[36] He notes the problems in reading the first chapter of Genesis sequentially, where three days pass, with three nights and days, before the creation of the sun and the moon on the fourth day. Such problems of sequence are resolved by his theory of simultaneous creation. He says of the seven days:

> And thus throughout all those days there is just the one day, which is not to be understood after the manner of these days that we see measured and counted by the circuit of the sun, but in a different kind of mode which has to allow for those three days that were mentioned before the fashioning of these lamps in the sky. This mode, you see, does not just operate as far as the fourth day, so that from then on we should be thinking of these usual ones, but right up to the sixth and seventh.[37]

The six days of creation are to be understood as the primordial act by which God creates the whole universe of creatures, either in their actuality or in their potential. Augustine points to the wonderful and inexpressible creativity of the Wisdom of God, "who reaches mightily from end of the earth to the other and she orders all things well" (Wis 8:1). Through Wisdom, all living things are fashioned together, in their specific potentiality, so that what we now see of all living creatures in time springs from "those implanted formulae or ideas (*rationes*) which God so to say scattered like seed in the very moment of fashioning them."[38]

These "ideas" are what Augustine also calls "seminal reasons" or "causal reasons," that God plants in creation from the beginning. These seminal reasons are not physical seeds, but God-given, invisible, seed-like powers in the created world.[39] In Augustine's interpretation, the opening chapter of Genesis is about divine Wisdom creating not just the universe, but also the seminal reasons for every living creature, simultaneously. He sees the seven days as a pedagogical structure that allows the reader to absorb over time what really happened all together:

> And consequently, the one who made all things simultaneously together also made simultaneously these six or seven days, or rather this one day six or seven times repeated. So then, what need was there for the six days to be recounted so distinctly and methodically? It was for the sake of those who cannot arrive at an understanding of the text, 'he created all things together simultaneously," unless Scripture accompanies them more slowly, step by step, to the goal to which it is leading them.[40]

When God rests on the seventh day, this is interpreted as the completion of the whole creation, of every entity and every living creature, in their seminal reasons. When the Eden story begins (Gen 2:4b) God's creative work continues, but it now takes the new form of the divine providential care that allows living creatures to exist and to develop in time. The first account of Genesis, then, tells of the first moment of creation in which God calls all things into existence, at least "in their inchoative state from which they were to develop gradually." The second account "no longer describes an event on the threshold between time and eternity," but describes events happening in time.[41]

Augustine's theory of seminal reasons provides a way of explaining why the second account describes the creation of the plants on earth and the first human beings, when according to the first account they are already created. After the Bible first tells us of simultaneous creation, he says, it then, from the description of the spring of water (Gen 2:6) onwards, informs us about the kinds of things that are made over intervals of time. Augustine notes that the author rightly begins from water, "that element from which all species, whether of animals or grasses or trees, take their rise."[42] He points out that "all the primordial seeds, I mean to say, from which every kind of flesh or fruit is born are moist and grow and develop out of moisture."[43]

In his discussion of the creation of the first man and woman, this structure is evident. Their original creation is different to their creation in time: the first is "in terms of a potentiality inserted as it were seminally into the universe through the Word of God when he created all things simultaneously"; the second is "in terms of the march of time, at which 'he is working until now'; and it was right and proper for Adam to be made now in his own time from the mud of the earth, and the woman out of the man's side."[44] In this "unwrapping" of primordial creation, human beings and other living creatures emerge in time through God's ongoing providential care and ordering of the whole creation. To express what is today called God's providence and ongoing creation, Augustine constantly quotes the text: "My Father works until now." (John 5:17)

He offers an image for the way animals, plants and human beings emerge in time from the simultaneous creation of all things.[45] He invites his readers to consider a beautiful tree, with its trunk, branches, leaves, and fruit. He traces the tree back to its origins as a tiny sprig, and back before that to the seed. He marvels that the whole tree is found in some way in the seed, not in its bodily mass, but in its potentiality and causative power. He notes that in order to grow, the tree needs a supply of earth and moisture. But it is the potential in the seed that enables it to use earth and water for the growth of the tree and its branches, leaves, and fruit. Seeds come from trees, and trees from seeds, and all come from the earth. In the seed is present all that will develop into a tree. It is this way, Augustine says, we can picture the world, when God created all things together, the sun, moon, and stars, but also the seeds, the seminal reasons, for all the creatures that would be brought forth from earth and water through intervals of time.

Augustine makes a three-fold distinction in talking about all the works of creation.[46] First, there are the eternal reasons or exemplars for all creatures in the Word of God. Second, there are the seminal reasons that God implants in the original creation that account for the generation and growth of living things. Third, there are all the living creatures that come forth in time from these seminal reasons because of God's creative and provident care: "Given the appropriate conditions of earth and moisture, these powers would produce the living creatures intended by God, which would come into being according to the plan of his providence."[47]

TRAJECTORIES

Augustine's theology centers on the human before God. It engages with a scientific and cultural worldview that differs greatly from those of the twenty-first century. His interpretation of Genesis, particularly of the second creation account, is far more literal than that of contemporary scholars.

Nevertheless, there are trajectories in this thought that are meaningful in today's context:

1. His view that every creature represents the beauty of its maker and exemplar, the Wisdom of God, has enduring significance in the wider tradition, and can have new meaning in the ecological context of today.
2. He offers a model for contemporary discussions between science and theology with his commitment both to the truth of Scripture and to the truth established by reason and experiment, and his conviction that both Scripture and reason spring ultimately from divine truth.
3. He exemplifies a theological method which, while committed to the truth of faith, nevertheless sees the theologian's interpretations as revisable in the light of new information from reason or the sciences, or from another's interpretations of the texts.
4. While it is anachronistic to cast Augustine as a supporter of Darwinism,[48] his commitment to engage with secular fields of knowledge and his development of a theology of seminal reasons offer a great deal of encouragement to contemporary theologians to be equally creative, brave, and humble, in engaging with contemporary science, particularly with evolutionary biology.

Notes

1. Augustine, *City of God*, trans. Marcus Dods, in *The Nicene and Post-Nicene Fathers* Series 1, Volume 2, 504. http://www.ccel.org/ccel/schaff/npnf102.toc.html.
2. Edmund Hill has translated all three of Augustine's commentaries, with introductions and notes, in his *On Genesis: A Refutation of the Manichees; Unfinished Literal Commentary on Genesis; The Literal Meaning of Genesis* (Hyde Park, NY: New York City Press, 2002). I will use Hill's translation of *The Literal Meaning of Genesis* throughout this chapter. I will also refer to the notes of John Hammond Taylor in his translation and annotation in the Ancient Christian Writers Series, 41 and 42, *Saint Augustine: The Literal Meaning of Genesis*, vols. 1 and 2 (New York: Paulist, 1982).
3. Augustine, *The Literal Meaning of Genesis*, 1.1.1. In the same paragraph he offers an example of figurative interpretation: "they become one flesh" of Gen 2:24 is understood as a sacrament of Christ and the Church in Eph 5:32.
4. Ibid.
5. Ibid., 8.4.8.
6. Ibid., 8.1.2.
7. Edmund Hill, *On Genesis*, 159.
8. Augustine, *The Literal Meaning of Genesis*, 5.5.12. See Simo Knuuttila, "Time and Creation in Augustine," in *The Cambridge Companion to Augustine*, eds., Eleonore Stump and Norman Kretzman (Cambridge: Cambridge University Press, 2001), 103–15.
9. Augustine, *Revisions*, 2.24, trans. Edmund Hill, *On Genesis*, 167.
10. Augustine, *The Literal Meaning of Genesis*, 1.21.41. Thomas Williams notes that for Augustine biblical exegesis is not simply about finding the author's intentions, not only because sometimes this is impossible, but also because the Scriptures are signs of realities that we learn only by seeing them for ourselves in eternal Truth. See his "Biblical Interpretation," in *The Cambridge Companion*, eds., Stump and Kretzmann, 59–70.
11. Augustine, *The Literal Meaning of Genesis*, 1.21.41. Thomas

Williams notes that for Augustine biblical exegesis is not simply about finding the author's intentions, not only because sometimes this is impossible, but also because the Scriptures are signs of realities that we learn only by seeing them for ourselves in eternal Truth. See his "Biblical Interpretation," in *The Cambridge Companion*, eds., Stump and Kretzmann, 59–70.

12. Bronwen Neil points out that, in his *De doctrina christiana*, Augustine ends up putting the onus on the reader to determine whether a biblical text should be taken in a literal or figurative sense, while insisting on the importance of the reader's experience, prayer for understanding and holiness. See her "Exploring the Limits of Literal Exegesis: Augustine's Reading of Genesis 1:26," *Pacifica* 19 (June 2006): 144–54.
13. See John Hammond Taylor, in the introduction to *The Literal Meaning of Genesis: Volume 1*, 6.
14. Augustine, *The Literal Meaning of Genesis*, 1.21.41.
15. Ibid.
16. Ibid., 1.19.39.
17. Ibid.
18. Ibid.
19. Ibid., 1.19.38.
20. Ibid.
21. Ibid., 1.19.39.
22. Ibid., 2.9.20.
23. Ibid.
24. See the Second Vatican Council's *Dogmatic Constitution on Divine Revelation* (*Dei Verbum*), par. 11.
25. Augustine, *The Literal Meaning of Genesis*, 2.9.21.
26. Ibid., 5.20.40.
27. Ibid., 2.6.12–13.
28. Ibid., 1.8.14.
29. Ibid., 1.18.36. Like Basil before him Augustine mentions this as the view of a learned Christian Syrian. As Edmund Hill points out, "This was very probably Saint Ephrem, a deacon of the Church of

Edessa, who founded a school of theology there, and died in 273" (note 22, in *On Genesis*, 185).

30. Edmund Hill, *On Genesis*, 13–14.
31. See Mary T. Clark, *Augustine* (London: Continuum, 1994, 2005), 39.
32. Carol Harrison, *Beauty and Revelation in the Thought of Saint Augustine* (Oxford: Clarendon, 1992).
33. Augustine, *The Literal Meaning of Genesis,* 6.12.20.
34. Ibid., 6.6.9.
35. Augustine has a unique place for angels in this story. He sees the word "heavens" in the opening of Genesis ("In the beginning when God created the heavens and the earth") as referring to the creation of the spiritual and angelic world. He understands the words "let there be light" (Gen 1:3) as referring to the illumination of angelic creatures. Because the angels contemplate the eternal Word they also know the forms of creatures before their creation, and then know them in their existence. See, for example, *The Literal Meaning of Genesis*, 2.8.17.
36. The Latin word behind "simultaneously" in the Old Latin and Vulgate versions is *simul* (at the same time), which seems a mistranslation of the Septuagint Greek word *koinē* (commonly). The NRSV translation is: "He who lives forever created the whole universe."
37. Augustine, *The Literal Meaning of Genesis*, 4.26.43.
38. Ibid., 4.33.51.
39. See John Hammond Taylor, *St. Augustine The Literal Meaning of Genesis*, vol. 1, 253, note 67. He points out that Augustine calls these seminal reasons not only *causales rationes* and *rationes seminales*, or simply *rationes*, but also *quasi semina futurorum*, *rationes primordiales*, *primordia causarum*, and *quasi seminalesrationes*.
40. Augustine, *The Literal Meaning of Genesis*, 4.33.52.
41. Edmund Hill, *On Genesis*, 160.
42. Augustine, *The Literal Meaning of Genesis*, 5.7.20.
43. Ibid.
44. Ibid., 6.6.8.

45. Ibid., 5.23.45.

46. Ibid., 5.12.28.

47. John Hammond Taylor, *Saint Augustine: The Literal Meaning of Genesis*, vol. 1, 253–54, note 67.

48. Since the 1920's the seminal reasons have been the occasion for a lively debate about whether Augustine should be invoked as in some way supporting the theory of evolution. See Hammond Taylor, *Saint Augustine: The Literal Meaning of Genesis*, vol. 1, 220–21, note 18.

5.

Hildegard of Bingen (1098–1179)

Life and Context: Hildegard was a Benedictine abbess of the twelfth century Rhineland, a visionary prophet, theologian, preacher, musical composer, dramatist, healer, and researcher in natural science and medicine. She received visions at a very young age, and while still a child she was placed by her parents in the care of a young woman committed to religious life named Jutta von Sponheim. They took up an anchorite life, attached to the Benedictine monastery of Disibodenberg. Jutta taught Hildegard to sing the divine office and the basics of Latin. They soon attracted others and became the center of a growing group of Benedictine nuns. When Jutta died in 1136, Hildegard was elected leader (*magistra*) of the nuns. In spite of opposition from Abbott Kuno, she succeeded in setting up an independent women's monastery at Rupertsberg in 1150, and then founding a second monastery at Eibingen in 1165. She had the support of Volmar, a monk of Disibodenberg, a spiritual advisor and friend who also served as her scribe. Hildegard was reluctant to share her visionary experience, but she says that in a vision in 1141, when she was 42, she was told by God to write down what she saw and heard. In the light of the divine instruction, she eventually wrote three major texts of visionary theology, the *Scivias*, between 1142 and 1151, *The Book of Life's Merits*, between 1158 and 1163, and *The Book of Divine Works*, between 1163 and 1174. She was confirmed in her visionary

> and prophetic vocation by Bernard of Clairvaux and by Pope Eugenius III, who read from part of her *Scivias* at the Synod of Trier in 1147.[1]

Hildegard experienced visions of light, and a voice from heaven, which she called the voice of the Living Light. She tells of a vision of extraordinary brilliance in which she was given an immediate grasp of the meaning of the Scriptures.[2] Sometimes there were complex visions, with radiantly beautiful figures, mountains, buildings, and strange animals. Hildegard insists that her visions are not experiences of the senses, and not the result of ecstasy, and that she sees them only in her spirit, when she is wide awake, and with her eyes open.[3] Her three major works offer theological interpretations of such visions.

In the *Scivias*, for example, Hildegard describes twenty-six visions and provides a theological interpretation of each of them. Her manuscript is illustrated with thirty-five brilliant illuminations, probably created in Hildegard's community under her supervision.[4] The theological interpretation of each vision, she insists, comes not from her, but from the Living Light. The title *Scivias* seems to be a contraction of the Latin for "know the ways" of God (*Scito vias Domini*). The ways of God she describes in this book cover a vast scope from the creation of angels and of the world, and the fall of Lucifer and Adam, to the incarnation, the church, the virtues, and to the end of the world, with the persecutions of the anti-Christ and the Last Judgment. The *Scivias* concludes with an expression of the celestial harmony of life in God, with hymns to Mary, and to the angels, patriarchs, prophets, apostles, martyrs, confessors and virgins.

Hildegard's medieval world is very distant from ours. Some of her images can seem alien, at least until one spends time with them. Some of her theological assumptions differ radically from those of many twenty-first century Christians, such as her vivid views of demons, her presumption that those beyond the church will be lost, her enthusiastic prioritizing of virginity and of monastic life in general, and her apocalyptic scenarios of the end of the world. While in such matters she was the product of her own religious culture, her major theological insights are deeply grounded in the Christian tradition, and her theology is radically incarnational and Trinitarian. Barbara Newman points out that in spite of the "outlandish" images found in Hildegard's *Scivias*, it is not far removed in substance from Hugh of St Victor's major theological work, *On the Sacraments of Christian Faith*, written only a decade or two earlier.[5] Hildegard's three major books constitute one of the great theological achievements of the twelfth century.

Hildegard's theology is not only traditional, but also highly original and fresh in its insights and expression, with a capacity to leap the centuries. There is a vividness and immediacy to her ideas, her images and her language that can be startling, challenging, and enriching. I will begin by exploring her view of creation, incarnation and the Trinity in the *Scivias*. Then I will take up her discussion of Divine Wisdom (*Sapientia*) and Divine Love (*Caritas*), from *The Book of Divine Works*. In the third section I will explore her concept of greenness, and in the fourth her view of human beings in relation to the wider creation. The chapter will conclude with a brief discussion of her view of music.

CREATION, INCARNATION, AND TRINITY

In the *Scivias*, as in all of Hildegard's works, the Word in whom all things are created is the Word made flesh. She moves quickly back and forth between creation and incarnation, and sees the incarnation as from the beginning the eternal counsel, or plan, of God, drawing on the text: "The counsel of the Lord stands forever" (Ps 33:11). She writes, at the beginning of book 3 of the *Scivias*: "Grant me to make known the divine counsel, which was ordained of old, as I can and should: how you willed your Son to become incarnate and become a human being within time; which you willed before all creation in your rectitude and the fire of the Dove, the Holy Spirit."[6]

In the second book of the *Scivias*, Hildegard describes a vision of the creation and redemption, as a blazing fire, with a sky-colored flame at its center.[7] The blazing fire, she tells us, represents the omnipotent God, a God who is "wholly living" and "wholly life," from whom everything that lives takes its life.[8] All creatures exist from, and are sustained by, this blazing fire of the Creator: "the sky holds light, light air, and air the birds; the earth nourishes plants, plants fruit and animals; which all testify that they were put there by a strong hand, the supreme power of the Ruler of All, who in his strength has so provided for them all that nothing is lacking to them for their use."[9]

The sky-colored flame at the center of the blazing fire, Hildegard explains, is the infinite Word of God. The Word is as inseparable from the blazing fire as the viscera are from the human being. In "the ardor of charity" the Word that is indivisibly in the Father becomes incarnate "by the Holy Spirit's sweet freshness (*per viriditatem suavitatis*) in the dawn of blessed virginity."[10] It is typical of Hildegard to see the incarnation as expressing the *ardor* of divine love, to speak of the sweet *freshness* or *greenness* of the Spirit, and to exult in the Spirit's work in the virginity of Mary as the beginning of a glorious new creation. She goes on to make the theological point that even after the Word assumed flesh, the Word also continued to remain inseparably with the Father. She points to the reason why the Son of God is called the Word: As in human life a word of command uttered by an instructor can be understood by those who hear it, so the Word of the Father can be known by creatures as the source of their creation.[11]

Hildegard points out that the sky-blue flame of the Word both sparks and blazes. She explains that the Word showers forth sparks in creating each creature, and blazes up in becoming incarnate. Reflecting further on the Word's role in creation, Hildegard speaks of the flame of the Word as hovering over the great sphere of creation, which is still formless and imperfect, and bringing forth all the diverse creatures, "shining in their miraculous awakening"; The Word is like a smith making forms out of bronze, "until each creature is radiant with the loveliness of perfection."[12]

Having made all the other creatures, the flame of the Word turns to the creation of the human. In the strong will of the Father, the Word looks upon the "poor fragile matter," the earthly mud, still unconscious, and not yet roused by the breath of life.[13] Hildegard tells how the Word warms this matter until it is made flesh and blood, and nourishes it with moisture as a mother gives milk to her children, and breathes upon it, and so, marvelously, draws forth the first human being.

In Hildegard's vision the flame "which burns ardently with a gentle breath" then offers the newly created Adam a white flower that hangs in the flame like dew on grass.[14] This symbolizes how the Father, through the Word and in the Holy Spirit, offers Adam the "the sweet precept of obedience" that in fresh fruitfulness hangs on the Word. In this way holiness is meant to drip down to Adam from the Father, in the Spirit and through the Word.[15] Adam, however, accepts the counsel of the Devil, rejects the divine offer, and turns away into the darkness of death, and this darkness spreads in the creation. Hildegard then shows briefly how the great prophets of Israel begin to drive back the darkness, how John the Baptist witnesses to the Son of God, how Christ's death brings liberation, and how by his resurrection we are led from death into life.

It is only after she has discussed the triune God engaged in the economy of creation and salvation that Hildegard focuses on the unity and fullness of life of the Trinity in itself, and then describes her beautiful vision of the Trinity:

> Then I saw a bright light, and in this light the figure of a human (*speciem hominis*), the color of a sapphire, which was all blazing with a gentle glowing fire. And that bright light bathed the whole of the glowing fire, and the glowing fire bathed the bright light; and the bright light and the glowing fire poured over the whole human figure, so that the three were one light in one power of potential.[16]

Hildegard explains what she knows from the Living Light: The bright light designates the Father; The sapphire-colored human form represents the Son, begotten of the Father in divinity before time began, and then in time become incarnate;[17] and the gentle glowing fire refers to the Holy Spirit by whom the only-begotten Son was conceived in the flesh and born of the Virgin, and poured true light into the world.

The interaction of the bright light, the figure of the human, and the glowing fire, their mutual "bathing," shows that the Father is not without the Son or the Holy Spirit; The Holy Spirit who kindles the hearts of the faithful is not without the Father or the Son; And the Son, who is the fullness of fruition, is not without the Father or the Holy Spirit. Hildegard insists that these three persons are one God and their unity is unbreakable. She says the Father is declared through the Son, and the Son through the creation, and the Holy

Spirit through the Son incarnate.[18] All creatures "declare" the Word in whom they were created.

DIVINE WISDOM AND DIVINE LOVE

As Barbara Newman points out, while Hildegard's visionary style and self-understanding are closely related to the prophets of the Old Testament, she also makes important use of the biblical Wisdom literature, above all in her imaging God in female form as *Sapientia* (Wisdom) and *Caritas* (Love).[19] The biblical wisdom tradition, and its personification of Wisdom as God's companion in creation, were widely embraced in the twelfth century, and found expression in Christology, in devotion to Mary, and in the liturgy. In Christology, the identification of the male Jesus with the female figure of Wisdom created a certain tension, as is evident when St. Martin of Léon points out that Jews might well ask: "If Christ is the Wisdom of God, why is he called a son and not a daughter?" His unconvincing reply is that the name of son is "more honorable."[20]

Hildegard often used the images of Wisdom and Love in speaking of the relationship between the Creator and the world of creatures. In Hildegard's usage Wisdom and Love are identical, so that she cans say simply "Wisdom and Love are one."[21] Her great presentation of Divine Love appears in the opening of the *Book of Divine Works*.[22] She tells of a vision in which she sees, within the mystery of God, a wonderfully beautiful image, of a human-like form, with a face radiant like the sun, a golden circlet on her head, carrying a lamb. The image speaks as the Creator:

> I am the supreme and fiery force who has kindled all sparks of life and breathed forth none of death, and I judge things as they are. Tracing the revolving orbits with my upper wings, that is

> with Wisdom, I have established true order there. I, the fiery life of the divine substance, blaze above the beauty of the fields, shine in the waters, and burn in the sun, moon and stars.
>
> With the all-sustaining force of the aerial wind, I bring all things to life. For the air lives in greenness and flowers; the waters flow as if living; the sun is also alive in its light, and when the moon has waned completely it takes light from the sun, as if it lived again; and the stars in their light also shine as if alive.[23]

The fiery force goes on to say "I am life entire, which is not struck from stones, nor budded from branches, nor rooted in the virility of the male, but all that is living is rooted in me. For Reason is the root, and the Word sounding in truth is its flower."[24] The voice from heaven, Hildegard says, has told her that the beautiful figure like a human being within the mystery of God is Divine Love, the love of the everlasting God. She appears like a human being because the Son of God came to us in the flesh to redeem our lost humanity in the service of divine Love. The brilliance of her face, beyond that of the sun, represents the incomprehensible Love of the God of creation and incarnation.[25]

In a letter to Abbot Adam of Ebrach, Hildegard describes another vision of Divine Love as a beautiful young woman with a brilliant, glowing face, in a cloak whiter than snow and brighter than a star, holding the sun and moon in her right hand and embracing them tenderly. Hildegard writes that she heard the voice from heaven say:

> The girl whom you see is Divine
> Love, who abides in eternity.
> For when God wished to create the world
> he bent down in tenderest love
> and foresaw every need,
> just like a father preparing an inheritance for his son.
> In this way he carries out all his works
> in a great burning fire of love.

> Thus all creatures in every species
> and form acknowledge their creator,
> Because Love was the primal stuff
> from which every creature was made.
> When God said: "Let it be done," it was done,
> because Divine Love was the matrix from which every creature was made,
> in the blink of an eye.[26]

Caritas, the burning fire of Divine Love, is the primal stuff, the matrix, from which all the creatures of the universe emerge. They are the fruits of the tenderness of this Love, and witness to this love by their very existence. In a vision in Book 3 of the *Book of Divine Works*, Love and Wisdom appear together, along with Humility, pictured as three brilliant women, two of them standing in a fountain of clear water with the third at its side. The first figure explains that she is Love and that Wisdom has performed her works with her, and Humility is her helper. Love says that the Living Fountain is the Spirit of God which brings life to all the works of God, and she says of Wisdom's work in creation:

> In the shadow, Wisdom metes out all things in equal measure. . . . And she herself and through herself constituted all things piously and gently. And they shall be destroyed by no enemy, since she sees most clearly the beginning and the end of her works who composed all things fully that all things may be ruled by her.[27]

Caritas goes on to say that Wisdom also revealed certain things to Hildegard, the same Wisdom that spoke through the prophets, the evangelists, and the disciples, so that the stream of Living Water might be spread throughout the world and bring salvation.[28] In her *Antiphon to Divine Wisdom*, Hildegard sings of Wisdom's universal creativity:

> O energy of Wisdom! You
> circled, circling encompassing all things,
> in one path possessed of life.
> Three wings you have:
> one of them soars on high,
> the second exudes from the earth and the third
> flutters everywhere. Praise to you, as befits you,
> O Wisdom![29]

Wisdom's wings, reminiscent of those of the seraph of Isaiah 6, suggest the realms of her creative action, in the heavens above, on the earth below, and everywhere. Newman suggests that the three wings can also be taken as emblems of the three divine persons, the Father in heaven, the Son on earth, and the Spirit everywhere.[30]

GREENNESS OF THE HOLY SPIRIT

One of Hildegard's key images is that of *greenness* (*viriditas*). She uses *greenness*, as well as *light* and *life*, to point to the interaction and the unity between different levels of reality. Greenness captures the life, the energy, the dynamic newness of things, in an abundance of multivalent resonances. Commentators note that at one level the origin of the image of greenness must lie in the "subtle, ever-changing and deeply affecting green of the hills that surround the Disibodenberg and Rupertsberg areas of the German Rhineland, where Hildegard lived and worked."[31] Greenness for Hildegard is the energy of life evident in grasses, trees, flowers and vineyards. It is the fruitfulness of the earth itself. Greenness is associated with moisture, with dew on the grass and with rainfall. Hildegard sees rivers and streams as sustaining the Earth by their greening power.[32]

Greenness also plays a part in Hildegard's anthropology, since she sees the human soul as the green life-force of the flesh.[33] In the life of faith, greenness expresses the God-given livingness of the spiritual journey. She speaks of the green vitality of the virtues, and the greening power of good deeds.[34] She begins her *Responsory for Virgins* with the line: "O most noble greenness."[35] Writing to Abbot Kuno, she speaks of Saint Rupert, patron of her monastery, as "the greenness of the finger of God."[36] She invokes the same image in her *Responsory for Saint Disibod*: "O living green of God's finger with which God planted a vineyard."[37] What this means, Newman explains, is that "God's life-creating finger, the Holy Spirit," works through the saint to establish a religious community.[38] Hildegard sees the church itself as spreading like blessed greennesss.[39] Greenness is brought forth by the mouth of the priest at the Eucharist.[40] In one of her songs to Mary, Hildegard hails her as the greenest branch.[41] She speaks of Jesus as the green wood who enables all the greening powers of the virtues.[42]

The greenness of nature gives symbolic expression to "the truly primordial vitality, the ultimately primal power that lies hidden in the ground of eternity" and "emanates from the fire of eternal life."[43] Hildegard associates this greenness particularly with the Holy Spirit. She speaks of the Spirit's gifts as green with the greenness of the Holy Spirit.[44] She describes the Holy Spirit as proceeding from the Father and the Son in eager greenness (*ardentissima viriditate*).[45] And, in a text mentioned earlier, she speaks of the Word becoming incarnate in the Virgin Mary through the Holy Spirit's sweet greenness (*per viriditatem suavitatis*).[46]

Hildegard's vision of the life-giving Spirit at work in the history of salvation is evident in the following passage, where, after reflecting on human sin as the loss of original greenness, she speaks of the work of the Spirit in bringing about the new deed of redemptive incarnation:

> And just as the flowers multiplied their fruits beyond their past yield, so also the knowledge of humankind, increased in wisdom by the Holy Spirit, advanced to a new star, which manifested the King of Kings. And this Wisdom blazed from the fire of the Holy Spirit, through which the Word of God was made flesh in the womb of the Virgin, as that star indicated, and by which the Holy Spirit announced the deed it had performed in the Virgin's womb to the peoples. And the brightness of the flame of the Holy Spirit is the sound of the Word which created all things. For the Holy Spirit made fertile the womb of the Virgin and came in tongues of fire over the disciples of the Son of God.[47]

For Hildegard the fiery Spirit is the source of revelation, the one who performs the deed of the incarnation in the womb of Mary, the brightness that accompanied the sounding Word in the creation of all things, and the one who empowered the disciples at Pentecost, enabling them and their successors to work marvels. The Spirit brings about a wonderful new greenness through the incarnation and Pentecost. In Hildegard's view, however, the strength of this greenness is much diminished in her own time, which she describes as a time of "womanly weakness," when justice is neglected, humans behave in stupid ways, and church authority fails disastrously.[48]

In Hildegard's theology, the Holy Spirit is the greening power of life. Her theology of the Spirit, as life that gives life in both creation and grace, is brought out succinctly in her *Antiphon for the Holy Spirit*:

> The Holy Spirit is a life-giving life,
> moving all things:
> it is the root of the whole creation
> and cleanses all things from impurity,
> scrubbing out sins
> and anointing wounds.
> So it is a glistening life and worthy of praise,
> arousing and resurrecting all.[49]

Sabina Flanagan suggests that Hildegard's description of the Holy Spirit as the root of the whole creation, on the one hand, and as the one who cleanses and anoints for healing, on the other, may not be the mixed metaphor it seems at first glance.[50] It may well be that Hildegard has two meanings of root (*radix*) in mind, the Spirit as root in the sense of the origin and foundation of the life of all creation, and also in the sense of being like the actual vegetable roots that Hildegard uses and advocates for healing.

For Hildegard, the Spirit is the life that gives life, the constant source of all greenness, the greenness of creation, saving incarnation, forgiving and healing grace, and resurrection. For her, the whole creation is radiant simply because it is God's creation: "For there is nothing in creation that does not have some radiance—either greenness or seeds or flowers, or beauty—otherwise it would not be part of creation."[51]

HUMAN BEINGS AND OTHER CREATURES

Alongside her visionary works, there are two books by Hildegard on scientific and medical matters, her *Physica* and her *Causes and Cures*. These are not based on visions and she does not attribute their descriptions of the natural world to a divine source. The *Physica* is a medieval encylopedia of natural history, opening with plants, followed by the elements (earth, water, and air), then trees, precious stones, fish, birds, animals, reptiles, and metals.[52] The comprehensive section on plants reflects Hildegard's interest in their healing qualities. She is particularly concerned to identify the humours of plants, as hot, cold, dry or moist, so as to indicate whether they might bring a patient to a balanced state.

The *Causes and Cures* gives far more space to medical conditions and their cures.[53] The first part of the book is a description of the creation of the world and of the human being in the cosmos. She follows Greek speculation in seeing both the human and the wider cosmos as constituted by the four elements of fire, air, water and earth. She offers detailed comments not only on treatments for ailments, but also on human sexuality, and women's health. Her advice seems to spring not only from established texts, like those of Galen and Isidore of Seville, but also from the Benedictine tradition of care for the ill, and from her own experience.

Hildegard's interest in the natural world involves not only the specific and practical cataloguing of healing herbs, but also her visionary images of the universe. In her *Scivias*, she envisions the universe in the shape of a cosmic egg, "a vast instrument, round and shadowed, in the shape of an egg, small at the top, large in the middle and narrowed at the bottom."[54] At the center is a globe of sparkling flame illuminating everything, showing that within God the Father is his ineffable only-begotten who becomes incarnate for the redemption and uplifting of the human race.

In her *Book of Divine Works*, Hildegard describes a different vision of the universe, which follows her exposition of the vision of Divine Love. Here the universe appears like a wheel, or a circle, positioned at the breast or heart of Divine Love. In the middle of the wheel is a human figure, whose head touches the circle above and whose feet touch it below. The figure's two hands are stretched out so that its finger tips touch the circle on left and right.

This image signifies, Hildegard says, that "in the structure of the world humanity is at the center."[55] The human person, then, is a microcosm of the universe. Though small in stature, the human is "great in strength of soul," with the head reaching to the elements above, and the feet to those below, and with the capacity for action symbolized by the two hands reaching out to the elements of the universe on left and right.[56]

Clearly, Hildegard has an exalted view of the human as at the center of God's plan of the creation and the incarnation. At the same time, as is evident from her medical and scientific works, she deeply values empirical knowledge of herbs, trees, and animals and the species of fish inhabiting the Rhine. She delights in the greenness of life in all its shapes, and she possesses a profound sense of the interconnection between human beings and the rest of the natural world.

CELESTIAL HARMONY

Hildegard's *Symphonia* is a collection of seventy musical texts, written to be sung in the celebration of the Divine Office and the Eucharist. It is made up of hymns, sequences, antiphons, and responsories, along with her musical drama, *The Play of the Virtues*.[57] She sees music as uniting earth and heaven, and can say that God is sound and life, as she does in her *Antiphon for the Trinity*: "To the Trinity be praise! / It is sound and life / and creator of all beings / in their life."[58]

Newman locates Hildegard within a broader theology of music that goes back to Clement of Alexandria almost a thousand years earlier, and his image of Christ as the New Song. Newman notes that "like all that Hildegard wrote, the *Symphonia* celebrates the mystery of God-become-man in the child of Mary."[59] Hildegard often speaks of the creative Word of God as sounding through the creation and, in her *Hymn to the Virgin*, she celebrates the celestial harmony sounding forth on Earth through the incarnation: "For your womb held joy/ when all the harmony of heaven (*celestis symphonia*) resounded from you."[60]

Hildegard's theology of music is outlined in a letter she

wrote to the clergy of Mainz. In the last year of her life, when she was eighty, she and her sisters were placed under interdict, which meant that they were not allowed to participate in the Eucharist or sing the Divine Office. She had buried a formerly excommunicated nobleman in consecrated ground at Rupertsberg. In Hildegard's view, he had been reconciled with the church, but the clergy disputed this and demanded his body be moved, something Hildegard refused to do. Her letter explains her actions, and points to her view of music in worship. As part of her argument, Hildegard speaks of Adam's singing in paradise, and presents him as possessing an extraordinary capacity for praising God in song:

> Adam was formed by the finger of God, which is the Holy Spirit . . . in Adam's voice before he fell there was the sound of every harmony and the sweetness of the whole art of music. And if Adam had remained in the condition in which he was formed, human frailty could never endure the power and the resonance of that voice.[61]

The devil, who hated the sound of such heavenly music, set out to lead Adam into sin, and ever since has been determined to destroy the beauty of divine praise. In case they have not got the message, Hildegard warns those who have stopped the music at Rupertsberg to beware lest they be ensnared in their judgment by Satan who had lured Adam away from celestial harmony. She tells them that if they do not repent they themselves may forgo the fellowship of angelic praise in heaven because they have unjustly taken from God the beauty of praise on Earth.

Hildegard sees humankind as musical by nature. After Adam's voice is stopped, the prophets, taught by the Spirit, still compose psalms and canticles, and invent musical instruments, by which the praise of God can go on. Hildegard thinks that humans are nostalgic for the celestial harmony, so that, when hearing some melody, they sometimes sigh or moan, recalling the heavenly music. She points to David, who "subtly contemplating the profound nature of the spirit, and knowing that the human soul is symphonic (*symphonialis*), exhorts us in his psalm to proclaim the Lord on the lute and play for him on the ten-stringed psaltery."[62] For Hildegard music is not simply an option, but something intrinsic to the praise of God, to the universe that is God's creation and to the human person.

TRAJECTORIES

Hildegard's twelfth-century cultural, scientific and theological context is so radically different to that of the twenty-first century that access to her work, and interpretation of it, becomes complex and difficult. And she has a strong view of the human as at the center of the universe that God creates. Nevertheless, the above exploration suggests rich trajectories for a contemporary theology of the natural world:

1. Hildegard envisions a profound connection between creation and incarnation in the eternal will of God, in a strong Trinitarian theology of Word and Spirit.
2. She sees God as life that gives life.
3. It is Divine Love that empowers the whole universe of creatures. Each creature exists from, and is held by, this Love.
4. All creatures declare the Word in whom they are created.
5. Hildegard has a highly original theological image of greenness (*viriditas*) that points to and unites all forms of life, biological, spiritual, and divine, and all that supports

life, as the work of the "green finger of God," the Holy Spirit.

6. Her twelfth-century attempt to see the universe in relation to God, suggests theological engagement with contemporary cosmology and biology.
7. Her active empirical engagement with the natural world of animals, plants, fish, rivers, and rocks suggests active theological engagement with sciences like biology and neuroscience.
8. Hildegard's theology of music invites new thinking about music in twenty-first century theology.
9. Hildegard offers a wonderfully holistic vision that includes all aspects of creation as integral to the journey of life in God.

Notes

1. For Hildegard's life see Anna Silvas, *Jutta and Hildegard: The Biographical Sources* (University Park: Pennsylvania State University Press, 1999); ed., Barbara Newman, *The Voice of the Living Light: Hildegard of Bingen and Her World* (Berkeley: University of California Press, 1998); Sabina Flanagan, *Hildegard of Bingen, 1098–1179: A Visionary Life* (London: Routledge, 1989); Heinrich Schipperges, *The World of Hildegard of Bingen: Her Life, Times and Visions*, trans. John Cumming (Collegeville, MN: Liturgical, 1998); Fiona Maddox, *Hildegard of Bingen: The Woman of Her Age* (London: Headline, 2001).
2. See her "Declaration" at the Beginning of the *Scivias*. For the critical edition see Adelgundis Führkötter and Angela Carlevaris, *Hildegardis-Scivias*, Corpus Christianorum: Continuatio Mediaevalis (Turnhout, Belgium: Brepols, 1978). I am using the translation of Columba Hart and Jane Bishop, introduction by Barbara J. Newman, preface by Caroline Walker Bynum, *Hildegard of Bingen:*

Scivias, The Classics of Western Spirituality (New York: Paulist, 1990).

3. See Hildegard's Letter 103, Response to Guibert of Gembloux, in *The Letters of Hildegard of Bingen*, trans. Joseph L. Baird and Radd K. Ehramm, 3 vols. (Oxford: Oxford University Press, 1994–98), Volume 2, 21.
4. The *Rupertsberg Scivias* was probably produced around 1175. Most scholars think that the illuminations were painted under Hildegard's supervision, or perhaps in her immediate tradition. This manuscript was lost in 1945, after it was evacuated to Dresden, and is now known only through photographs, and a copy made by the nuns of Eibingen in the later 1920s.
5. Barbara Newman, *Sister of Wisdom: Hildegard's Theology of the Feminine* (Berkeley: University of California Press, 1987, 1997), 16.
6. Hildegard, *Scivias* 3.1. Prologue.
7. Ibid., 2.1.1.
8. Ibid.
9. Ibid., 2.1.2.
10. Ibid., 2.1.3.
11. Ibid., 2.1.4.
12. Ibid., 2.1.6.
13. Ibid., 2.1.7.
14. Ibid., 2.1.8.
15. Ibid.
16. Ibid., 2.2. Prologue. In this instance, I have modified the translation of Columba Hart and Jane Bishop, replacing the "the figure of a man" with "the figure of a human," as the translation of Hildegard's "*speciem hominis*." For a good summary of Hildegard's theology of Trinity see Anne Hunt, *Trinity: Insights from the Mystics* (Collegeville, MN: Liturgical, 2010), 23–47.
17. Barbara Newman points to the heavenly sapphire stone of Exodus 24:10, and notes that sapphire blue is a hue that Hildegard associates with the divinity and predestination of the Word (Newman, *Sister of Wisdom,* 57).
18. Hildegard, *Scivias*, 2.2.2.

19. Newman, *Sister of Wisdom*, 42.

20. Ibid., 43.

21. Ibid., 49.

22. For the critical edition see *Liber divinorum operum*, eds., Albert Delorez and Peter Dronke Corpus Christianorum: Continuatio Mediaevalis vol. 90 (Turnhout, Belgium: Brepols, 1996). There is an abridged English translation in Matthew Fox, ed., *Book of Divine Works, with Letters and Songs*, trans. Robert Cunningham (Santa Fe: Bear & Company, 1987).

23. Hildegard, *The Book of Divine Works*, 1.1.2. Translation of this and following quotations by Sabina Flanagan, in *Secrets of God: Writings of Hildegard of Bingen* (Boston & London: Shambhala, 1996).

24. Ibid.

25. Ibid., 1.1.3.

26. Translation by Sheryl A. Kujawa-Holbrook, in *Hildegard of Bingen: Essential Writings and Chants of a Christian Mystic—Annotated & Explained* (Woodstock, Vermont: Skylight Paths Publishing, 2016), 37.

27. Hildegard, *The Book of Divine Works*, 3.8.2.

28. Ibid.

29. The Latin text and this translation are found in Barbara Newman, *Saint Hildegard of Bingen: Symphonia: A Critical Edition of the Symphonia armonie celestium revelationum*, second edition (Ithaca: Cornell University Press, 1988, 1998), 101. I am quoting from Newman's literal translation, which she offers with her interpretative translation.

30. Newman, *Symphonia*, 268.

31. Fiona Bowie and Oliver Davies, *Hildegard of Bingen: An Anthology* (London: SPCK, 1990), 31. I am following their lead in this section.

32. Hildegard, *The Book of Divine Works*, 1.4.59.

33. Ibid., 1.4.21.

34. Ibid., 2.18.

35. Hildegard, *Symphonia*, no. 56.

36. Hildegard, Letter 38, in *The Letters of Hildegard*, 1, 107.
37. Hildegard, *Symphonia*, no. 42.
38. Newman, *Symphonia*, 291.
39. Hildegard, *Scivias*, 2.5.26.
40. Ibid., 2.6.11.
41. Hildegard, *Symphonia*, no. 19.
42. Hildegard, *The Book of Divine Works*, 3.10.19.
43. Heinrich Schipperges, *The World of Hildegard of Bingen: Her Life, Times and Vision* (Collegeville, MN: Liturgical, 1998), 111.
44. Hildegard, *Scivias*, 3.6.33.
45. Ibid., 3.7.9.
46. Ibid., 2.1.3.
47. Hildegard, *The Book of Divine Works*, 3.10.8.
48. Ibid. Hildegard, a woman of enormous influence in her own time, and an outspoken prophetic critic of the failures of church leaders, also took for granted the contemporary cultural and religious view of men as strong and women as weak.
49. Hildegard, *Symphonia*, no. 24.
50. Flanagan, *Hildegard of Bingen*, 110.
51. Hildegard, *The Book of Divine Works*, 1.4.11.
52. See the translation of Priscilla Throop, *Hildegard von Bingen's Physica: The Complete English Translation of Her Classic Work on Health and Healing* (Rochester, VT: Healing Arts, 1998).
53. See the translation of Patrick Madigan, *Holistic Healing [Causae et Curae]* (Collegeville, MN: Liturgical, 1994).
54. Hildegard, *Scivias*, 1.3. *Prologue.*
55. Hildegard, *The Book of Divine Works*, 1.2.15.
56. Ibid.
57. In Hildegard's time, the word *symphonia* could have the general sense of music or harmony.
58. Hildegard, *Symphonia*, no. 26.
59. Newman, *Symphonia*, 45. Clement speaks of the "supermundane

Wisdom, the celestial Word" who is "the all-harmonious, melodious, holy instrument of God," and he sees the human as a beautiful, breathing instrument made in the divine image (Newman, *Symphonia*, 21).

60. Hildegard, *Symphonia*, no. 17.

61. Hildegard, "Letter 47," trans. Robert Carver in Bowie and Davies, *Hildegard of Bingen: An Anthology*, 151.

62. Ibid.

6.

Bonaventure of Bagnoregio (1221–1274)

Life and Context: Born in Bagnoregio in Tuscany, Bonaventure joined the Franciscan Friars Minor in 1243. He was sent to study at the University of Paris, where Franciscan theology had flourished under Alexander of Hales and John of Rochelle. In 1253, Bonaventure took up the Franciscan chair at the university, and lectured on the *Sentences*, a work written by Peter Lombard that had become a standard text upon which theologians were expected to comment. He received the degree of Master (the equivalent of a doctorate), along with Thomas Aquinas, in 1257. He was elected as Minister General of the Friars Minor in the same year. In 1273 he was made Cardinal Bishop of Albano. He took a leading role in the Council of Lyons (1274), in its attempt to reach reconciliation with the Orthodox. He died while the council was still in session. Bonaventure wrote widely on Scripture, theology, and philosophy. He drew on the Christian Neo-Platonic tradition, and also on Aristotle. His theology was deeply influenced by Augustine, and he took up themes from Richard of St. Victor, and Pseudo-Dionysius. His major systematic work is his commentary on Peter Lombard's *The Four Books of the Sentences*, written when he was twenty-seven.[1] Other well-known works are his *Breviloquium* (meaning a summary), his *On the Reduction of the Arts* *to Theology*, his *Disputed Questions on the Mystery of the Trinity*, and his *The Mind's Journey into God*. His late work, *Collations on the Six Days*, is based on a series of talks given in Paris between Easter and Pentecost 1273.

The influence of the Christian Neo-Platonic tradition on Bonaventure is apparent in the way he speaks of the journey into God as a movement upwards, frequently using the language of ascent and the image of the ladder. While it is not necessarily the case, this approach to Christianity can result in a flight-from-the-world rather than a down-to-earth spirituality. And in his eschatology, he adopts the medieval view that, in the end, while humanity and the universe will be transformed and renewed, there will be no place for plant and animal life, since they do not possess the capacity for eternal life. He sees them as consumed by the transforming fire, although he acknowledges a limited future for them: "They will be preserved as ideas; and in a certain manner they will survive also in their likeness, humankind, who is kin to creatures of every species."[2] In this way, Bonaventure adds "one can say that all things will be made new."[3]

However Bonaventure is also a deeply committed follower of Saint Francis of Assisi. And so, in spite of Bonaventure's Neo-Platonism and eschatology, it is important to ask how his theology witnesses to Francis's love and respect for the creatures of Earth, and to discern whether it can have new meaning in the Anthropocene epoch. I will begin this exploration with Bonaventure's *The Mind's Journey into God*, exploring the place he gives to the experience of God in the natural world. Then I will turn to three major themes in his work that may be resources for a contemporary theology of creation: the first person of the Trinity as the Fountain Fullness, the Word as Exemplar, and the idea of the Book of Creation.[4]

THE EXPERIENCE OF GOD IN CREATION IN *THE MIND'S JOURNEY INTO GOD*

The inspiration of Francis of Assisi is far more evident and explicit in Bonaventure's *The Mind's Journey into God* than it is in other major texts, such as his *Commentary on the Sentences of Peter Lombard.* In the *Journey*, Bonaventure is less constrained than in his other works by the methods and traditions of scholastic theology, so that a highly regarded interpreter of Bonaventure can say that, when we open this text, "we discover a new Bonaventure, the true Franciscan, who has learned from Saint Francis not only the rules and forms of life, but his whole outlook, his ideal."[5]

In his prologue to the *Journey*, Bonaventure describes how he had come to write the book. Near the thirty-third anniversary of Francis's death, Bonaventure, seeking peace in God, felt moved by divine inspiration to follow Francis to Mount Alverna. While pondering the vision Francis had received at this holy place, the vision of the crucified Christ in the form of a six-winged Seraph, and while meditating on Francis's burning love for Jesus crucified, which found expression in the marks of the passion on his body, Bonaventure comes to two conclusions. The first is that on the journey into divine peace and wisdom, the only way is Christ crucified: "There is no other way but through the most burning love of the Crucified."[6]

Bonaventure's second conclusion is that the six wings of the Seraph can be understood as symbols of six levels of illumination and six stages on the journey into God. He describes a contemplation that takes place at each level. He calls this contemplation a *speculatio*, related to the word for a mirror (*speculum*). It refers to a kind of mirroring or reflection by the mind of divine truth. The six steps are arranged in groups of two. In the first and second steps, the mind contemplates God in the sense experience of the world of creation, and at this level discovers vestiges (footprints) of the triune God. In the third and fourth levels, Bonaventure sees the mind as contemplating God by turning inward and finding within the image of God and, in the grace-filled soul, the likeness of God. Having contemplated God in the world around it, and then in the inner world, the mind, in the fifth and sixth steps, moves to the world beyond creation and beyond itself, to contemplate God first as Being itself, and then as pure Goodness, as the self-communicating love of the Trinity.

But even in such contemplation, Bonaventure points out the mind is not yet satisfied. It desires not only to know God, but to be united with God. But how can such union with the Absolute God be possible for a creature? It is possible, says Bonaventure, *only* through the one Mediator, who is the crucified Jesus. At this level the mind waits upon the Beloved and, by God's gift of the Holy Spirit, is drawn beyond itself, and beyond all knowing, into the burning love of Christ crucified in mystical union. As Francis was carried out of himself in contemplation and passed over into the peace of God, so Bonaventure concludes: "God invites all truly spiritual persons through Francis to this sort of passing over, more by example than by words."[7]

From beginning to end, Francis is the model for the journey. At the beginning of his first chapter Bonaventure writes: "Here begins the contemplation (*speculatio*) of the Poor One in the Desert."[8] The whole theme of the journey or pilgrimage reflects the restless journey that was Francis's own life. And the journey of the soul culminates not directly in the Trinity, as it does for Bernard and other authorities on the spiritual life, but in the particularly Franciscan vision of Christ crucified. The culmination in the cross is an indication that

Bonaventure's *Journey* is not finally about a world up there, a world beyond, but rather it is about this world, the place of the incarnate and crucified Jesus.

While Bonaventure's third and fourth chapters, on the mind's search within, echo Augustine in finding the image of the triune God in the mind's remembering, understanding, and loving God, his first two chapters on encountering the vestiges of God in the world outside us reflect Francis's love and profound respect for the natural world as the place of God. These are the focus of my exploration here. How does Bonaventure see the natural world around us as mirroring its Creator? He tells us that it can happen in two ways, which he spells out in the first two steps on the journey into God.

THE FIRST STEP: FINDING GOD THROUGH CREATION

In the first step, the mind finds God *through* creation, while in the second, the mind finds God *in* creation. In the first step, then, Bonaventure says that we "put the whole world of sense-objects before us as a mirror through which we may pass to God, the highest creative Artist."[9] In this step, Bonaventure points consistently to three divine attributes, the power, the wisdom, and the goodness of the Creator. These three attributes, he says, "shine forth" in created things, as we experience the world around us through our bodily senses and our minds.

He describes us as seeing God in creatures in three ways. First, we contemplate things as they are *in themselves*, in their orientation, their distinctiveness, and their finite limits.[10] From seeing things as they really are in themselves, Bonaventure says, "we can rise as from the vestige to an understanding of the immense power, wisdom, and goodness of the Creator."[11] Second, we see creation in the light of *faith*, and attend to its origin, development, and end. We know that this world we see around us is fashioned by the Word of Life—and are led to see the power, providence, and justice of God. Third, we investigate creation with our *reason*, and discover that some things simply exist, some are living, some are rational, some are bodily, and some are both bodily and spiritual. In such explorations by way of reason, Bonaventure writes, "from visible realities, the soul rises to the consideration of the power, wisdom and goodness of God, in so far as God is existing, living, and intelligent, purely spiritual, incorruptible and immutable."[12]

The vestige of God that we find in creation reflects something of the Trinity: the Father, the Source of All, is reflected as the Power that enables creatures to exist (efficient causality); the Word is reflected as the Exemplar for each creature (exemplary causality); and the Spirit is reflected as the Goodness, which brings creatures to their consummation (final causality). This way of thinking links each creature to the Triune Creator in immediacy. Leonard Bowman comments: "This sets his world-view apart from a Neoplatonic exemplarism which sees the universe as a hierarchical chain of being. . . . For Bonaventure, every single creature from the angel to the grain of sand has its direct model and foundation in the Word. . . . Each being is equally close to God, though the model of relationship differed according to the capacity of the creature."[13]

This contemplation of God through creatures can be extended, Bonaventure says, through the seven-fold properties of creatures, their origin, greatness, multitude, beauty, fullness, activity, and order. He sees the work of the six days of creation as proclaiming "the power that produces all things from nothing, the wisdom that clearly distinguishes all things, and the goodness that richly adorns all things." All of this points, he says, to the "immensity of the power, wisdom, and goodness of the triune God who, though uncircumscribed, exists in all things by virtue of power, presence and essence."[14]

The number and diversity of creatures, beyond all human knowing, points to the immensity of these same three attributes of power, wisdom, and goodness. And the beauty of creatures marvelously proclaims the same attributes: "The beauty of things in terms of the diversity of light, shape and color in bodies that are simple, inorganic and organic, as in the heavenly bodies and in minerals, in stones and in metals, in plants and in animals clearly proclaims the three attributes mentioned above."[15] Bonaventure concludes his treatment of the first step in the journey where God is found through the mirror of creation with a ringing declaration:

> Therefore, any person who is not illumined by such great splendors in created things is blind. Anyone who is not awakened by such great outcries is deaf. Anyone who is not led from such effects to give praise to God is mute. Anyone who does not turn to the First Principle as a result of such signs is a fool. Therefore open your eyes, alert your spiritual ears, unlock your lips, and apply your heart so that in all creation you may see, hear, praise, love and adore, magnify and honor your God lest the entire world rise up against you.[16]

THE SECOND STEP: FINDING GOD IN CREATION

Bonaventure's second step on the journey into God is the contemplation of God *in* other things in so far as God is truly present in them by essence, power, and presence. In this step the focus is on the way that other creatures are received into the mind through the bodily senses. Bonaventure reflects on three aspects of the process by which we know external objects through the doors of the five senses.

The first is apprehension: a likeness of the external object is generated in the medium (such as light), passes to the sense organ, and from there passes to the interior organ and then to the faculty of awareness. The second aspect is pleasure: the object is seen as beautiful, sweet, or wholesome. The third is judgment (or abstraction): in perceiving something specific through the senses, the mind abstracts its universal and timeless content, thus forming an idea. Through these three operations, Bonaventure tells us, "the entire world enters into the human soul through the doorways of the senses."[17]

Bonaventure then sets out to show how each of these three actions are "vestiges in which we can see our God."[18] First, in apprehension of objects around us, we become aware of a likeness generated in the medium and impressed on the organ, which points to its source in the external object that is known. It is because creatures around us generate a likeness of themselves through light or sound that we can know them. "This suggests," Bonaventure says, "something about a far more wonderful generation in God: the eternal Light generates an Image that is coequal, consubstantial, and coeternal. If it is in the nature of knowable objects to generate a likeness of themselves, then in this they are like mirrors in which we can glimpse the eternal generation of the Word, the Image of the Father."[19]

Second, the pleasure by which external objects give us delight in their beauty, sweetness, and wholesomeness, can be understood as pointing to this eternal divine generation, where there is supreme equality and proportion between the Image and the One who generates. It points to supreme beauty and delight in God: "it can be seen clearly that it is in God alone that the true fountain of delight is to be found."[20] From all the delights we experience in our knowing of creatures through our senses, "we are led to seek this one delight."[21]

The third way of judgment, Bonaventure tells us, is "more excellent" and "more immediate" and "leads us to see the eternal truth with greater certainty."[22] When we form a concept we abstract from place, time, and change. In this context, following Augustine's theory of illumination, Bonaventure sees the mind as forming a concept against a standard that transcends the object, and which has no limits. We judge them in light of eternal truth. The standard is "immutable, unlimited, and unending."[23] It is not that we have direct vision of the light of God. But, nevertheless, it is only in this light that we grasp the ideas of things which are contingent in time and space.[24] We judge them against laws that are uncreated and exist eternally "in the eternal Art from which, and through which, and in accordance with which all beautiful things are formed."[25] It is this eternal Art, Bonaventure says, by which all things are produced, conserved and distinguished. It is this eternal Art that sustains the form in all things and is the rule that directs them.[26] The very process of abstraction leads us into a profound closeness to God, and God is in some way known in our knowledge of objects of sense experience.

Bonaventure concludes the first two steps of journey by saying that "all creatures in this world of sensible realities lead the spirit of the contemplative and wise person to the eternal God."[27] All of these creatures are "shadows, echoes, and pictures" of the first Principle, and of the "efficient, exemplary and ordering Art."[28] While every creature is by nature a sign of its Exemplar and "a kind of copy and likeness" of eternal Wisdom, Bonaventure points out that there are also instances where creatures can be taken up to represent God in a special way.[29] This happens in the Scriptures when creatures like the burning bush signify and prefigure what is to come. And in our life as church, God has given us the signs that are instituted to be not simply signs but sacraments of the church.

THE FOUNTAIN-FULLNESS

The early Franciscan theologians, including Alexander of Hales, were deeply influenced by St. Francis's experience of God as a good and loving Father. They gave expression to this view of God by taking up from the Greek tradition Pseudo-Dionysius's insight that goodness is self-diffusive (*bonum diffusivum sui*). Bonaventure fully embraces this concept and builds on it as the point of departure for his theology of the triune God. In his view, such emphasis on the primal goodness of God is fully in accord with the New Testament revelation of the divine name as good: "No one is good but God alone" (Luke 18:19; Luke 19:17). He sees the First Testament as witnessing to the first name of God as the "One who is" (Exod 3:14), as pure being, and the New Testament as revealing God as the supreme good.

By taking supreme goodness as his starting point along with the conviction that goodness is self-diffusive, Bonaventure is able beautifully to unite metaphysics and Christian Trinitarian theology. If God is supreme goodness, God is always and necessarily self-communicating. Uniting the philosophical idea of the self-diffusive good with the concept of the triune God of Christian revelation leads Bonaventure to conclude that there is always and necessarily self-communication in the triune God. Self-communication belongs to the divine nature. Because God is self-diffusive goodness, Bonaventure argues, the emanation of the Word occurs by nature. It is natural, in the sense of being in accord with the divine nature, for divine goodness to communicate itself in the Word.

But the New Testament defines God not only as goodness but also as love (1 John 4:8, 16). This insight into the divine nature as love prompts Bonaventure to borrow from Richard of St. Victor's analysis of Trinitarian love, and to see the procession of the Spirit as an emanation by way of love or by way of the divine will. The first emanation, the generation of the Word, brings out the necessary self-communication of the fully fecund divine nature. The second, the spiration of the Spirit, expresses the loving freedom of the fecundity of the divine will. The Father is the fruitful source of both the generation of the Word by nature, and the breathing forth of the Spirit by way of liberality or love. In taking up what is distinctive of the Father, Bonaventure writes:

> For it is proper to the Father to be the one without an originator, the Unbegotten One; the Principle who proceeds from no other; the Father as such. "Unbegottenness" designates him by means of a negation, but this term also implies an affirmation, since unbegottenness posits in the Father a fountain-fullness. The "Principle that proceeds from no other" designates him by an affirmation followed by a negation. "Father" designates him in a proper, complete, and determinate way, by affirmation and the positing of a relation.[30]

In an evocative phrase, Bonaventure often speaks of the Source of All, the Father, as the *Fountain Fullness* (*fontalis plenitudo*). The image is of an abundant, overflowing spring or fountain of life-giving water. This Fountain Fullness is not begotten from any other. Unbegottenness (or innascibility) is in itself a negative concept, but with Bonaventure it is always linked to the positive characteristic of the generative fecundity of one who is Principle, Source, and Fountain Fullness. Zachary Hayes speaks of it as a bipolar concept—the Father is generative precisely as unbegotten.[31] For Bonaventure, then, the Father, the Fountain Fullness, possesses priority in the Trinity, because the Father is the principle of fecundity with regard to the other persons of the Trinity:

> But as much as anything is prior, so much is it more fecund and the principle of others; therefore, as the divine essence, because

> [it is first], is the principle of other essences, so the person of the Father, since he is first, because [he is] from no one, is the principle and has fecundity in respect of persons.[32]

The priority of the Father is such that while the divine essence is the source of creation, the Father is prior in the divine life, and therefore ultimately also the principal of creation. Although the idea of the Father as the Source of triune life can be found in Augustine,[33] it becomes far more of a systematic principle for Bonaventure, and operates in a way that is closer to the priority given to the first person in Eastern theology. Bonaventure is perfectly clear that the three persons are coequal, coeternal, and consubstantial, and that the Trinity as such is the principle and source of creation. Supreme primacy, he says, requires the highest actuality, fontality, and fecundity. God must be "eternally principle, most perfect, most actual, most productive, prior to the production of the world."[34] This demands the two emanations of divine life, the emanation from the first person of the Word by way of nature, and the emanation of the Spirit by way of the will or of love.[35]

For Bonaventure, then, the primacy of the first principle in the order of essence is found equally in all three persons. But in terms of personal origin, it is the unbegotten one, the Father, who is the Fountain Fullness for the processions of the Word and the Holy Spirit. This means that the Fountain Fullness of the divine life is the origin of the divine fecundity at work in the whole creation: "For since the Father brings forth the Son, and together with the Son brings forth the Holy Spirit, God the Father through the Son and with the Holy Spirit is the principle of everything created."[36] It is only because the Father produces the Word and the Spirit eternally, Bonaventure says, that the Father is the productive source of creatures in time. Thus the Father is rightly called the "Fountain of Life" (Ps 36:9).[37]

The person of the Father, then, is the Fountain Fullness in both triune life and in creation, "the source and origin of all, within and without the Godhead."[38] It is from this Fountain Fullness that all things come and it is to them that they all return. In Bonaventure's metaphysics of *exitus* (going forth) and *reditus* (returning), the Father is not only the source but also the goal of all created reality.[39] Zachary Hayes, then, can say: "Creation itself is but the radiation in space and time of the eternal inner-Trinitarian life."[40]

THE EXEMPLAR

Bonaventure considers the second person of the Trinity under three titles, as Son, Image, and Word. The title Son brings out the fully personal and relational nature of the divine generation: the person of the Father eternally generates the person of the Son. The title Son, while appealing in its reference to biological and human begetting, is also limited in that it points only to the Son in relation to the Father. The second title, Image, brings out the idea that the Image generated is the perfect likeness of the Father. While this likeness does not include the Father's personal property of unbegottenness, it does include the Father's character of being the source of others.[41] The perfect Image of the Father is, with the Father, an active source of the Spirit. Bonaventure does not see the Spirit as Image because the Spirit proceeds from the two persons, and gives expression to both.[42]

While Bonaventure makes frequent use of the titles Son and Image, he has a preference for the third title, Word. He finds this title rich in meaning because it expresses the relationship of the second person both to the Father and to creation.[43] It can express not only the Word's relationship to the entire mystery of creation, but also divine revelation and incarnation.[44] The Word is, then, the perfect expression of the Father who is Fountain Fullness and, as such, the Word is simultaneously Exemplar of all creation. As the full expression of God's fecundity, the Word of God is also the expression of all that God can be in relation to finite creatures.[45]

Bonaventure sees the Word as uniquely proceeding from the Father by way of exemplarity as the very "reason for exemplifying."[46] Being the Exemplar is not simply an appropriation to the second person of the Trinity, but is proper to the Word.[47] The Word is the principle of expression and manifestation in the Trinity.[48] Because of the unity of the divine nature, the whole Trinity is exemplary with regard to creation, but this is focused and expressed in the Word: "Thus, while at one level the whole of the Trinity is exemplary with respect to the world, at another level the mystery of exemplarity is concentrated in a unique way in the Son . . . as the Word is the inner self-expression of God, the created order is the external expression of the inner Word."[49] Bonaventure sees the Word as the inner self-expression of God, and creation as the external expression of this inner Word: "Hence the Word expresses the Father, and the things he made, and principally leads us to union with the Father who brings all things together; and in this regard he is the *Tree of Life*, for by this means we return to the very *fountain of life* and are revived in it."[50]

Hayes points to the importance of the theme of Christ as the centre in Bonaventure's thought, above all in the *Collations on the Six Days*, where the idea of the centre is applied to all levels of the mystery of Christ: "The eternal Son who is the center of the Trinity and who mediates all the divine works of creation and illumination, in becoming incarnate assumes his place as the center of the created universe and its history. . . . Not only does all emanate from the Father through the Word; but the return of all things back to the Father can take place only through the same Word, who stands at the very center of reality."[51] The Word of God is the metaphysical center of the movement out from God (the *exitus*) and the return of all things to God (the *reditus*):

> Such is the metaphysical Center that leads us back, and this is the sum total of our metaphysics: concerned with emanation, exemplarity, and consummation, that is, illumination through spiritual radiations and return to the Supreme Being. And in this you will be a true metaphysician.[52]

Bonaventure builds his theology of the Word on the analogy of human consciousness, and on the distinction in human thinking and speaking between the inner word of conscious knowledge, and the outer word of communication and speech. In God's inner Word, God knows not only God's self, but also all the ways in which God might possibly communicate God's self in creatures. The external word is the creation, which is not God but God's expression in a universe of creatures.[53] All of these creatures reflect the mystery of God, since the inner Word of God is the Exemplar for every creature.

THE BOOK OF CREATION

For Bonaventure, like Augustine and others,[54] the natural world is a book that tells us of God, as he says in his *Breviloqium*:

> From all we have said, we may gather that the created world is a kind of book reflecting, representing, and describing its Maker, the Trinity, at three different levels of expression: as a vestige, as an image, and as a likeness. The aspect of vestige ("footprint") is found in every creature; the aspect of image, only in intelligent creatures or rational spirits; the aspect of likeness, only in those spirits that are God-conformed.[55]

Every creature is related to, dependent upon, and conformed to its Creator as the principle of its existence. The conformity as a vestige, found in all creation, Bonaventure sees as "remote": each creature is configured to its Creator in the way it partakes of unity, truth, and goodness. The conformity to God as an image, found in human beings, he considers to be "proximate": it is found in intelligent creatures that are made to attain God, in knowledge and love, by means of memory, understanding, and will. The third level of conformity, found in those transformed by grace, he finds "most intimate": it is the possession of the gift of the Holy Spirit as an infused gift, by which the person is conformed to God in faith, hope and love.[56]

Clearly the three levels of the book of creation stand behind the first four of the six steps described in *The Mind's Journey into God*. As Bonaventure sees it, before sin entered the world this book of creation effectively revealed divine Wisdom: "when the image was not yet spoiled but rendered God-like through grace, the book of creation sufficed to enable human beings to perceive the light of divine Wisdom."[57] But in spite of sin, all is not lost. The capacity for contemplation of God through the book of nature that is lost by sin can be recovered by grace and faith, through the book of the Scriptures, and through Christ. For Bonaventure the book of Scripture and the grace of God are necessary if fallen human beings are to reach a full understanding of what lies before them in the book of nature.

Bonaventure has a special word, "contuition," to describe seeing something in itself and at the same time seeing it as the expression of the Eternal Art. He writes: "all creatures in this world of sensible realities lead the spirit of the contemplative and wise person to the eternal God. . . . They are vestiges, images, and spectacles proposed to us for the contuition of God."[58] The creatures of our world, then, are signs that point beyond themselves: "For every creature is by nature a kind of copy and likeness of that eternal Wisdom."[59]

By contuition we not only know other creatures, but in truly knowing them in their specificity and uniqueness, we also know something of their Exemplar. And all these creatures, in their variety and diversity, represent the divine light, each in its own way: "As you notice that a ray of light coming in through a window is colored in accordance with the shades of the different panes, so the divine ray shines differently in each creature and in the various properties."[60]

TRAJECTORIES

While Bonaventure owes a good deal to the Neo-Platonic tradition, and his eschatology is not inclusive of other forms of life, his Franciscan inheritance is obvious in his commitment to the creatures of this world and in his central focus on Jesus Christ, and on his cross. I see his theology as offering these trajectories towards a contemporary theology of the natural world:

1. The Trinity is radically dynamic, fruitful, and self-communicating by nature.
2. Creation is the free overflow of this inner-Trinitarian fruitfulness and divine self-communication in a world of creatures.
3. The Father is the Fountain Fullness, the Source of all fecundity in the triune life, and in creation.
4. The Word is the self-expression of the Fountain Fullness in revelation and incarnation. And the Word is the Exemplar for all creatures, and each is the expression of the eternal Art.

5. All creatures reflect the Trinity, witnessing to the power, wisdom, and goodness of their Creator.
6. Creation is a book of God that we can read in the light of the biblical book, and in the light of Christ.
7. Every creature, every eco-system, every grain of sand, every great galaxy, is the self-expression, and the place of divine presence: "Open your eyes, alert your spiritual ears, unlock your lips, and apply your heart so that in all creation you may see, hear, praise, love and adore, magnify and honor your God."[61]

Notes

1. For the Latin text, see *Doctoris seraphici S. Bonaventurae opera omnia* (Rome: *Ad claras Aquas* [Quaracchi], 1882). I will use the English translation of the first book of the *Sentences* in *Commentaries on the Four Books of Sentences: Book I – On the One & Triune God* (Mansfield, MA: The Franciscan Archive, 2014); *Works of St. Bonaventure IX: Breviloquium*, trans. Dominic V. Monti (St. Bonaventure, NY: Franciscan Institute Publications, 2006); *Works of St. Bonaventure III: St. Bonaventure's Disputed Questions on the Mystery of the Trinity*, trans. Zachary Hayes (St. Bonaventure, NY: Franciscan Institute Publications, 2000); *Works of St. Bonaventure II: Itinerarium Mentis in Deum*, trans. Zachary Hayes (St. Bonaventure: Franciscan Institute Publications, 2002); *Works of Bonaventure, V. Collations on the Six Days*, trans. Jose De Vinck (Paterson, NJ: St. Anthony Guild, 1970).
2. Bonaventure, *Breviloquium*, 7.4.7.
3. Ibid.
4. I am not, then, focusing attention on Bonaventure's theology of the Spirit, which is an important aspect of his Trinitarian theology.
5. Philotheus Boehner, "Introduction," in *Works of St. Bonaventure: Itinerarium Mentis in Deum*, eds. Philotheus Boehner and Zachary

Hayes (Saint Bonaventure, NY: Franciscan Institute Publications, 2002), 9. (I will use Zachary Hayes's translation in this publication, henceforth referred to as *Itinerarium*).

6. Bonventure, *Itinerarium*, Prologue, 3.
7. Ibid., 7.3.
8. Ibid., 1.1.
9. Ibid., 1.9.
10. Bonaventure follows Augustine using the ternary "weight, number, and measure" from Wisdom 11:21 (*Itinerarium* 1.11).
11. Bonaventure, *Itinerarium* 1.11.
12. Ibid., 1.13.
13. Leonard Bowman, "The Cosmic Exemplarism of Bonaventure," *The Journal of Religion* 55:2 (1975), 181–98, at 187.
14. Bonaventure, *Itinerarium*, 1.14.
15. Ibid.
16. Ibid., 1.15.
17. Ibid., 2.6.
18. Ibid., 2.7.
19. Ibid.
20. Ibid., 2.8.
21. Ibid.
22. Ibid., 2.9.
23. Ibid.
24. See Philotheus Boehner, *Itinerarium*, 179n10.
25. Bonaventure, *Itinerarium* 2.9.
26. At this point Bonaventure builds on Augustine to reflect on numbers: "since there is no beauty of delight without proportion; and since proportion resides first of all in number; it is necessary that all things involve number. From this we conclude that *number is the principal exemplar in the mind of the Creator*, and in creatures it is the principal vestige leading to wisdom" (*Itinerarium* 2.10).
27. Bonaventure, *Itinerarium* 2.11.

28. Ibid.
29. Ibid., 2.12.
30. Bonaventure, *Breviloquium*, 1.3.7.
31. Zachary Hayes, "Introduction," in *St Bonaventure's Disputed Questions on the Mystery of the Trinity*," trans. Zachary Hayes (St. Bonaventure, NY: Franciscan Institute, 1979), 41–43.
32. Bonaventure, *Sentences*, d.2, a.u., p.2, a.1, fund.4.
33. See his *De Trinitate*, 4.20.29.
34. Zachary Hayes, "Introduction," in *Mystery of the Trinity*, 101.
35. Bonaventure, *Mystery of the Trinity*, 8, Conclusion.
36. Ibid., 8. Replies, 7.
37. Ibid.
38. Hayes, "Introduction," in *Mystery of the Trinity*, 101.
39. See Hayes, "Introduction," *Mystery of the Trinity*, 41. The whole structure of Bonaventure's *Breviloquium* is built on this structure of *exitus* and *reditus*. See the comments of Dominic Monti in his "Introduction," *Breviloquium*, xlviii.
40. Hayes, "Introduction," 102.
41. Bonaventure, *Breviloquium*, 1.3.7.
42. Bonaventure, *Sentences*, d.31, p.2, a.1, q.2, resp.
43. Ibid.
44. Zachary Hayes, "Introduction," *Mystery of the Trinity*, 51.
45. Ibid., 47.
46. Bonaventure, *Sentences*, d.6, a.u., q.3, resp.
47. Ibid., d.6, a.u., q.3, ad.4.
48. "*ratio exprimendi et manifestandi*" (Bonaventure, *Sentences*, d.27, p.2, a.u., q.3, resp.).
49. Zachary Hayes, "Introduction," *Mystery of the Trinity*, 47.
50. Bonaventure, *Collations on the Six Days*, 1, 17.
51. Zachary Hayes, "Introduction," *Mystery of the Trinity*, 54. See *Collations on the Six Days*, 1, 10–39.

52. Bonaventure, *Collations on the Six Days*, 1, 17.
53. Bonaventure, *Sentences*, d.27, p.2, a.u., q.1, resp.
54. See Augustine, *Contra Faustum*, 32.20; *Enarrationes in Psalmos*, 45.7; *Sermones*, 68.6.
55. Bonaventure, *Breviloquium*, 2.12.1.
56. Ibid., 2.12.3.
57. Ibid., 2.12.4.
58. Bonaventure, *Itinerarium* 2, 11.
59. Ibid., 2.12.
60. Bonaventure, *Collations on the Six Days*, 12.14.
61. Bonaventure, *Itinerarium* 1.15.

7.

Thomas Aquinas (1225–1274)

Life and Context: Like Bonaventure, Aquinas lived in a time of religious renewal epitomized in the formation of the Franciscan and Dominican orders, and a period of intense intellectual life associated with the newly-founded universities of Europe, such as those of Paris, Oxford, Cambridge, and Salamanca. One of the issues that confronted theologians of the time was the renewal of interest in Aristotle, stimulated by thinkers from Spain, including the Muslim scholar Ibn Rushd (1126–1198), known to the Latin world as Averroes, and the Jewish philosopher Maimonides (1135–1204). The Aristotelian revival presented a challenge to Christian theologians, many of whom were inclined to Neo-Platonism rather than Aristotle's this-worldly philosophy. Thomas came from the district of Aquino, in the Lazio region of today's Italy. In spite of strong opposition from his family he joined the Dominicans, and was sent in 1245 to study at the University of Paris with the Dominican now called Albert the Great, a theologian deeply engaged with Aristotle and the physical sciences of his day. When Albert was transferred to Cologne in 1248, Aquinas followed him, and began his first lectures on the Scriptures. Aquinas returned to Paris to complete his studies, culminating in his *Commentary on the Sentences of Peter Lombard*. He taught in Paris, in Naples, in Orvieto, and in Rome. He wrote as a Christian theologian, fully committed to biblical revelation, but as one who also embraced philosophical exploration, and was able to enter into critical and constructive engagement with Aristotle, whom he called "the Philosopher." His works include commentaries on Scripture, and on texts of Aristotle, as well as major theological works, including his *Summa contra Gentiles* and his masterpiece the *Summa theologiae*.[1] He died on the way to the Second Council of Lyons in 1274.

Aquinas has a positive, open, view of the natural world, based firmly on the biblical view of the goodness of creation. He is a thinker who learns much not only from the Bible, but also from the approach to nature of his empirically-minded teacher, Albert the Great, and from the down-to-earth philosophy of Aristotle. He has a high view of the human as created in the image of God, and at times he writes of other creatures as given for human use.[2] But he is not inclined to disparage nature, nor to see it as an impediment on the way to God. For Aquinas the world of nature is always God's good creation and to demean creation is to demean the Creator.

He sees the natural world as a place of divine presence. For him, God is intimately present to every creature, to every plant and to every sparrow. In response to the question whether God is in all things he writes:

> God exists in everything; not indeed as part of their substance or as an accident, but as an agent is present to that in which its action is taking place. . . . Now since it is God's nature to exist, he it must be who properly causes existence in creatures, just as it is fire itself sets other things on fire. And God is causing this effect in things not just when they begin to exist, but all the time they are maintained in existence, just as the sun is lighting up the atmosphere all the time the atmosphere remains lit.[3]

Aquinas's metaphors bring out the continuous nature of God's creative act. Creatures exist because they are continually ignited by the *fire* of God. As the *sun* continuously radiates light and illumines the day, so God continuously pours forth being on creatures enabling them to exist. He insists that this creative presence of God is deeply immanent to each creature. Existence, he points out, is what is most "intimately and profoundly interior" to each creature, and it is at this most interior place of existence that God is present to each thing enabling it to be: "So God must exist and exist intimately in everything."[4] And because God is not only interior to all things, but is also uncontained by anything, and is completely beyond all things, it is equally true to say that God is most intimately interior to things as it is to say that all things are in God.[5]

In the introduction to his treatment of creation in his *Summa theologiae*, Aquinas makes an explicit link to what he has written about God as Trinity.[6] He says that, having earlier discussed the "coming forth" (*processio*) of the divine persons in the Trinity, he will now take up the task of discussing the "coming forth" (*processio*) of all creatures from God. In his work, *procession* is a technical term for the eternal coming forth of the Word and Spirit in the divine life. These intra-divine processions, he now suggests, are to be seen as the source and model of the free act of creation, by which a universe of creatures now comes forth from God in all its abundance and diversity.

In the same introduction, Aquinas points out that his treatment of creation will be divided into three parts, discussing first the production of creatures, then their distinction, and, finally, their preservation and guidance. This outline makes it abundantly clear that creation involves not just the original production of a world of creatures, but their ongoing existence, flourishing and governance. For Aquinas, these various aspects are united in God, in the one divine act of creation. Creation, then, is not simply an event of the past, but a continuous relationship. From God's side it is the ongoing conferring of existence, and of the capacity to be and become, in an inter-relational world. From the side of the creature, it is the permanent condition of receiving existence from another.

Aquinas's discussion of creation draws not only on theology, but also on philosophy, specifically on metaphysics. In the first section of this chapter, I will focus on his metaphysical approach to creation through the concept of participation. Then, in the second section, I will take up his theological insights into creation as an act of the Trinity. Finally, I will explore how Aquinas's notion of God's creative act sets creation free to be itself, and enables the laws of nature, and the empirical sciences, to have their own integrity.

CREATION AS A RELATIONSHIP OF PARTICIPATION

The biblical doctrine of creation, that God alone is the Creator of all things in heaven and on earth, sets the scene for Aquinas's philosophical exploration. As I have already suggested, Aquinas thinks through this biblical idea that God is the source of every entity by exploring the philosophical idea of existence. What is it that accounts for the actual existence of things? What is it that enables this tree in front of me to actually exist? What is it that enables me to be?

Aquinas's project had to face the limits of language available in his time. The Latin word *ens* was used to refer to a specific being. The word *essentia* referred to a thing's essence or nature. But there was no word available to speak of the actual existence of an entity—to focus on the fact of this entity's existence.[7] So Aquinas takes up the word *esse* (literally 'to be'), with the meaning of the real existence or 'is-ness' of a thing. He sees God as the one whose very nature is to be, to exist, to possess *esse*. God's essence is to be.

To express the relation between God whose very nature is

to be, and creatures who do not possess in themselves the reason for their existence, Aquinas takes up the notion of participation from the Neo-Platonic tradition. He thinks of creation as the relation of participation by which entities continually receive their being from the one, unique, divine source who possesses the absolute fullness of being. He writes that "all other than God are not their own existence (*esse*), but participate in existence (*esse*)."[8] The concept of participation enables him to speak of God as the absolute fullness of being, who enables all creatures to participate in existence as a sheer gift. Using this concept of participation, he is able not only to point to the Creator as constant Source and giver of being, but also to show the fundamental goodness of creatures, in so far as they constantly receive their existence, identity, and integrity from their good Creator.

A creature that participates in being points beyond itself to the source of all being. It exists from the God who is sheer to-be (*esse*). Aquinas says that God is *esse*, subsisting through God's own self.[9] To possess existence by nature is absolutely unique to God, since all the entities of the universe, all creatures, are not their own existence, but participate in existence. Aquinas's thinking thus moves from creatures who participate in existence to God whose essence is to be, whose very nature is to exist.

Aquinas never includes God and creatures under a general concept of being. God is never thought of as a being amongst other beings. Rather, Aquinas sees all the creatures we observe empirically, including ourselves, as participating in existence, and thus as pointing beyond themselves to the transcendent first cause. In his view, God is not known directly from creatures, but only as the first cause of the being of all things, and thus as the mysterious and wonderful fullness of being and life, the Creator.

Rudi Te Velde points out that Aquinas's concept of participation has the connotation that the finite creature embodies in its own particular way a likeness of the divine being from which it exists: "That which exists in a finite manner, so as to be a particular being of a certain kind, must therefore be intrinsically and positively related to the infinite fullness of being in such a way that it expresses something of this fullness in itself (*similitudo*)."[10] The concept of participation expresses the idea that the creature has a form of identity with the infinite Creator, such that the creature *is* the infinite in a limited, particular, creaturely way. The creature expresses something of the fullness of God. While Aquinas does not see creatures as participating in the divine essence, he does see each creature as possessing a divine *likeness* by which it is constituted in its immediate relationship with God.[11] Each creature is a kind of composition, of the thing it is in itself such as a tree, and of the tree's participation in absolute being. It is not as if existence is added to the essence of a tree. Rather the essence of the tree exists only in and from its participation. It becomes the tree it is only by participating.

Each creature is in the likeness of God because of its participation in being (*esse*), but this does not mean that all participate in being in the same way. There is a hierarchy of participation, with creatures distinguished by the different ways in which they participate in absolute being. But in Aquinas's concept of creation, human beings, other animals, birds, trees, mountains and rivers, and the stars of distant galaxies, all exist, in their own distinct ways, "in communion with the universal source of being."[12] This universal source of being is, in Aquinas's Christian theology, God the Trinity.

A FULLY TRINITARIAN THEOLOGY OF CREATION

Recent scholarship has once again made it clear that Aquinas's theology of creation is fully Trinitarian, with each of the divine persons involved in the one act of creation in specific ways. This was not always been clear in earlier accounts. Twentieth-century theology was marked by the artificial and misleading opposition, introduced by Theodore de Regnon in 1892, between two types of Trinitarian theology: a Latin conception of the Trinity grounded in the one divine essence and a Greek conception focused on the divine persons. The result was a false stereotype of Augustine and Aquinas as almost exclusively focused on the one divine essence in their theology of creation, and of Greek theologians, such as the Cappadocians, as focused on persons and relationships.

In the light of this, it has been a necessary corrective to insist on the one hand, that the great theologians of the East, like those of the West, hold that the divine actions of creation and salvation are common to all the divine persons, and belong to the one divine essence. And it has been equally necessary, on the other hand, to show how Western theologians, like Aquinas, in their own distinctive ways, see God's creative and saving acts as personal, in that each of the divine persons brings something properly their own to the work of creation and salvation.

It is worth noting another misconception of Aquinas's view. In the middle of the twentieth century, Karl Rahner criticized the scholastic theology of the standard manuals for the way they treated the one God philosophically and speculatively before turning to the Trinitarian God of revelation, broadly following Aquinas's pattern. Rahner opposed the scholastic theology of the Trinity for what he rightly saw as a damaging tendency to speculate on "the immanent

Trinity" (the inner life of God) in a way that is completely separated from the "economic Trinity" (the biblical God revealed in the economy of creation and salvation).

In his view, the way back to a life-giving theology of the Trinity was to ground all theology about the inner life of God in what we know from the biblical economy of creation and salvation. Rahner's critique was an important protest against the sterility of much theology that found its way into textbooks after Aquinas, but it is not a critique that applies to Aquinas himself. As Aquinas expert Jean-Pierre Torrell has said, "The famous Rahnerian axiom—'The Trinity of the economy of salvation is the immanent Trinity and vice versa'—is nowhere better verified than in St. Thomas."[13] Biblical faith is the starting-point for Aquinas, and his theology of creation is fully informed by this faith.

At the beginning of this chapter I drew attention to the way Aquinas's introduction to his treatment of creation explicitly grounds the coming forth of a world of creatures in the processions of Word and Spirit in the triune life of the Trinity. Gilles Emery has shown how Aquinas consistently understands these Trinitarian processions of Word and Spirit as the exemplary cause and reason for the further free procession of all things in creation.[14] Emery points to a theological principle that can be found in all the major works of Aquinas: the dynamic, eternal, coming forth of the Word and Spirit in the divine life is the model, source, and cause of the production of the world of creatures.[15]

Aquinas also locates what is distinctive to the divine persons in the act of creation in their personal properties. He points to the personal property of the Son as the Word, the *Logos*, and to the personal property of the Spirit as Love. He explains how these distinctive personal properties come into play in the one Trinitarian act of creation:

> For, as was shown when we were discussing God's knowledge and willing, God is the cause of things through his mind and will, like an artist of works of art. An artist works through an idea conceived in his mind and through love in his will bent on something. In like manner God the Father wrought the creature through his Word, the Son, and through his Love, the Holy Spirit. And from this point of view, keeping in mind the essential attributes of knowing and willing, the comings forth (*processiones*) of the divine Persons can be seen as types for the comings forth of creatures.[16]

What is specific, in the divine life, to the Son as Word, and to the Spirit as Love, determines what is specific to their distinct roles in the one act of creating a universe of creatures. Each creature, each star in our galaxy, each bird, is an expression of an idea in the mind of God the divine artist. Each is an expression of the Word, the *Logos*. And each is the product of the divine will, the fruit of divine Love, the Holy Spirit.

Aquinas has another, closely related, way of specifying the distinct roles of the divine persons in the one act of creation, in his understanding of the proper order in the Trinity found in their relations of origin. Because the Father is the principle of the Word, the Father is also the ultimate principle and source for all creation. Because the Word receives creative power from the Father, the Father is understood as creating through the Word. And because the Spirit is the Love that comes from both the Father and the Word, the Holy Spirit has creative power from both, and brings life and completion to the creation. The order of the relations of origin of the Trinity is also the order that determines what is distinctive of the Three in the common act of creation of a universe of creatures. Aquinas writes:

> As the divine nature, while common to all three persons, is theirs according to a certain precedence, in that the Son receives it from the Father, and the Holy Spirit from them both,

> so it is with creative power, for it is common to them all; all the same the Son has it from the Father, and the Holy Spirit from them both. Hence to be the Creator is attributed to the Father as to one not having power from another. Of the Son we profess that through him all things were made, for while yet not having this power from himself, for the preposition "through" in ordinary usage customarily denotes an intermediate cause, or a principle from a principle. Then of the Holy Spirit, who possesses the power from both, we profess that he guides and quickens all things created by the Father through the Son.[17]

Each divine person has a distinct mode of existence. The Father eternally exists as the Source without origin, who is the principle of the Word, with whom the Father breathes forth the Holy Spirit. The distinct mode of existence of each divine person springs from these relations. And as each person has a distinct mode of existence, so each has a distinct mode of action, in the one act of creation.[18] The Father acts in the world through the Son who is Word and Wisdom, and creates and gives life through the Holy Spirit who is Love in person; the Son acts "insofar as he is personal expression of the wisdom of the Father—that is to say in so far as he is God the Word from whom bursts forth Love"; the Holy Spirit acts as "the Communion and Love of the Father and the Son," bringing life to creatures as "Love and Gift proceeding from the Father and the Son."[19]

For Thomas Aquinas, then, the Trinity acts in a single action, by the one power, from the one divine nature, but according to the distinct personal mode that is proper to each person. The diversity and distinction of creatures is an expression and reflection of the abundance of divine life. The exemplar for all creatures is found in the Word and Wisdom of God: "divine wisdom holds the originals of all things, and these we have previously called the Ideas, that is the exemplar forms existing in the divine mind."[20] In the divine Word, God comprehends the one divine essence, and also the diverse exemplars of creatures by which they participate in the likeness of the one divine essence.

This means that, for Aquinas, as for Augustine and Bonaventure, a trace of the Trinity can be found in all creatures. Because Aquinas sees the processions of the divine persons according to the model of the Word of the mind and the Love of the will, he sees in human beings, endowed with mind and will, a representation of the Trinity that is more than a trace and that can be called an image. As he says, human beings image the Trinity "when they conceive an idea and love springs from it."[21]

What of other creatures? According to Aquinas, each of them possesses a likeness of the Trinity by way of a trace. Each creature has a form that makes it what it is, and each of them is ordered to other creatures. Each creature exists in its own identity and exists as related to other creatures. So in Aquinas's view, each entity, as a created substance, points to its principle and cause, "and so indicates the Person of the Father, who is the beginning from no beginning."[22] And because of its particular form, "it tells of the Logos, for form in a work of art is from the artist's conception."[23] And because each creature goes out from itself in relationships, "it tells of the Holy Spirit as Love."[24] Each entity, each kangaroo, is a trace of the Trinity because it points to is source and principle (the Father), it possesses its own specific form and identity that points to the divine artist (the Word), and participates in an inter-relational world that points to the divine will that orders creatures to one another (the Spirit who is Love).

The abundance and diversity of creatures is needed, according to Aquinas, to give expression to the fullness and beauty of the Trinity. The plurality of creatures and their distinctiveness spring from the divine intention. God brought creatures into existence to communicate and express divine goodness, which necessarily requires a diversity of creatures:

> For he brought things into existence so that his goodness might be communicated to creatures and re-enacted through them. And because one single creature was not enough, he produced many and diverse, so that what was wanting in one expression of the divine goodness might be supplied by another, for goodness, which in God is singular and all together, in creatures is multiple and scattered. Hence the whole universe less incompletely than one alone shares (*participat*) and represents his goodness.[25]

The full, uncreated Image of God, the eternal Word, is singular. But no one creature can adequately express and represent this divine Image and Exemplar. Many diverse creatures are needed to better represent the divine goodness, with each a partial expression of divine goodness. For Aquinas, many creatures are needed to contribute to the perfection of the universe,[26] and the whole universe as ordered to God as its end.[27] "This implies," says William French, "that a world with humans, snail-darters, whales, mountain gorillas, and ferns of all sorts is better than one simply filled with humans."[28]

In today's world, human actions are destroying many such expressions of divine goodness. Species of animals, insects, and plants are made to go extinct. Ancient forests are logged and burnt. Land is degraded. Rivers are used as dumps. Great areas of mountain range and farming land are disfigured and made sterile by mining operations. The oceans are not only warming because of human-induced climate change, but are being filled with plastic. Aquinas's concept of the diversity of creatures as representing the sheer abundance and beauty of God has a prophetic word to speak in our time.

CREATION SET FREE: THE INTEGRITY OF NATURAL CAUSES

Both the atheistic scientists of recent times and fundamentalist Christians see the scientific account of origins and the biblical account of creation as in competition with one another. Either science is right or the Bible is right. In this context, Aquinas's theology of creation has much to offer, because it shows not only the possibility of, but also the necessity for, different levels of explanation.[29] Furthermore, in his theology it becomes clear that these different levels of explanation are non-competing and mutually enriching.

Earlier in this chapter, I discussed how Aquinas sees God as present to all creatures, continually conferring existence (*esse*) upon them: he writes that "God acts interiorly in all things," since "for all things God is properly the universal cause of *esse*, which is innermost in all things."[30] In language from Aristotle, but informed by his own theological convictions, Aquinas speaks of God's creative act of conferring existence on all things as *primary causality*, and of all the interacting causes found in the creaturely world as *secondary* causes. But God is never to be seen as a cause among other causes in the world, as a cause like creaturely causes, but only as the Creator who enables all creaturely causality. When God is referred to as primary cause, the word *cause* is being used analogously to point to the absolutely unique relationship of creation. For Aquinas there is an infinite difference between God's creative act and the interacting secondary causes we find at work in the world around us. These secondary causes include all the patterns of relationship found in the natural world, all the interactions of the empirical world, and everything studied by the sciences.

In Aquinas's view, apart from the case of a miracle, God

acts in and through secondary causes. He rejects the extreme view that God acts directly as the cause of all events in nature in such a way that there is no real role for created causes (called *occasionalism* in the history of philosophy). Equally, he rejects the view that God acts in the beginning to set things up, but takes no further part in the action (often called *deism*). His view is that God continually acts in and through creatures being truly causal in their own right. He completely opposes the idea that creaturely causes do not possess their own reality and integrity:

> But this is impossible, and first because it would deprive creation of its pattern of cause and effect, which in turn would imply lack of power in the creator, since an agent's power is the source of its giving an effect a causative capability. It is impossible, secondly, because if the active powers that are observed in creatures accomplished nothing, there would be no point to their having received such powers. Indeed if all creatures are utterly devoid of any activity of their own, then they themselves would seem to have a pointless existence, since everything exists for the sake of its operation.[31]

Aquinas's view is that God enables creatures to be fully causal in their own right. He sees God acting in this profoundly respectful way "from the abundance of his goodness, imparting to creatures also the dignity of causing."[32] In the divine goodness, God so upholds the dignity of creatures that God wants them to be fully causal, with their own integrity and proper autonomy. In terms of contemporary science this would mean that God respects the integrity of the laws of nature, including all that is involved in the emergence of the universe over the last 13.8 billion years and the evolution of life on Earth over the last 3.7 billion years.

God's act of creation establishes the natural world in its own real distinction from God. The concept of participation enables Aquinas to think of the relationship between God's creative action and the working of natural causes in a non-exclusive and non-competitive manner. In his view, then, since divine action and creaturely causality operate at different levels, there is nothing to prohibit the one and same action, such as the causing of a creature to exist, "issuing from a primary and secondary agent."[33] God's creative act is precisely the kind of causality that enables a universe of creatures to exist in their own proper being with their own proper operations. God creates in such a way that creation is "set free" in its own natural being.[34]

The causality of God as Creator, then, enables nature to function with its own proper system of cause and effect. God is not to be found as a cause like others in the natural world. God's action is not to be found by the methods of science. What the empirical sciences explore is what Aquinas calls secondary causes—all the interacting relationships, causal connections, and systems to be found in the natural world.

For one who thinks like Aquinas, it is not only nature that possesses its own integrity but also the sciences. It is not the role of theology to step in to answer unanswered scientific questions. God should never be invoked to fill the gaps in scientific knowledge. There is never a need to engage in a strategy like "intelligent design"—attempting to find complexity in nature that cannot be accounted for by current evolutionary science with the implication that it must be due to the intervention of an Intelligent Designer. The role of theology, and philosophy, is to ask the deeper question as to why there is anything at all. What is it that accounts for the very existence of the natural world with all its evolutionary interconnections? What is it that enables and empowers a universe of creatures to exist, to interact, and to evolve? And what is the meaning of the existence of galaxies, of Earth and its living creatures, and of me and all those I love? Is all ultimately meaningless, or the gift of unthinkable Love, as Aquinas holds, and biblical faith teaches?

TRAJECTORIES

It requires some effort for twenty-first century people to get inside Aquinas's way of doing theology. And it is important to acknowledge that he writes of other animals as ordered to human use,[35] and shares the medieval view that there is no place for animals and plants in God's fulfillment of creation.[36] Nevertheless, he offers important insights that can be fundamental in a twenty-first century theology of the natural world.

1. It is God's nature to exist, and God is interiorly and intimately present in all creatures, enabling their existence.
2. Creatures possess existence by participation. Each expresses something of the fullness of God and possesses a divine *likeness.*
3. The dynamic, eternal, coming forth of the Word and Spirit in the divine life is the model, source, and cause of the production of the world of creatures.
4. Because the Father is the principle of the Word and the Spirit, the Father is also the ultimate principle and source for all creation. Because the Word comes from the Father, the Word receives creative power from the Father, and the Father creates through the Word. Because the Spirit is the Love that comes from both the Father and the Word, the Holy Spirit has creative power from both, and brings life and completion to the creation.
5. Each creature, each star in our galaxy, each bird, is an

expression of an idea in the mind of God, the divine artist. Each is an expression of the Word. Each is the product of the divine will, the fruit of divine Love, the Holy Spirit.

6. The variety and diversity of creatures express the divine goodness better than any one creature could ever do.
7. God acts in and through natural causes, such as the laws of nature that science discovers.
8. God's creative action and the laws of nature operate at different levels in a non-exclusive and non-competitive way.
9. God fully respects the integrity of natural causes.

Notes

1. The edition of the *Summa theologiae* I am using is the Blackfriars edition, 61 volumes, Latin and English translation, with notes, introductions, and commentaries (New York: McGraw-Hill Book Company, 1964–1980).
2. Aquinas, *Summa contra Gentiles*, 3.112.12.
3. Aquinas, *Summa theologiae*, 1.8.1.
4. Ibid.
5. Ibid., 1.8.1 ad 2.
6. Ibid., 1.44. Preface.
7. The Latin word *existentia* had the slightly different meaning of standing out.
8. Aquinas, *Summa theologiae*, 1.44.1.
9. "*Deus est ipsum esse per se subsistens*," often shortened to *ipsum esse subsistens*. To "subsist" means that something exists as a substance in its own right.
10. Rudi Te Velde, *Aquinas on God: The "Divine Science" of the Summma*

Theologiae (Aldershot: Ashgate, 2006), 140.

11. Ibid., 146, no. 49. He notes that Aquinas speaks of creatures participating in the divine nature only in his theology of grace.
12. Ibid., 141.
13. Jean-Pierre Torrell, "Preface" in Gilles Emery, *Trinity in Aquinas* (Ypsilanti, MI: Sapientia Press, 2003), xx.
14. Emery, *Trinity in Aquinas*, 69, 172. See also Gilles Emery, *The Trinitarian Theology of Saint Thomas Aquinas* (Oxford: Oxford University Press, 2007).
15. Thomas spells out this principle in his *Commentary on the Sentences*: "processiones personarum aternae sunt causa et ratio productionis creaturarum" (I *Sent.*, d.14, q.1, a.1, sol.). For examples of this principle in the *Summa theologiae*, see 1.45.6 at 1, and 1.45.7 at 3.
16. Aquinas, *Summa theologiae*, 1.45.6. In his *Commentary on the Gospel of John* (1.2.76) Aquinas says that if "through" denotes causality from the standpoint of the thing produced, then the statement that "The Father does all things through the Son" is "not simply appropriated to the Word, but is proper to the Word" ("*non est appropriatum verbo, sed proprium eius*").
17. Ibid., 1.45.6 at 2.
18. See Gilles Emery, *The Trinity: An Introduction to the Catholic Doctrine of the Triune God* (Washington, DC: The Catholic University of America Press, 2011), 163.
19. Ibid.
20. Aquinas, *Summa theologiae*, 1.44.3.
21. Ibid., 1.45.7.
22. Ibid.
23. Ibid.
24. Ibid.
25. Ibid., 1.47.1.
26. Ibid., 1.22.4.
27. Ibid., 1.65.2.
28. William C. French, "Grace is Everywhere: Thomas Aquinas on Grace and Salvation," in *Creation and Salvation, Volume 1: A Mosaic*

of Selected Classic Christian Theologies, ed. Ernst M. Conradie (Zurich: LIT, 2012), 147–72, 159.

29. On the levels of explanation, see John F. Haught, *Making Sense of Evolution: Darwin, God, and the Drama of Life* (Louisville, KY: Westminster John Knox, 2010), 23–27.
30. Aquinas, *Summa theologiae*, 1.105.5.
31. Ibid.
32. Ibid., 1.22.3.
33. Ibid., 1.105.5 ad 2.
34. See Te Velde, *Aquinas on God*, 141. See also Elizabeth Johnson, *Ask the Beasts: Darwin and the God of Love* (London: Bloomsbury, 2014), 154–80.
35. See Aquinas, *Summa contra Gentiles* 3.112.12.
36. See Aquinas, *Summa theologiae supplementum*, 3.91.5.

8.

Martin Luther (1483–1546)

Life and Context: Martin Luther lived in a period of church life when there was a culture of intense anxiety about one's eternal salvation, a concern exacerbated by the widespread preaching of indulgences. He was born in Eisleben, Saxony, the son of a miner. Luther was a good student who graduated as a Master of Arts from the University of Erfurt in 1505. Suffering anguish about where he stood before God, Luther joined the Augustinian community at Erfurt, and was ordained a priest in 1507. He was invited to study and teach at the new University of Wittenberg, and after a short time back at Erfurt, became professor at Wittenberg in 1512. He rejected scholastic theology, embraced the thought of Augustine, and focused his academic teaching entirely on the Bible. Working through his lectures on the Psalms and the letters of Paul, Luther found profound liberation and a radical reorientation of his life in the insight that we are saved not by what we do, but by faith in Jesus Christ. On October 31, 1517, he posted his ninety-five theses at the Castle Church of Wittenberg, creating enormous interest, but also arousing suspicion in Rome that he was rejecting papal authority. After a dispute with Cardinal Cajetan, and after publically burning an ultimatum from Pope Leo X, Luther was excommunicated in January 1521. He abandoned his religious habit in 1524, married a former nun, Katharina von Bora in 1525, and together they established a hospitable home in the

> former Augustinian monastery at Wittenberg. Luther continued to preach powerfully, to teach, write and publish widely throughout his life, translating the Bible, revising the liturgy, writing hymns, and engaging in controversy with Rome and with others in the wider Reformation movement. He completed his translation of the Bible into German in 1534, and in 1535 began his *Lectures on Genesis*, completed only a short time before his death on February 18, 1546.[1]

There can be little doubt that the focal point for Luther's life's work was his discovery of a gracious God. He found profound liberation in the biblical teaching that we are justified by the grace of Christ alone, and in the conviction that what is required of us is not any form of self-justification, but simply faith in Christ alone. Having found this God of grace in the reading of the Scriptures, he labored long and hard to put the Bible into the hands of ordinary Christians.

Bernhard Lohse points to what is original in Luther's theology: "What is new is that of all the questions with which theology must deal, the aim and goal in any instance is the question of salvation. Questions about the doctrine of God, about the sacraments, about ecclesiology, can be dealt with only when this aspect is seen from the outset."[2] In a similar way, his theology of creation is directed towards and serves his theology of salvation. But, nevertheless, as Paul Althaus says, Luther's theology is summed up in the phrase "God is God," and for him God is God in both creation and salvation, so that "being God and creating are identical."[3] It is God and only God who creates. Thus while Luther never attempts the kind of systematic theology found in Aquinas or in Calvin, he nonetheless offers rich theological insights into God's creative act and into the world around us understood as God's good creation. I will focus first on Luther's particularly personal sense of being created, then on his theological view of the creative Word of God. In the third section I will take up his comments on the presence of God in creatures and, finally, point briefly to his view of the risen Christ at the heart of the creation.

CREATION AS PERSONAL

In Luther's thought creation is not an abstract doctrine, nor is it about something that simply happened in the past. It is God's constant action, which takes place in a three-fold way, in original creation, in ongoing preservation, and in re-creation in Christ.[4] It is always creation out of nothing, completely underserved and unmerited by the creature. God creates simply out of freedom and love. The priority in Luther's thought about creation is on the way the human creature stands receptively before creation and before the Creator. For Luther creation is a doctrine that is always personal, or in the language of a later time, existential. This is fully evident in his explanation of the first article of the Creed in the *Small Catechism*:

> I believe that God has created me together with all that exists. God has given me and still preserves my body and soul: eyes, ears and all limbs and senses; reason and all mental faculties. In addition, God daily and abundantly provides shoes and clothing, food and drink, house and farm, spouse and children, fields, livestock, and all property—along with all the necessities and nourishment for this body and life. God protects me against all danger and shields and preserves me from all evil. And all this is done out of pure, fatherly, and divine goodness and mercy, without any merit or worthiness of mine at all! For all of this I owe it to God to thank and praise, serve and obey him. This is most certainly true.[5]

Luther's creation theology, then, is that of one who is convinced that we stand before a God who freely cares for each of us and provides for each of us personally. God constantly gives gifts from the divine abundance, gifts that are directed to me as an individual believer. His theology of creation is about everyday life, the life of marriage, children, home, friends, eating and drinking, farm, or other work, as the good place of God. One of his constant themes, one that would have an enormous impact on future generations, is his vigorous rejection of the monastery as the ideal, or prime way to God, and his rediscovery of Christian vocation in the daily life of ordinary Christians. It is a theology that fully embraces bodily existence.

While Luther certainly makes it clear that he accepts the historicity of Adam and Eve, he resists the idea of seeing the Genesis texts as referring only to the beginning of things. As Johannes Schwanke points out, for Luther the events of creation are happening in his own history. For him, primordial history is present history:

> Luther does not allow himself to be distanced from God's creative work by any isolated, past original history, by any "beginning of things," but instead sees himself placed in the most radical fashion in the creative event of primordial history, which he interprets as a history of the present. Luther's personal and present environment is the effective sphere of divine creativity. It is not Adam who is ultimately relevant here, but Luther. In an interlacing of times, past, present, and future come together in a single moment; pervading time, God's living creative Word is without end and remains ever "effective" to this very day, is *verbum efficax*.[6]

Each human being is addressed personally by the creative Word. Each receives the abundance of his or her life as a sheer gift. Each is called to personal response. For Luther, God's creation and preservation of creatures are one: "We Christians know that with God creating and preserving are identical."[7] He sees the Word of God as creating and conserving humanity in three estates, in the church, the family and the state.[8] In each of these estates human beings are called to be co-operators with the creating and sustaining Word. There is no separation between sacred and profane in any of these areas. So Luther writes: "Hence when a maid milks the cows or a hired hand hoes the field—provided that they are believers, namely, that they conclude that this kind of life is pleasing to God and was instituted by God—they serve God more than all the monks and nuns, who cannot be sure about their kind of life."[9]

Along with humans, all other creatures also depend upon God who continually enables them to be born and to live, and provides for them each day. Luther speaks of wonderful natural events as miracles.[10] He sees the birth of a child, for example, as taking place only through God's creating and sustaining Word. But this Word is profoundly linked with the love and generativity of the parents, so that the creative act of the Word is mediated through the parents in bringing a new life into existence. God's power and care extend continually to all God's creatures. In Luther's view, the constant miracles of the natural world, such as the plant growing from a seed, or a chick hatching from an egg, should lead us to wonder and praise: "If you should examine a kernel of grain on the field minutely, you would die of wonder."[11]

THE WORD OF SALVATION IS THE CREATIVE WORD

Luther links creation and salvation together and sees both as completely underserved and unmerited gifts. The absolute gratuity that characterizes Luther's theology of grace also applies to the experience of being a creature of a gracious God. Niels Gregersen has argued that Luther's theology of creation is modelled on his doctrine of salvation, and that there is a parallel between the indwelling of Christ in the believer by grace and the work of Father, Son and Spirit creatively at work in the life of the creature in the divine blessing.[12] Luther unites creation and grace in one large view of God's gratuitous action:

> For we believe that God, who is the almighty Creator, produces all things from nothing, the best things from those that are evil, and salvation out of what is despaired of and lost. This is attributed to Him in Rom 4:17, when it is stated that He "calls into existence the things that do not exist." And 2 Cor 4:6 speaks of God who ordered light to shine out of darkness–not a spark from a coal, but light out of darkness, life from death, righteousness from sin, the kingdom of heaven and the liberty of the children of God from enslavement to the devil and hell.[13]

The God who creates new things out of nothing, who brings bright light out of darkness, is also the one who saves, bringing life out of death, righteousness out of sin, and liberation out of slavery.

For Luther, our life, our justification, our liberation is found only in Jesus Christ, who is the Word made flesh. This is the same creative Word that speaks in the opening chapter of Genesis. It is the Word in whom all things are made (John 1:3). Luther's whole theology can be characterized as a sustained and powerful theology of the Word of God, the Word that addresses us, the Word that reveals, the Word that saves.[14] This Word is mediated to us through the Scriptures, and is encountered and known in the life of the church, in the Word proclaimed and the Sacraments of baptism and eucharist. It is a Word from outside ourselves, an external or alien Word, rather than simply an interior experience.

In his commentary on first chapter of the Gospel of John, particularly in his reflections on the words "And the Word was made flesh" (John 1:14), Luther celebrates the incarnate Word not only as the Word of creation, but also as the Word continually involved in the preservation of creatures:

> God the Father initiated and executed the creation of all things through the Word; and now He continues to preserve His creation through the Word, and that forever and ever. . . . For just as we were created by Him without our own aid and agency, so we cannot maintain ourselves with our own might. Hence as heaven, earth, sun, moon, stars, man, and all living things were created in the beginning through the Word, so they are wonderfully governed and preserved through that Word.[15]

As long as creatures exist, they exist only from the continuously creative Word. Not only the existence of creatures, but also all their actions, interactions, and wonderful fruitfulness, evident in the birth of children and the begetting of new life throughout nature, are completely dependent on this constant creative act:

> How long, do you suppose, would the sun, the moon, the entire firmament keep to the course maintained for so many thousands of years? Or how would the sun rise and set year after year at the same time in the same place if God, its Creator, did not continue to sustain it daily? If it were not for the divine power, it would be impossible for mankind to be fruitful and beget children; the beasts could not bring forth their young, each after its own kind, as they do every day; the earth would not be rejuvenated each year, producing a variety of fruit; the ocean would not supply fish.[16]

Luther brings home the existential meaning of this theology for his congregations: "If God were to withdraw His hand, this building and everything in it would collapse."[17] If God were to stop enabling the whole process then there would be nothing at all: "The sun would not long retain its position and shine in the heavens; no child would be born, no kernel, no blade of grass, nothing at all would grow on the earth or reproduce itself if God did not work forever and ever."[18] But instead, what we observe is the wonderful newness of the creation:

> Daily we can see the birth into this world of new human beings, young children who were nonexistent before; we behold new trees, new animals on the earth, new fish in the water, new birds in the air. And such creation and preservation will continue until the Last Day.[19]

In this quotation, Luther speaks of us *seeing* new babies, new young trees, new animals, new fish and young birds, and recognizing that all of this is the work of the ever creative Word of God. Because of his strong theology of the Word, Luther usually gives priority to hearing the Word over seeing. In his understanding we do not see God in the creatures and people around us, because God, who is certainly present to them, is also hidden in them, so that all creatures are like masks of God. And it is fundamental for the Christian to distinguish between God and the masks of God. We need the Word to speak the truth of God, to illuminate what is hidden. God is known not simply, then, through what we see, which is always a creature, but through the revelatory Word. Luther insists that he could find God in a stone, in fire, in water, or in a rope, but, he says, God "does not wish that I seek him there apart from the Word."[20] So Luther does not encourage the idea that we can know the Word through creation alone. Even when we are filled with wonder at the creation, we need the illumination of the gospel Word. We need to hear and not simply see. As Paul Santmire says, "Luther champions the sensibility of hearing, on the one hand; and often (but not always) rejects the sensibility of seeing."[21]

God is not fully self-evident in nature, but is a hidden God. Robert Jenson points out that Luther knows of three ways in which God is hidden, in creation, in the cross of Jesus, and in the darkness of faith itself.[22] With regard to the first hiddenness, God hides Godself in the way that God rules the creation, which often defies out understanding. Jenson notes the continued relevance of this theology in the light of the extreme suffering evident in our world. Holding to the Christian view of the goodness and providence of God, he asks, how can we explain the terrible suffering of even one child? Of course, if God is considered as a distant or disengaged Creator, then God's responsibility for suffering might seem less evident. But such a disengaged God is not the biblical God, and not the God of Luther—"But the real God, the Creator, whose omnipotent agency is closer to every grain of sand than it is to itself, cannot so easily be excused."[23] In Jenson's view, we must not pretend that we can make God's providence morally comprehensible. He says bluntly that sheer anger, or atheism, are in fact reasonable responses to the way God governs the creation. If we are to proclaim the biblical teaching of the goodness of creation it must be accompanied by an anguished "Nevertheless!" Jenson says that we need to face more honestly the ways in which the natural world does not show forth divine goodness. It would be a great apologetic advance, Jenson states, if the church were to speak this kind of truth in its address to the world.[24]

In 1518, Luther attended a chapter of his Augustinian order at Heidelberg, and presented his theses, called the "Heidelberg Disputation," where he outlined the distinction between a theology of the cross and a theology of glory. A theologian of the cross is one whose knowledge of God comes through God's self-revelation in the Word made flesh, and above all in the cross of Jesus. A theologian of glory is one whose knowledge of God builds upon rational speculation. A theology of the cross contradicts human expectations, while a theology of glory sees more continuity between human expectations and God. In his critique of theologians of glory, Luther attacks scholastic theology, and its dependence on philosophers like Aristotle, and the method of arguing from creation to God. What he defends in all this is the conviction that we are justified by grace alone, by faith in Christ alone. Victor

Westhelle writes that "the theology of the cross is the doctrine of justification and vice versa."[25] Luther's theology of the cross, then, stands as a challenge to theological arguments that would argue rationally from creaturely life to the nature of God. What matters is the liberating Word that God speaks to us in the cross of Christ, which challenges our rational assumption and ways of thought.

Luther's emphasis on hearing rather than seeing, his teaching on the hiddenness of God in creation, and his embrace of the theology of the cross and rejection of the theology of glory, all taken together suggest that Luther might not have much to contribute to today's discussion of the presence of God in the creatures around us. But in fact Luther very often expresses a lively conviction of the immanence of God to even the tiniest of creatures.

THE PRESENCE OF GOD IN CREATURES

Luther sees the whole creation as fundamentally good, and as the place of divine indwelling. He sees God as wholly present, and immediately present to all creatures. Because he is committed to the idea that God cannot be contained by any creature and is always the transcendent one, he is not inclined to a pantheistic position. But he consistently sees the God beyond all creatures as interiorly present to each of them. He explores his theology of divine presence in various places, including his eucharistic theology where, against Zwingli, he articulates his view of the real presence of Christ.

In speaking of God's presence, Luther protects the divine transcendence, in part, by the diverse multitude of prepositions he uses. God, then, is in, with, and under, but also above, outside, and beyond all things. God can be fully and deeply present in a creature and at the same time be radically beyond it. In Luther's view, then, God is not limited to a creaturely way of inhabiting space. He writes:

> God is substantially present everywhere, in and through all creatures, in all their parts and places, so that the world is full of God and He fills all, but without His being encompassed and surrounded by it. He is at the same time outside and above all creatures. These are exceedingly incomprehensible matters; yet they are articles of our faith and are attested clearly and mightily in Holy Writ.[26]

Luther's position, then, is fully consistent with the mainstream of Christian theology on the indwelling of God to each creature and on God's utter transcendence of all creaturely limits. These are not opposites for him, as they were not for the great patristic and medieval theologians. It is precisely because God is beyond all human reason, and beyond all the spatial limits of creatures, that God can be fully and interiorly present to each creature. What is unique to Luther is the vigorous, existential and engaging way he expresses this long-standing conviction of Christian faith. He does this with typical power with the image referred to earlier of a grain of wheat:

> For how can reason tolerate it that the Divine Majesty is so small that it can be substantially present in a grain, on a grain, through a grain, within and without, and that, although it is a single Majesty, it is entirely in each separately, no matter how immeasurably numerous these grains may be.[27]

How can God be so small as to be *in* a single grain of wheat? How can God be both within and without a grain? Luther uses paradox to point to what is beyond comprehension in his own form of apophatic theology.[28] After speaking of a God who is small enough to be in a grain of wheat, he goes on immediately to ask how we might understand that the majesty of this God "is so large that neither this world nor a thousand worlds can encompass it."[29] Luther then encapsulates his own theology on divine presence:

> His own divine essence can be in all creatures collectively and in each one individually more profoundly, more intimately, more present than the creature is to itself, yet it can be encompassed nowhere and by no one. It encompasses all things and dwells in all, but not one thing encompasses it and dwells in it.[30]

For Luther it is "vulgar and stupid" to think of the divine presence as filling creation in the way that finite creatures fill a space, as if "God is a huge, fat being who fills the world similar to a sack of straw filled to the top and beyond."[31] No. God's presence is of another kind, a kind that is appropriate only to the Creator: God is "a supernatural, inscrutable being able to be present entirely in every kernel of grain and at the same time in all, above all, and outside creatures."[32] Luther uses all his rhetorical skill to bring out the reality of the Creator's inner presence to every kind of creature, but his continual use of paradox and his explicit statements always guard God's unspeakable otherness:

> Nothing is so small but God is still smaller, nothing so large but God is still larger, nothing is so short but God is still shorter, nothing so long but God is still longer, nothing is so broad but God is still broader, nothing so narrow but God is still narrower, and so on. He is an inexpressible being, above and beyond all that can be described or imagined.[33]

Because God is present in the tiniest creature, Luther can embrace in his preaching the idea that the natural world speaks to us of God. It is full of Bible! He writes: "Thus our house, farm, field, garden, and everything is full of 'Bible'; there God not only preaches through His miracles, but also strikes out eyes, touches our senses, and illuminates our very hearts if we are willing to receive it."[34] Like Bonaventure, and others in the Christian tradition, Luther thinks that if it were not for the sin of Adam, God's power, grace, and wisdom would have been easily recognized in the smallest blossom. He speaks of "the power and wisdom of God in even the smallest flowers," and of God creating "out of the parched soil, such a variety of flowers, such pretty colors, such sweet vernal grass, beyond anything a painter of an apothecary could make."[35] In spite of Luther's emphasis on hearing, he clearly believes that seeing properly does matter. He challenges those who see, but don't see, who take the miracles of creation for granted:

> They say, "Oh is that such a great thing the sun shines, or fire warms, or water gives fish, or the earth yields grain, or a cow calves, or bears children, or a hen lays eggs? That happens every day." My Mr Simpleton, is it a small thing just because it happens every day? If a magician could make an eye that would live or that would be able to see one cubit, great God, he would be a lord on earth! Yet whoever could make a real leaf or a blossom on a tree would be above God and would have a world of admiration, praise and thanks. But it is a discouraging damnably ungrateful and blind that God showers upon them such great and rich miracles, and they do not consider even one of them or thank Him for it![36]

The upright, however, have a different response: They "think about those works, consider them, admire them, with pleasure, so that they must gratefully say: 'Surely this is an excellent, great, beautiful and glorious work!'"[37]

CREATION AND THE RISEN CHRIST

Luther's focus on salvation in Christ does not lead him to an other-worldly view of creatures around him, but to a new perception of God's presence and action at the heart of nature and to new relationship with other creatures.[38] The consciousness of being saved by the grace of Christ, Luther proposes, can lead to a view of nature deeper than that found in Erasmus, or those who follow Rome:

> We are now living in the dawn of the future life; for we are beginning to regain a knowledge of the creation, a knowledge forfeited by the fall of Adam. Now we have a correct view of the creatures, more so, I suppose, than they have in the papacy. Erasmus does not concern himself with this; it interests him little how the fetus is made in the womb.[39]

The awareness of divine mercy at work in our lives, of grace abundantly and freely given, means, Luther says, that "by God's mercy we can begin to recognize his wonderful works and wonders also in flowers when we ponder his might and goodness."[40] If we ponder the meaning of the Word embracing creaturely life in the incarnation, we will look at other creatures with far more appreciation:

> Now if I believe in God's Son and bear in mind that He became man, all creatures will appear a hundred times more beautiful to me than before. Then I will properly appreciate the sun, the moon, the stars, trees, apples, pears, as I reflect that he is Lord over and the Center of all things.[41]

When the risen Christ ascends to the right hand of the Father, Luther says, he is present to the whole universe of creatures. The right hand of God is everywhere; it is the creative power of God present to the whole creation, creating and sustaining all things. This right hand is now the place of Christ: "Christ's body is everywhere because it is at the right hand of God which is everywhere, although we do not know how that occurs."[42] Calvin opposes this theology because he sees it as undermining the humanity of the risen Christ.

Although Santmire recognizes that Luther's position is controversial, he suggests that it could contribute to a renewed theology of the cosmic Christ for an ecological age. It could mean, he suggests, that we "could possibly tell of encountering the presence of Christ when we contemplate the lilies of the field or when we respond to the faces of the poor as well as when we receive the bread and wine of the Eucharist."[43] It is notable that Pope Francis takes up precisely this position in his recent encyclical *Laudato Si'*.[44]

When Luther looks towards the final fulfillment of things, he imagines it as an embodied transformation of human beings participating in resurrection life, and as a new heavens and earth. He does not think of the wider creation as having sinned or fallen, but he sees it as suffering the effects, the curse, of the human fall.[45] So while human beings are saved both in the sense of being radically forgiven and also as participating in final fulfillment in Christ, for the wider creation salvation means only the second of these—overcoming of decay and death and sharing in final fulfillment with human beings. We do not find in Luther any developed thinking about the future of creation in God. But in light of the biblical promise of the new heavens and the new earth (Isa 65:17–18; 2 Pet 3:13), Luther states:

> That will be a broad and beautiful heaven and a joyful earth, much more joyful than the Paradise was.[46]

TRAJECTORIES

It needs to be acknowledged that the other side of the focus on individual salvation, associated with the Reformation and its Roman Catholic response, has been Western Christianity's extreme neglect of God's creation and its failure to protect the natural world. But this does not express Luther's own position. Luther not only reflects a general Christian anthropocentrism, but also can be very interested in and sympathetic to God's other creatures.[47] Here are some trajectories in his thought can have new meaning in today's context:

1. The Word of God who is made flesh is the Word of Creation.
2. Being justified by the grace of God leads to a new, far more developed, appreciation of the natural world.
3. Luther represents a lively, personal, existential sense of being a creature among the other creatures of our world.
4. He has a stance of radical receptivity before the Creator for all the things of everyday life—all is a gift.
5. Luther advocates a revolutionary view of vocation in ordinary life, of marriage, family, home, work, meals, the body, sexuality, and nature as the place of God.
6. God can be so small as to be in a single grain of wheat and yet God's majesty is so large that neither this world nor a thousand worlds could ever encompass it.
7. The conviction that God is hidden in the creation can be meaningful in facing up to the violence, suffering, and loss built into the natural world.
8. Luther argues that the risen Christ who is at the right hand of God is mysteriously present and at work in the whole creation.

Notes

1. For Luther's writings, see Jaroslav Pelikan et al., eds., *Luther's Works* (Philadelphia: Fortress Press and St. Louis: Concordia, 1958–1986), hence *LW*, and *D. Martin Luthers Werke. Kritische Gesamtausgabe* (Weimar: Böhlau, 1883–1993).
2. Bernhard Lohse, *Martin Luther's Theology: Its Historical and System-*

atic Development (Minneapolis: Fortress Press, 1999), 35.

3. Paul Althaus, *The Theology of Martin Luther* (Philadelphia: Fortress Press, 1966), 105.
4. In this section, I draw on Johannes Schwanke, "Luther's Theology of Creation," in *The Oxford Handbook of Martin Luther's Theology*, eds., Robert Kolb, Irene Dingel, and L'Ubomír Batka (Oxford: Oxford University Press, 2014), 201–11.
5. *The Small Catechism*, in *The Book of Concord: The Confessions of the Evangelical Lutheran Church*, eds., Robert Kolb and Timothy J. Wengert (Minneapolis: Fortress Press, 2000), 354–55.
6. Schwanke, "Luther's Theology of Creation," 202–3.
7. Luther, *Lectures on Genesis*, 22:13, *LW* 4,136.
8. Schwanke, "Luther's Theology of Creation," 207–9.
9. Luther, *Lectures on Genesis*, 22:2, *LW* 3, 321.
10. Luther, *Psalm 111* (1530), *LW* 13, 369.
11. Luther, *Sermon von dem Sakrament*, cited in Heinrich Bornkamm, *Luther's World of Thought* (Saint Louis: Concordia, 1958), 182.
12. Niels Henrik Gregersen, "Grace in Nature and History: Luther's Doctrine of Creation Revisited," *Dialog* 44:1 (March 2005), 19–25.
13. Luther, *Lectures on Genesis* 45:7, *LW* 8, 39.
14. See Jaroslav Pelikan, *Luther the Expositor: Introduction to the Reformer's Exegetical Writings* (St. Louis: Concordia, 1959).
15. Luther, *Sermons on the Gospel of St John*, 1:3, *LW* 22, 26.
16. Ibid.
17. Ibid.
18. Ibid.
19. Ibid.
20. Luther, *The Sacrament of the Body and Blood of Christ Against the Fanatics (1526), LW* 36, 342.
21. H. Paul Santmire, "Creation and Salvation according to Martin Luther: Creation as the Good and Integral Background," in *Creation and Salvation, Volume 1: A Mosaic of Selected Classic Christian Theologies*, ed. Ernst M. Conradie (Zurich: LIT, 2012), 173–202,

180.

22. Robert W. Jenson, "Luther's Contemporary Theological Significance," in *The Cambridge Companion to Martin Luther*, ed. Donald K. McKim (Cambridge: Cambridge University Press, 2002), 272–88, 278.
23. Jenson, "Luther's Contemporary Theological Significance," 279.
24. Ibid.
25. Victor Westhelle, "Luther's *Theologia Crucis*," in *The Oxford Handbook of Martin Luther's Theology*, ed. Kolb, et al., 156–67, 164.
26. Luther, *Dass diese Worte Christi* (1527), cit., Bornkamm, *Luther's World*, 189. Throughout this section I engage with ideas and examples found in the work of H. Paul Santmire: *The Travail of Nature: The Ambiguous Promise of Christian Theology* (Minneapolis: Fortress Press, 1985), 121–43; "Martin Luther, The Word of God and Nature; Reformation Hermeneutics in Context," in *Ecological Hermeneutics: Biblical, Historical and Theological Perspectives*, eds., David G. Horrell, Cherryl Hunt, Christopher Southgate, and Francesca Stavrakopoulou (London: T&T Clark, 2010), 166–80; "Creation and Salvation according to Martin Luther," in Conradie, *Creation and Salvation*, 173–202.
27. Luther, *Dass diese Worte Christi* (1527), cited in Bornkamm, *Luther's World*, 189.
28. Santmire, "Creation and Salvation," 183–84.
29. Luther, *Dass diese Worte Christi* (1527), cit., Bornkamm, *Luther's World,* 189.
30. Ibid.
31. Luther, *Vom Abendmahl Christi* (1528), cit., Bornkamm, *Luther's World*, 188.
32. Ibid.
33. Luther, *Confession Concerning Christ's Supper* (1528), *LW* 37, 228.
34. Luther, *Second Sermon on the Resurrection of the Dead* (May 25, 1544), *LW* 58, 126.
35. Luther, *Table Talk*, *LW* 54, 327.
36. Luther, *Psalm 111* (1530), *LW* 13, 366–67.

37. Ibid.

38. Santmire, *The Travail of Nature*, 131.

39. Luther, *Table Talk*, 1, 1160, cit., Bornkamm, *Luther's World*, 184.

40. Ibid.

41. Luther, *Sermons on the Gospel of John*, 3:35, *LW*, 496.

42. Luther, *Confession Concerning Christ's Supper*, *LW* 37, 214.

43. Santmire, "Creation and Salvation according to Martin Luther," in *Creation and Salvation*, ed., Conradie, 199.

44. See, for example, *Laudato Si'*, par. 100: "Thus the creatures of this world no longer appear to us under merely natural guise because the risen One is mysteriously holding them to himself and directing them towards fullness as their end. The very flowers of the field and the birds which his human eyes contemplated and admired are now imbued with his radiant presence."

45. Luther, *Lectures on Genesis 3:17*, *LW* 1, 204.

46. Luther, *Psalm 8:3*, *LW* 12, 121.

47. See David Clough, "The Anxiety of the Human Animal: Martin Luther on Non-human Animals and Human Animality," in *Creaturely Theology: On God, Humans and Other Animals*, eds., Celia Deane-Drummond and David Clough (London: SCM, 2009), 42–60.

9.

John Calvin (1509–1564)

Life and Context: Calvin was born in Noyon, not far from Paris. As a law student in Paris, Calvin was exposed to the Christian humanism of Erasmus and Budé, and to various currents of thinking about church reform. By 1533, he had read and been influenced by Luther's works. It is not clear when Calvin broke finally with Rome, but in 1534, fearing persecution from King Francis I, he left Paris for Basel, where he completed the first edition of his *Institutes of the Christian Religion* (1536). He was persuaded to assist in the reform of the religious and civic life of Geneva, which had achieved independence and aligned itself with the Protestant cause as a free republic. In 1538, after conflict with the city council, Calvin was expelled from Geneva and went to Strasbourg where he lectured on the New Testament, published a commentary on Romans, brought out a developed edition of the *Institutes*, and was married. In 1541 he was invited back to Geneva, where he developed his *Ecclesiastical Ordinances*, seeking to organize the church in Geneva in the light of the Word of God and the model of the early church. The church would be administered by pastors, teachers, elders, and deacons, and overseen by a consistory made up of pastors and lay elders. Eventually, not only the church but also the city were transformed by Calvin's work. He continued to preach, teach, and write, publishing his final revision of the *Institutes* in 1559.[1] Towards the end of his life he formed an Academy in Geneva that would train ministers, some of whom would carry his understanding of Christian faith beyond Geneva to other parts of Europe and the world.

Calvin has a strong sense of the creative and providential action of God in the natural world as well as in human lives. Novelist Marilynne Robinson describes Calvin as integrating God's cosmic power with God's intimate kindness for each of us. She refers to Calvin's words: "The whole world is preserved, and every part of it keeps its place, by the will and decree of Him, whose power, above and below, is everywhere diffused. Though we live on *bread*, we must not ascribe the support of life to the power of *bread*, but to the secret kindness, by which God imparts to bread the quality of nourishing our bodies."[2] In her reflection on this text, Robinson writes: "Kindness is uttered again in everything that nourishes."[3] In Calvin's thought, she says, God's attributes, such as the divine kindness, are understood as present and intentional, as if the bread were given to us from Christ's own hands. She adds: "Calvin would say, And it is."[4]

I will begin this chapter with a discussion of Calvin's concept of the knowledge of God through creation, before taking up his metaphors for creation. Then I will focus on his interest in the starry heavens above, offer a brief account of his understanding of the eschatological future of creation, and conclude with his view of human responsibility for creation.

THE KNOWLEDGE OF GOD THE CREATOR

A recent commentator lists ten distinctive contributions Calvin makes to Christian theology, the first being his positive appreciation of the natural order, and his insistence that we are to find delight and enjoyment in the sight and the smell of flowers, grasses, trees, and their fruits, and to see them as the mirror of God's glory.[5] The second is Calvin's conviction of God's provident care for the universe and all its inhabitants. God sustains and governs the whole universe by the divine power, wisdom, and goodness, as God acts providentially in the life of believers. Calvin says: "Nothing is more profitable than the knowledge of this doctrine."[6]

Calvin was at one with the great theologians of the patristic and medieval eras in holding that God creates the whole universe *ex nihilo*, and that God continues to provide existence for all things, and to care for them in divine providence. Like his predecessors, such as Augustine, he understands creation as an act of God the Trinity, with the Father creating the universe of creatures through the eternal Word. He sees God as creating over six days so that "our human minds might more easily be retained in the meditation of God's works."[7] And, he notes, God waited to fashion the human being on the sixth day because God wanted to first prepare all that would be useful and helpful for humanity.[8]

Calvin's *Institutes* are structured around our human knowledge of God. He takes up the knowledge of God as Creator in Book 1, and the knowledge of God as Redeemer in Books II–IV.[9] He sees the knowledge of God as shining forth in the universe that God creates, sustains, and governs. Creatures proclaim the wisdom of God: "There are innumerable evidences both in heaven and on earth that declare his wonderful wisdom."[10] These evidences, he says, are revealed in the sciences, such as astronomy and medicine, but are also available to ordinary people, who "cannot open their eyes without being compelled to witness them."[11] They cannot be unaware "of the excellence of divine art" for it reveals itself in the countless, but well-ordered, stars of heaven.[12] And the human body itself is so remarkably ingenious that "its Artificer is rightly judged a wonder-worker."[13]

But because sin has perverted their vision, humans can fail

to see creation for what it is and instead are filled with errors, superstition, and idolatry. This means that humanity is in need of further and more effective help to direct it truly to the Creator. This help has been given in the saving Word of God, who is revealed in God's gift of the Scripture. We need the biblical Word to interpret rightly and fully God's presence and action in the wider creation. It is Scripture that provides the "spectacles" by which we can see the true God in creation:

> Just as old or bleary-eyed men and those with weak vision, if you thrust before them a most beautiful volume, even if they recognize it to be some kind of writing, yet can scarcely construe two words, but with the aid of spectacles will begin to read distinctly; so Scripture, gathering up the otherwise confused knowledge of God in our minds, having dispersed our dullness, clearly shows us the true God.[14]

Calvin consistently claims that God created the world for the use and comfort of humanity: "God himself has shown by the order of creation that he created all things for man's sake."[15] And Calvin's views were significant in the emergence of the modern world, as a commentator on Calvin points out: "Calvin is arguably the most influential theologian of the English-speaking world, in which the scientific and industrial revolutions developed."[16] Does this mean that we should see Calvin's theology of creation as supporting the ruthless exploitation of the natural world that has led to our current ecological crisis? I think that a response to this question needs to take into account what Calvin actually says about the meaning of creation, which is taken up in what follows.

THREE METAPHORS FOR THE NATURAL WORLD

Randal Zachman helpfully brings together various aspects of Calvin's teaching on the theological meaning of the universe of creatures, by highlighting three of Calvin's metaphors for the created order, as the theatre of God's glory, the living image of God, and the beautiful garment of God.[17]

THE THEATRE OF GOD'S GLORY

Calvin writes of the natural world not only as a book, but also as a painting from which believers can learn of the Creator, and often also as the theater of the divine glory.[18] The metaphor of a painting occurs, for example, when he proposes that while all people can see God's creation displayed before them like a beautiful painting, it is only in relation to Christ that the true and full meaning of the divine work of art is understood:

> We must therefore admit in God's individual works—but especially in them as whole—that God's powers are actually represented *as in a painting*. Thereby the whole of mankind is invited and attracted to recognition of him and from this to true and complete happiness. Now those powers appear most clearly in his works. Yet we comprehend their chief purpose, their value, and the reason why we should ponder them, only when we descend into ourselves and contemplate by what means the Lord shows us in his life, wisdom and power; and exercises in our behalf his righteousness, goodness and mercy.[19]

Calvin conveys a similar message with his image of the creation as a glorious theatre: "Therefore however fitting it may be for man seriously to turn his eyes to contemplate God's works, since he has been placed in *this most glorious theater* to be a spectator of them, it is fitting that he prick up his ears to the Word, the better to profit."[20] In this metaphor, we are invited to imagine humans assembled as an audience in a great and beautiful theater, the theater of the universe, in which all the wonderful works of God are on stage before them. Impacted by sin, however, they can easily misunderstand what they see, and draw false conclusions, and end up in idolatry. They need the clear teaching of the one true God, given in the Scriptures, in order to see that it is truly the glory of God that is revealed in the theatre of the universe.

Calvin's insistence on the need for biblical revelation does not lead him to neglect God's self-manifestation in creation, which he sees as the first way in which we meet God, with the Scriptures being the chief way:

> Meanwhile, let us not be ashamed to take pious delight in the works of God open and manifest in *this most beautiful theater*. For as I have said elsewhere, although it is not the chief evidence for faith, yet it is the first evidence in order of nature, to be mindful that wherever we cast our eyes, all things that they meet are works of God, and at the same time to ponder to what end God created them.[21]

In Calvin's view, sin not only means humans do not see creation rightly or clearly, but also that creation itself suffers the curse brought by human sin, so that sin "defrauds" God of glory.[22] But God's will to communicate God's self is not defeated. Since humans fail to know the wisdom of God, which should be evident to them in the creation, God sends Wisdom in the flesh to lead them to the fullness of truth: "We must, for this reason, come to Paul's statement: 'Since in the wisdom of God the world did not know God through wisdom, it pleased God through the folly of our preaching to save those who believe (1 Cor 1:21).' *This magnificent theater* of heaven and earth, crammed with innumerable miracles, Paul calls the wisdom of God."[23]

Creation for Calvin, then, is the "most glorious," "most

beautiful," and the "magnificent" theater of the divine glory, in which humans can see the works of God and come to know God. Zachman sums up Calvin's theological metaphor of the theater: "by our contemplation, feeling and enjoyment of the powers of God that we behold in the theater of the world, we are invited, allured, and attracted to seek the God who is the source and author of all these powers, in whom alone is found human happiness and blessedness."[24]

IMAGE AND MIRROR OF GOD

In his interpretation of Hebrews 11:3, and in reference to Romans 1:20, Calvin speaks of the universe that we see around us as offering a clear image of God and as making visible the invisible things of God: "These words contain the very important teaching that in this world we have a *clear image of God*, and in this passage our apostle is saying the same thing as Paul in Rom 1:20, where he says that the invisible things of God are made known to us by the creation of the world, since they are seen in his works."[25] In a metaphor very closely interrelated to that of image, Calvin goes on to call the natural world the mirror of God, since God shows us evidence of God's self in the works of creation:

> In the whole architecture of his world God has given us clear evidence of his eternal wisdom, goodness, and power, and though he is invisible in himself he shows himself to us in some measure in his work. The world is therefore rightly called *the mirror of divinity*.[26]

Although Calvin lists other powers of God that can be discovered in the universe as the mirror and the image of God, such as mercy, truth, righteousness and life, he identifies the three in the quotation above with the three persons of the

Trinity, linking goodness to the Father, wisdom to the Son, and power to the Holy Spirit.[27]

In his commentary on Romans, Calvin repeats his concept of creation as the image of God, and says that we human beings are called to lift our minds to God in contemplating God's image in creation: "By saying 'God manifested it,' he means that man was formed to be a spectator of the created world, and that he was endowed with eyes for the purpose of his being led to God himself, the Author of the world, by contemplating *so magnificent an image*."[28]

When Calvin describes the human, however, it is clear that in his view humans are made in the divine image in a unique way. He sees the primary seat of the divine image in the human as "in the mind and heart, or in the soul and its powers," but there is no part of the human, in which "some sparks did not glow."[29] In this context, he speaks like others in the tradition, of the *traces* of God in the wider creation: "even in the several parts of the world some traces of God's glory shine."[30] He insists that when God places the divine image in the human a "tacit antithesis" is introduced that raises the human above other creatures and separates them from "the common mass."[31] In my view, the fact that Calvin gives a unique place to humans as image of God should not stop theologians today from building upon his theology of the universe as itself a magnificent image and mirror of God.

THE BEAUTIFUL GARMENT OF GOD

The image of the garment appears particularly in Calvin's commentaries on the psalms. When Psalm 104:1–2 speaks of God as being clothed with glory and being arrayed with light as with a garment, Calvin writes:

> In respect of his essence, God undoubtedly dwells in light that is inaccessible; but as he irradiates the whole world by his splendor, this is *the garment* in which he, who is hidden in himself, appears in a manner visible to us. . . . That we may enjoy the sight of God he must first come forth to view with his clothing; that is to say, we must first cast our eyes upon the *very beautiful fabric* of the world in which he wishes to be seen by us.[32]

The response to God's beautiful garment, the array of creatures, can only be that of astonishment and overwhelming admiration. Calvin says that we ascribe to God due honor when, "seized with astonishment, we acknowledge that our tongues and all our senses fail in doing justice to so great a subject."[33] Our astonishment at the sheer beauty and splendor of God's beautiful garment can lead us, then, beyond what we see to the invisible God, so that our hearts are moved to praise of the true living God.

Zachman notes that this metaphor allows Calvin to speak of God's intimate care for creatures, and of God's providence at work even in the desert wilderness. He points to Calvin's words: "Rivers run through the great and desolate wildernesses, where the wild beasts enjoy some blessings of God; and no country is so barren as not to have trees growing here and there, on which birds make the air to resound with the melody of their singing."[34]

Calvin, of course, sees the God who provides for the whole creation as caring wonderfully for the human being who is God's special creature, but he also sees humans as called to take care of other creatures of God. So he writes: "For if there is one drop of compassion in us, it will never enter our minds to kill an unhappy little bird, which so burns either with the desire of offspring, or with love towards its little ones, as to be heedless of life, and to prefer endangering itself to the destruction of its eggs or its brood."[35] Calvin opposes the destruction of trees in warfare not only because they and their fruits are manifestations of God's blessing to us, but also because killing trees destroys the beautiful ornamentation that God has given to the earth.[36]

THE STARRY HOST OF HEAVEN

Calvin teaches that Christian believers ought to be constantly attentive to God at work in the whole creation. He even suggests that such contemplation should occupy every waking moment: "There is indeed no moment which should be allowed to pass in which we are not attentive to the consideration of the wisdom, power and goodness, and justice of God in his admirable creation and government of this world."[37] But, even if constant attention is beyond us, we have the Sabbath, a time designed by God so that we might attend to the glory of God revealed in our universe: "And certainly God took the seventh day for his own and hallowed it, when the creation of this world was finished, that he might keep his servants free from every care, for the consideration of the beauty, excellence, and fitness of his works."[38]

It is clear from Calvin's many references to the beauty of heaven above that he takes great delight in the night sky. In Ernst Conradie's exploration of Calvin's legacy for Christian ecotheology, he focuses attention on Calvin's view of the stars of heaven, even as he acknowledges that this is counter-intuitive in the light of the obvious need for ecotheology to focus on the community of life on Earth.[39] Conradie notes that Calvin's views of the universe were pre-Copernican (but not necessarily anti-Copernican) and geocentric, and that he sees God as playing an essential role in regulating the movements of the heavenly bodies, and in holding Earth securely in its place.[40] He points to Calvin's two-fold rule in contemplating the glory of the stars: first to contemplate gratefully God's power at work in the wonders above, then to be led to contemplate God's power and grace at work in ourselves. With regard to the first act, contemplating the stars, he writes:

> The first part of the rule is exemplified when we reflect upon the greatness of the Artificer who stationed, arranged, and fitted together the starry host of heaven in such wonderful order that nothing more beautiful in appearance can be imagined; who set and fixed some in their stations that they cannot move; who granted to others a freer course; who so adjusted the motion of all that days and nights, months, years, and seasons of the year are measured off; who so proportioned the inequality of days, which we daily observe, that no confusion occurs. If it is so too when we observe his power in sustaining so great a mass, in governing the swiftly revolving heavenly system and the like. For these few examples make it sufficiently clear what it is to recognize God's powers in the creation of the universe.[41]

If he were to list all the wonders of creation, Calvin says, there would be no end to it because there are "as many miracles of divine power, as many tokens of goodness, as many proofs of wisdom" as there are kinds of things in the universe, and as there are things great or small.[42] While it is easier to see the reflection of God in the starry heaven above than in the struggle and chaos of the earthly realities around us, God is still to be found in these realities: "There is certainly nothing so obscure or contemptible, even in the smallest corners of the earth, in which some marks of the power and wisdom of God may not be seen; but a more distinct image of him is engraven on the heavens."[43]

As Conradie notes, a shift in focus becomes possible when "we are ravished with admiration" and are "overwhelmed with ecstatic admiration by the immensity and beauty of God's work." A movement of transcendence can then allow us to focus on the divine Artist in thanksgiving, praise and love.[44] And the glorious experience of the starry heaven can enable us to see God's glory in the more mundane things of our life on Earth. According to Calvin, when David sings "The heavens are telling the glory of God" (Ps 19:1), he particularly selects the heavens for contemplation, so that their extraordinary splendour might lead us to contemplate God "on the face of the earth, not only in general, but in the minutest plants."[45]

Again in this context, Calvin spells out that the knowledge of God that we might find from the stars alone is unstable, unclear, and insufficient. Sin has created disorder, and as a result, nature can have a chaotic and threatening character.[46] But despite the chaos caused in the natural world by human sin, there remains a glorious beauty and order in nature. When the Word of God provides the "spectacles" to heal our sight, we can see the glory of God revealed in the theater of the universe with far greater clarity.[47]

In discussing the Lord's Prayer, Calvin asks what it means to speak of the Father as in heaven. He makes it clear that God transcends all place, and is beyond all creation whether heaven or earth. The Scriptures tell us that the heaven of heavens cannot contain God (1 Kgs 8:27). And God tells us through the prophet that heaven is God's seat and the earth God's footstool (Isa 66:1). Calvin comments on this text: "By this he obviously means that he is not confined to any particular region, but is diffused throughout all things. But our minds, so crass as they are, could not have conceived his unspeakable glory otherwise. Consequently it has been signified to us as "heaven," for we can behold nothing more sublime or majestic than this."[48] God's utter transcendence means that God cannot be limited to any place, including the glorious starry heaven above us. Because of the majesty and sublimity of the heaven above, it functions as a symbol, the best available symbol, for the place of God.[49] But for Calvin God is present everywhere, and confined nowhere.

FUTURE LIFE

In attempting to help his people and their pastors to face the trials of life, including the real possibility of persecution and death, Calvin encourages the idea that this earthly life is far inferior to the life to come, which he images as the life of heaven. In his pastoral outreach he portrays an attitude to life in this world as characterized by "contempt for its fragility and brokenness, but not by hatred towards that which is earthly, bodily and material."[50] Our destiny is the fullness of happiness in the heavenly life of God, "heavenly immortality."[51] He can say that "heaven is our homeland," and earth is "our place of exile."[52]

This attitude to the future life, which Calvin shares with many other Christian thinkers, does not lead in his thinking to any lack of engagement with this world. On the contrary he encourages a positive and balanced attitude to everyday life, encouraging his readers to use the good things of this world "with a clear conscience, whether for necessity or for delight."[53] He proposes the principle that God's gifts are rightly used when directed to the end for which they were created, and God created them for our good and not for our ruin.[54] He encourages frugality and moderation, and the idea that earthly possessions are held in trust.[55] And he teaches every person to see their life in its particularity as a calling: "The Lord bids each one of us in all life's actions to look to his calling."[56]

In discussing the resurrection of the dead, Calvin puts emphasis on believers participating in a fully bodily way in Christ's ascension into heaven.[57] This raises the important question about his thinking on the rest of creation. Do other creatures have a future in God? Calvin never treats this issue in detail, and is cautious about the dangers of eschatological speculation. However, Susan Schreiner tracks his comments on particular texts. Commenting on Romans 8, Calvin shows that he holds that the universe, damaged by sin and in need of renovation, shares in "the longing with which everything in this world aspires to the hope of resurrection," and that he sees the universe as awaiting its share in the freedom from corruption that the resurrection promises.[58] Interpreting 2 Peter 3:10–13, Calvin says that God will not abandon or destroy creation; it is only corruptions that will be purified and melted by fire. Commenting on 1 Corinthans 15:28, Calvin writes that all things will be brought back to God who is their beginning and their end.[59] Schreiner concludes that Calvin sees God as faithful to God's original creation: "Just as God brought the cosmos into being, closely governs and restrains its natural forces, so too he will renew and transform its original substance."[60]

HUMAN RESPONSIBILITY FOR GOD'S CREATION

Calvin could not be aware, as we are in the twenty-first century, of the limits to the resources of our planet, but he is fully aware of the danger of being trapped in ever-increasing consumption of the good things offered in this world. Human beings can fail to acknowledge the Creator, and remain trapped in the endless attempt to find fulfillment in creatures. The ungodly, who do not see beyond the good things around them to the Creator shining forth in them, can seek to find happiness only in possessing more and more things. Yet their desire is never satisfied: "However great the abundance of the ungodly, yet their covetousness is so insatiable, that like robbers, they plunder right and left, and yet are never satisfied."[61]

On the other hand, Calvin thinks that those who see the beauty of creation as the theater of God's glory can attain a certain freedom in their approach to possessing things.

They will also feel the attraction of things that bring joy and comfort, but will not be trapped in this attraction: "And although the faithful also desire and seek after worldly comforts, yet they do not pursue them with immoderate and irregular ardour; but they patiently bear to be deprived of them, provided they know themselves to be the objects of divine care."[62] Knowing oneself as the object of divine care creates the possibility of moderation and frugality, as well as the possibility of enduring times of deprivation. Calvin's theology of divine providence is always in evidence. In this context it can provide a foundation for a Christian approach to a less possessive way of life, and to a certain freedom in today's consumerist society.

Perhaps the most detailed advice Calvin can offer us today in the midst of a crisis in our use and abuse of creation is found in his remarkable commentary on Genesis 2:15:

> The custody of the garden was given in charge to Adam, to show that we possess the things which God has committed to our hands, on condition, that being content with a frugal and moderate use of them, we shall take care of what shall remain. Let him who possesses the field, so partake of its yearly fruits, that he many not suffer the ground to be injured by his negligence; but let him endeavour to hand it down to posterity as he received it, or even better cultivated. Let him so feed on its fruits, that he neither dissipates it by luxury, nor permits it to be marred or ruined by neglect.
>
> Moreover, that this economy and this diligence, with respect to those good things which God has given us to enjoy, may flourish among us; let everyone regard himself as the steward of God in all things which he possesses. Then he will neither conduct himself dissolutely, nor corrupt by abuse those things which God requires to be preserved.[63]

So much of this text has striking relevance in today's world, the language of custodianship and stewardship, the emphasis on virtues of frugality, moderation, economy, and diligence, the idea that we possess things only conditionally, the idea that we are required to hand on the gifts we are given to posterity, and the insistence that we must not destroy or damage what God requires us to preserve. Randall Zachman rightly asks: "If we had followed the teaching of Calvin about creation, would we really have been led to exploit and defile the earth with a good conscience or even with indifference?"[64] And he asks a further question: "Is the ecological crisis, at least in the Western world, due to the fact that too many people followed Calvin's teaching about creation, or is it due to the fact that his teaching was apparently ignored?"[65]

TRAJECTORIES

Calvin's theology of creation is undoubtedly centered on the human. And historically his theology has played a major role in the English-speaking world in which the scientific and industrial revolutions first developed, and in some cases may have functioned to support exploitative attitudes to nature. But this function was not Calvin's intent, and stands in contradiction to some of his theological positions which may be helpful trajectories in today's world:

1. The knowledge of God shining forth in the universe that God creates, sustains, and governs.
2. The strong sense of providence both in the natural world and as directed intentionally to us: "Kindness is uttered again in everything that nourishes" (Marilynne Robinson).
3. Creation as the first revelation of God.
4. The positive appreciation of the natural world, and of finding delight and enjoyment in birds and animals, in the sight and the smell of trees and flowers.

5. Amazement and delight in the glorious starry heavens above—possibilities of connection with contemporary cosmology and astronomy.
6. Metaphors for the universe of creatures as the theater of the divine glory, the image of God, and the beautiful garment of God.
7. Humans as custodians and stewards, exercising of moderation, frugality, and freedom from possessiveness.
8. The necessary relation between creation and the "spectacles" of the Word of God.
9. The conviction that we must not damage or destroy what God requires us to preserve.

Notes

1. Calvin's works are found in *Joannis Calvini opera quae supersunt omnia*, ed. Wilhelm Baum, Edward Cunitz, and Edward Reuss, 59 vols., Corpus reformatorum 29–87 (Brunisvigae: Schwetschke [Bruhn], 1863–1900). For Calvin's *Institutes*, I will use the translation by Ford Lewis Battles, *Institutes of the Christian Religion*, 2 vols., Library of Christian Classics (Philadelphia: Westminster, 1960).
2. John Calvin, *"The Whole World is Preserved": John Calvin, Commentary on a Harmony of the Evangelists: Matthew, Mark, and Luke*, trans. William Pringle (Edinburgh, 1985; Grand Rapids, MI: Baker Book House, 1996), 24.
3. Marilynne Robinson, *The Givenness of Things: Essays* (London: Virago, 2015), 263.
4. Ibid., 263–64.
5. I. John Hesselink, "Calvin's Theology," in *The Cambridge Companion to John Calvin*, ed. Donald K. McKim (Cambridge: Cambridge University Press, 2004), 74–92, at 85.

6. Calvin, *Institutes* 1.17.3.
7. John Calvin, *Commentary on Genesis*, in *The Commentaries of John Calvin on the Old Testament* (=*CTS*), 30 vols. (Edinburgh: Calvin Translation Society, 1843–48), 1.96.
8. Calvin, *Institutes* 1.14.22. See Susan E. Schreiner, *The Theater of His Glory: Nature and the Natural Order in the Thought of John Calvin* (Durham, NC: Labyrinth, 1991), 15–16.
9. See Edward A. Dowey Jr., *The Knowledge of God in Calvin's Theology* (Grand Rapids: Eerdmans, 1994).
10. Calvin, *Institutes*, 1.5.2.
11. Ibid.
12. Ibid.
13. Ibid.
14. Calvin, *Institutes*, 1.6.1.
15. Ibid., 1.14.22.
16. Randall C. Zachman, *John Calvin as Teacher, Pastor and Theologian* (Grand Rapids, MI: Baker Academic, 2006), 233.
17. Zachmann, *John Calvin as Teacher*, 231–42.
18. See also Schreiner, *The Theater of His Glory*, 65, 107, 121.
19. Calvin, *Institutes*, 1.5.10. In this section I am adding italics to highlight Calvin's key metaphors.
20. Ibid., 1.6.2.
21. Ibid., 1.14.20.
22. Calvin, *Institutes*, 2.6.1.
23. Ibid.
24. Zachmann, *John Calvin as Teacher*, 235.
25. Calvin, *Commentary on Hebrews* 11:3, in *Calvin's New Testament Commentaries* (=*CNTC*), ed. David W. Torrance and Thomas F. Torrance, 12 vols. (Grand Rapids: Eerdmans, 1959–72), 12:160. For a full treatment of the universe as the living image of God see Randall C. Zachman, *Image and Word in the Theology of John Calvin* (Notre Dame, IN: Notre Dame University Press, 2007), especially 25–72.

26. Ibid.
27. See Zachman, *Image and Word*, 27.
28. Calvin, *Commentary on Romans* 1:19, *CNTC* 8:31.
29. Calvin, *Institutes*, 1.15.3.
30. Ibid.
31. Ibid.
32. Calvin, *Commentary on Psalms*, 104:1, *CNTC* 11:145.
33. Ibid., 104:24, *CTS* 11:164.
34. Ibid., 104:10, *CTS* 11:154.
35. Calvin, *Commentary on Deuteronomy*, 22:6, *CTS* 5:56.
36. Zachman, *John Calvin as Teacher*, 238.
37. Calvin, *Commentary on Exodus*, 20:8, *CTS* 4:436. See Zachman, *John Calvin as Teacher*, 239.
38. Ibid., 20:8, *CTS* 4:437.
39. Ernst M. Conradie, "John Calvin on Creation and Salvation: A Creative Tension," in *Creation and Salvation. Volume I: A Mosaic of Selected Classic Christian Theologies*, ed. Conradie (Zurich: LIT, 2012), 203–24.
40. Ibid., 212–14. On this see Susan Schreiner, "Creation and Providence," in *The Calvin Handbook*, ed. Herman J. Selderhuis (Grand Rapids: Eerdmans, 2009), 267–75.
41. Calvin, *Institutes*, 1.14.21.
42. Ibid.
43. Calvin, *Commentary on Psalms*, 19:1, *CTS* 8:808.
44. Conradie, *John Calvin on Creation*, 209.
45. Calvin, *Commentary on Psalms,* 19:1, *CTS* 8:808.
46. See Schreiner, *The Theater of His Glory*, 22–30.
47. Conradie writes that this suggests "a hermeneutical spiral moving from the contemplation of the heavens above to knowledge of God in Christ in order to return to the praise of the Creator by using the spectacles of God's self-revelation in Christ to detect God's presence in God's works." ("John Calvin on Creation," 211).

48. Calvin, *Institutes*, 3.20.40.

49. Conradie, "John Calvin on Creation," 212.

50. Ibid., 214.

51. Calvin, *Institutes*, 3.9.1.

52. Ibid., 3.9.4.

53. Ibid., 3.10.1.

54. Ibid., 3.10.2.

55. Ibid., 3.10.5.

56. Ibid., 3.10.6.

57. Ibid., 3.25.7. Calvin insists that Christ's ascended body remains human and finite, and thus he rejects the ubiquity of the resurrected body of Christ (held by Luther) as "monstrous" (*Institutes* 4.17.30).

58. Schreiner, *The Theater of His Glory*, 97–98.

59. Ibid.

60. Ibid., 99.

61. Calvin, *Commentary on Psalms*, 37:21, *CTS* 9:36. See Zachman, *John Calvin as Teacher*, 240–42.

62. Calvin, *Commentary of Psalms*, 4:7, *CTS* 8:49.

63. Calvin, *Commentary on Genesis*, 2:15, *CTS* 1:125.

64. Zachman, *John Calvin as Teacher*, 242.

65. Ibid.

10.

Pierre Teilhard De Chardin (1881–1955)

Life and Context: Pierre Teilhard de Chardin was born near Orcines, among the extinct volcanoes of the Auvergne region of central France.[1] Influenced by his father, an amateur naturalist, Teilhard became fascinated from an early age by animals, plants, rocks, and geological formations. Under his mother's influence, he developed a Christ-centred mysticism and, in 1899, he entered the Jesuit novitiate at Aix-en-Provence. Between 1905 and 1908 he taught physics and chemistry at the Jesuit college in Cairo. He studied theology at Hastings in England between 1908 and 1912, was ordained a priest in 1911, and served as a stretcher bearer during the First World War. Teilhard received his doctorate in geology in 1922 at the Institute Catholique in Paris, and worked closely with paleontologist, and specialist on Neanderthals, Marcellin Boule at the Natural History Museum. Teilhard's essays connecting evolution and Christian faith alarmed Catholic Church authorities, with the result that he was moved from Paris. Between 1926 and 1946 he did important geological and paleontological work in China. His theological works include his *Mass on the World* (1918), *The Divine Milieu* (1927), and *The Human Phenomenon* (1940). Roman authorities refused Teilhard permission to publish his theological works, but multiple copies were made and circulated. He worked in Paris from 1946 until 1951, before taking a position at the Wenner-Gren Foundation in New York City, where he died on Easter Sunday, 1955. Teilhard left his theological writings in the care of his secretary Mademoiselle Jeanne Mortier, who enabled their publication.

Pierre Teilhard de Chardin was a talented and widely published geologist and paleontologist, closely involved with the team that discovered and studied the *Homo erectus* fossils (*Sinanthropus pekinensis*) at Zhoukoudian, thirty miles south-west of Beijing.[2] Marcellin Boule said of the young Teilhard that he possessed all the qualities of a first rate naturalist: "an aptitude for work, penetrating observation, a combination—valuable as it is rare—keenness for minute analysis and a gift of wide synthesis, and great independence of mind."[3] Ursula King paints a picture of him later in his life, during a ten month expedition in the Gobi desert: "He had been tirelessly active along the whole journey, never without his geologist's hammer, his magnifying glass, and his note book."[4]

Teilhard also worked tirelessly towards an integrated vision of the inner relationship between evolution and Christian faith. He was not only an accomplished empirical scientist, but also a theological visionary, a mystic who wrote of himself as encountering the living God at the heart of matter and of life. Near the end of his life, he describes how the whole universe came to be for him like the burning bush of Moses: "the World gradually caught fire for me, burst into flames . . . this happened all *during* my life, and *as a result of* my whole life, until it formed a great luminous mass, lit from within, that surrounded me."[5]

By Teilhard's own account, there are three universal aspects at work in his understanding of reality, the cosmic, the human, and the Christic. He says that the cosmic and the Christic were with him from the first moment of his existence, but it has taken him his whole life to see how these three are progressively outlining the one fundamental reality.[6] In sketching Teilhard's theology of creation, I will follow this threefold pattern, with the first section on matter and evolution, the second on his view of the human and what he terms the noosphere, and the third on his theology of Jesus Christ at work in the whole creation.

MATTER AND ITS EVOLUTION

Teilhard tells of being drawn by matter, or by something that shone from the heart of it, from the age of six of seven. He loved iron, its strength, hardness, durability, and its consistency. He had a need for the essential, for what gave a sense of fullness, of necessary reality. He says that when as a child he realized that iron can become pitted and rust, he was near despair. He turned to the finely colored rocks, such as chalcedony, that he could collect from the countryside. He describes this leading to a transition: the substitution of quartz for iron led the young Teilhard towards the solid form of geological formations, then to the structures of the planet, and ultimately to the universe itself. As he taught basic physics and explored astronomy as a young Jesuit, it slowly began to become clear to him that the only real that could satisfy him was on the scale of the universal.

As a child, attracted by the variety of vegetable and animal forms around him, he was disconcerted by the perishability of a flower or an insect. He became passionate about finding new and rare species, but also felt the attraction of what lies behind all the manifestations of reality. He says of himself that he was in danger of seeking to submerge himself in the All, to be fused with the All.[7]

He says that what rescued him from the tendency towards a kind of pantheism was the emergence in his own consciousness of the idea of evolution during his theological study at Hastings. The idea of evolution was already like a fire consuming his heart and mind by the time he eagerly read Bergson's *Creative Evolution.*[8] His love for matter, life, and energy could now be combined in a synthesis, in a view of the world that was no longer that of a fragmented and static cosmos but of an organic process of cosmogenesis. Teilhard says that the word evolution was like a tune that haunted him, an unsatisfied hunger, a promise held out to him, a summons to be answered.[9]

While his own early focus had been very much on matter, in the light of his new-found evolutionary understanding Teilhard came to see matter and spirit as two states or aspects of the same cosmic stuff. He began to give more priority to spirit, and to the future. What paleontology had demonstrated for him, in the evolution of matter into life and of life into consciousness, was the progressive spiritualization of matter. He no longer saw spirit as the opposite of the tangibility of matter that he had loved so much. Rather spirit was the heart of matter, and the future of matter.

This vision of a universe that is in the state of evolution, and evolution directed towards self-conscious spirit, meant a complete turnabout in Teilard's pursuit of what is most fundamental and consistent in reality. It was no longer the smallest physical particle, such as the atom, that was foundational. What provided the real basis for reality was evolution towards complexity. The solid basis of everything was now identified with "extreme organic complexity."[10] The happiness that the young Teilhard had formerly looked for in iron, he now found in matter that through the evolutionary process of increased complexity becomes spirit.

Teilhard had begun to reflect on the immense unity of life

on Earth, of all that springs from biological evolution. His own experiences as a biologist both in the field and in the laboratory led him to consider the whole of life, and all that supports life, as forming a living envelope around Earth. Following Edwin Suess, he called this envelope the "biosphere." Closely related to this, he began to ponder the growth in shared consciousness of the planetary community of human beings. Teilhard came to the proposal that alongside the biosphere, there is emerging another immense planetary unity, that of human thought, and ultimately of human love, that he called the noosphere.[11]

Teilhard saw that increasing complexity is at the heart of biological evolution, enabling the formation of molecules, cells, and living organisms. His paleontological work, including his doctoral thesis, convinced him of the importance of the development of the brain, evident in the fossil record, which points to a further increase in complexity that enables increase in consciousness. At the end of *The Human Phenomenon,* Teilhard articulates the law that he sees as operating in the whole emergence of the biosphere and the noosphere, the cosmic law of complexity-consciousness.[12] Taking up what was at the time the still controversial idea of an expanding universe, he writes that as the universe appears to be expanding, it also appears to be becoming physiochemically more complex. On Earth, this increase in complexity is evident in chemistry, in the appearance of life, in the further evolution of diverse species, and in the emergence of humans with their highly complex brains and their capacity for thought. Increasing complexity is linked to an increase in "interiority" or the capacity for consciousness.

"This structural relationship between complexity and consciousness," Teilhard says, "has always been known and remains experimentally incontrovertible."[13] It is supported by the evidence of the fossil record. What he sees as original to his own position is that he proposes that "consciousness, defined experimentally as the specific effect of organized complexity, extends far beyond the ridiculously small interval over which our eyes manage to distinguish it directly."[14] In Teilhard's vision, the whole universe is involved in the process of increasing complexity and consciousness. This is because, on the one hand, he attributes some level of rudimentary "psyche" or interiority to even tiny particles.[15] And, on the other hand, he proposes that the increase in complexity-consciousness will ultimately result in the full emergence of the noosphere.

THE NOOSPHERE

According to Teilhard, his first insight into the idea of communal human consciousness occurred during the First World War, when he was a participant in the masses of humanity that opposed each other in the trenches of France.[16] He began to become aware of the global nature of the human, and to see human evolution ("anthropogenesis" or "hominization") as now leading in the direction of the emergence of global human consciousness. Around the membrane of life stretched like film over the surface of Earth, another envelope was becoming clear to him, like a luminous aura around the planet. This envelope, the noosphere, was not simply consciousness, but a real unity of thought.[17]

Once he had grasped the idea of a universe in which matter had evolved into the biosphere of Earth, and was now being transformed into a noosphere around the planet, Teilhard concluded that there is a tidal force inherent in the matter of the universe that leads towards increased complexity, to life, to human consciousness, and finally to a shared world of thought. In his view, the apparent rarity of life in the universe does not diminish its importance or quality. The rarity of the appearance of life can be understood as the expression of the difficulties presented by the play of chance in the evolution of complexity. But once life establishes a foothold in one part of the universe, as it has on Earth, then it can quickly expand and develop. Teilhard sees evidence for this view in the fossil record, particularly in the increase in brain capacity found in different geological eras.

The key moment in the process of hominization is what Teilhard calls "reflection," the moment when life reaches a level of complexity, and "psychic temperature," when it crosses over into self-conscious thought.[18] He sees this as open to experimental observation at the point of discontinuity, and of take-off, between the biosphere and the noosphere. This is the point where matter and life become transformed into mind, or as Teilhard says, into spirit. This means that he can declare: "Matter is the matrix of Spirit. Spirit is the higher form of matter."[19] Matter falls forward into light:

> At that time my position was firmly and permanently established: I had seen, once for all, that when the World is left to itself it does not fall in the direction of obscurity; with all its vastness and all its weight it falls forward in equilibrium, towards the light. And in future nothing can make me swerve from this irrevocable conviction that it is in the form, I do not say of Concepts, but of Thought that the Stuff of things gradually concentrates in the pure state, in a cosmic peak: and this it does in its most stable form, which means in the form that has become the most completely irreversible.[20]

Teilhard notes that, while an increasing number of people agree about the evolutionary movement from matter to life, and from life to the human, there is not yet agreement on whether evolution has come to a stand-still in the human.[21] Teilhard's position is that the human is still evolving into something new. He sees the human as like a vast flower now folding in upon itself. Production, nutrition, technology, research, and the legacy of heredity, are all building up to planetary dimensions. It is increasingly impossible for the individual to claim economic or intellectual self-sufficiency. In Teilhard's view, this is a continuation of the process of hominization that gave rise to thought on Earth. He proposes this is not simply a new vision of the human, but a transformation in the very organ of the vision. The human itself is being transformed into a collective, a collective of reflection and of increasing unitary organization. Complexity is still rising, but now on the scale of the planet. The trajectory that gave rise to the human, involving matter, life, and thought, is still at work in the transformation of the noosphere as a whole. Teilhard sees this evolutionary process as still at an embryonic stage. Looking ahead he sees the outline of what he calls the ultra-human, where the individual ego goes beyond itself into the unity of the collective consciousness of the noosphere.[22]

In *The Human Phenomenon*, Teilhard points out that the union of consciousness of which he speaks is a unity in which each becomes more conscious of itself, and more fully itself. He points to a principle he sees at work not only in the cells of a body, and in the members of a society, but also in the unity of the spiritual synthesis of the noosphere that "union differentiates."[23] He distinguishes his position from pantheism, where individuals become dissolved in the whole, on the one hand, and from the collapse into individualism, on the other. To become truly and fully oneself, he argues, we must advance towards the other: "The end of ourselves and the culmination of our originality is not in our individuality but in our person; and according to the evolutionary structure of the world, the only way we can find our person is by uniting with one another."[24]

In this whole vision, priority lies not with the past but in what lies ahead. This suggests to Teilhard the need to understand that there is a focal point, or pole, to which the whole process of cosmogenesis is directed. He names this pole of attraction, and of consolidation, the Omega Point of evolution. He speaks of the Omega as experientially real for him. The incorruptible and substantial which he had pursued from his childhood has now become simultaneously universalized and personalized:

> The "piece of iron" of my first days has long since been forgotten. In its place is the Consistence of the Universe, in the form of Omega Point, that I hold now concentrated (whether above me or, rather, in the depths of my being, I cannot say) into one single indestructible center, WHICH I CAN LOVE.[25]

The Omega, then, is not simply a fusion of elements of the universe, but is that which draws the universe forward into the personal. It radiates the energy of love: "Omega in its ultimate principle can only be a distinct Center radiating at the core of a system of centers."[26] The increasing personalization that takes place in the union of consciousness and thought is "under the influence of a supremely autonomous focal point of union."[27] The union to which the Omega draws us is a union in interpersonal love. Teilhard has no time for collectives that debase and enslave human consciousness. He writes:

> Love alone is capable of completing our beings in themselves as it unites them, for the good reason that love alone takes them and joins them by their very depths—this is a fact of daily experience. For actually is not the moment when two lovers say they are lost in each other the moment when they come into the most complete possession of themselves? Truly, in the couple and in the team, and all around us at every moment, does love not accomplish that magic act, reputed to be so contradictory, of "personalizing" as it totalizes? And if it does this on a daily basis on a reduced scale, why should it not someday repeat it in the dimensions of the Earth?[28]

In Teilhard's view, the internal propensity to consciousness and union is present in a rudimentary way in all that exists, all the way down to the molecule and the atom, and it is this that forms the evolutionary ground for love to appear in the human.[29] At the level of the human, he says, we are being led not only to the love of spouse, children, friends, and country, but to a love that embraces the entire universe.

For this kind of love to grow, Teilhard proposes, we need to see the universe ahead of us leading to the personal, leading to "Someone." So he writes: "Let the universe take on ahead of us a face and a heart, become personified, so to speak."[30] This center of love that draws us into the future must be acting already, and must be loving and lovable here and now: "For the noosphere to be actual and real, the center must be actual and real. To be supremely attractive, Omega must be already supremely present."[31] It must also, Teilhard proposes, be capable of drawing us beyond the limits of the transient, beyond death and decay, into a new form of life that he calls superlife. Omega for Teilhard, then, is not only supremely personal, but also has the qualities of autonomy, actuality, irreversibility, and transcendence.[32]

THE CHRISTIC

Theologian Christopher Mooney has pointed out that Teilhard identifies the Omega and the Christ of Christian faith by three distinct but connected levels of argument.[33] First, arguing as an empirical scientist, Teilhard finds evidence in the history of evolution, particularly in the fossil record, for the evolution of life and consciousness, and understands this in terms of the law of complexity-consciousness. He situates this evolution in the context of what is known of the expanding universe, and thus sees the universe as crossing major thresholds, as it gives rise to life, and then to consciousness, in the process he calls cosmogenesis.

On this empirical basis, Teilhard then predicts that humankind is in the process of crossing a new threshold of reflection to the noosphere. The second level identified by Mooney, then, is that of a philosophical argument, where Teilhard proposes that evolutionary progress now takes the shape of higher forms of interpersonal communion. Thinking philosophically, Teilhard argues for a Center, an Omega, a personal source and object of love, capable of drawing the human community to embrace the whole universe in love. This Center would not only be drawing us into the future, but would need to be also already present and at work in the world, radiating and activating the love energy of the universe.

On top of these scientific and philosophical lines of thought Teilhard then adds a third, that of a theology based on Christian revelation. At this third level, Teilhard proposes that the risen Christ proclaimed by the New Testament, the cosmic Christ in whom all things hold together (Col 1:17), can be identified with the Omega of evolution. The data of science and philosophy are brought into a unity with Christian revelation, so that Teilhard speaks of the risen Christ as the prime mover of evolution, and as Christ-Omega and Christ the Evolver.[34] Cosmogenesis now takes the shape of the Word incarnate. What Teilhard proposes, then, is a genesis of the universe, life, and consciousness that is truly Christic, and which can now be understood as a Christogenesis.

In Jesus Christ, the Word made flesh, Teilhard sees God as partially "immersing" God's self in the world of matter, and becoming an "element" in it. And then, from the heart of matter, the incarnate Christ, through his death and resurrection, takes leadership of, and becomes head of, what we now call evolution. Christ, "the principle of universal vitality" is now transforming the reality into which he is inserted in the incarnation, and by "a perennial act of communion and sublimation, he is aggregating the entire psyche of Earth to himself."[35] When Christ has gathered everything together and transformed everything, then, all will be united in God who is all in all.

> If the world is convergent and if Christ occupies the center of it, then the Christogenesis found in Saint Paul and Saint John is no more and no less than both the expected and the unhoped for prolongation of the noogenesis in which cosmogenesis culminates for our experience. Christ is organically clothed in the very majesty of his creation. And, accordingly, without metaphor, it is through the whole length, thickness, and depth of the world in movement that human beings see themselves capable of experiencing and discovering their God.[36]

In Teilhard's view, Christianity has received from Christ the mission of already expressing in our world a new state of consciousness, that of Christian love. And so he points to the thousands of mystics over twenty centuries who have lived such love with passion and brilliance. He sees all Christians called to participate in this work, as a phylum of love in the world, love for the whole universe directed to Christ-Omega.

Looking back on the development of his thought, Teilhard traces the convergence of two streams of thought, the first concerned with the evolutionary emergence of matter, life, and the human, and the second to do with what he calls the Christic, the presence of Christ to all things.[37] The first, beginning with his early love of matter, leads him ultimately to see the universe, the whole world of matter, as in the process of becoming fully personalized in the Omega Point. In the second, Teilhard reflects on the emergence of the "Christic" in his life, beginning from his initiation through his mother into the symbol of the heart of Christ. He describes the discovery that the fire of love symbolized in this heart permeates everything in the universe. This coincides, in his life, with a view of God not simply as the God above, but as the God ahead, the God who draws all things to their completion in Christ. The incarnation reveals a God who is radically involved with matter. The risen Christ, in Teilhard's vision, shares in the divine immensity, and therefore is able to be at work in the whole of creation, drawing it to its culmination and transfiguration. In this way the cosmic and the Christic not only converge, but are one:

> The cosmic sense and the christic sense: these two axes were born in me quite independently of one another, it would seem, and it was only after a long time and a great deal of hard work that I finally came to understand how, through and beyond the Human, the two were linked together, converged upon one another, and were in fact one and the same.[38]

Based on his science Teilhard saw a vision of a universe that was becoming personalized through convergence. Based on his theological commitment, he saw a vision of a person, Christ, who was becoming universalized. The result was his conviction of Christ as the very heart of the evolving matter of the universe: "To Christify matter: that sums up the whole venture of my innermost being."[39] This process of christification happens through the energy of incarnation, flowing into, illuminating and giving warmth to the universe of matter.

Just two months before his death, Teilhard began to write his final essay on "The Christic," which he saw as bringing together the quintessence of *The Divine Milieu*, *The Mass on the World*, and *The Heart of Matter*. In this essay, he argues that there is more in the total Christ than humanity and divinity. There is also the whole creation. He speaks of creation as a third "aspect," or "function" of Christ, even as a third "nature" of Christ.[40] Teilhard asks himself how such an "immensified" view of the Christ avoids depersonalizing him. He finds the answer to this precisely in the union between the Omega of evolution and the Christ, since this constitutes a Divine Milieu in which all opposition between the universal and the personal is wiped out, so that what is most cosmic is now most personal and what is most personal is most cosmic.

Teilhard's work was resisted by some other biologists, and not simply because of his bold linking of evolution with Christ. The philosopher of science Ernan McMullan has pointed to Teilhard's embrace of the idea of radial energy at work in the universe as one explanation for the violent opposition to him by some leading neo-Darwinian biologists.[41] Teilhard divides the energies that propel the universe forward into two types, tangential and radial.[42] Tangential energies are those that are normally associated with the natural sciences, including those involved in Darwin's account of evolution by means of natural selection. But Teilhard introduces another form of energy, the radial, as necessary to account for the evolutionary process. This is fundamentally psychic in nature, attracting the universe towards complexity, and a more centered state. It can be discerned by seeing the larger patterns of evolutionary process, rather than through the normal modes of inference at work in biology. Some biologists resist not only the idea of such radial energy, but even the very idea that there is direction in the evolutionary process.

Most theologians have been slow to address the issues taken up by Teilhard. Heather Eaton says of Teilhard that he was "one of the first scientists and still one of the few theologians to realize that the human and the universe are part of the one reality; immersed in the same process, the same creative energies, the same evolutionary dynamics and orientation."[43] His views have been criticized as not taking enough account of sin, and as uncritically progressive and optimistic. But his work was defended by Henri De Lubac,[44] and many of his ideas had an important influence on Karl Rahner's theology.[45] Teihard's work is an important influence on some contemporary theologians, including John Haught and Ilia Delio.[46] John Haught points to the importance of Teilhard's insistence that the universe is still coming into being, and that the centre of reality is not the past, nor the eternal present, but the future:

> What does it really mean for Christian faith, then, that we live in an unfinished universe? At the very least it means an end to the idea that God's creation has at any time been perfect or paradisal. Once we have full absorbed the scientifically incontestable fact that Earth was not Eden in the beginning, serious reflection on Christian faith can have the effect of ennobling and adding new zest to faith and life. How so? It may do so by making us realize that our lives are tied into a universe that still has a future, a universe that can become much "more" than it is now.[47]

Haught says that Christians who profess to love God and to be saved by Christ have nothing to lose and everything to gain by transplanting their devotion to the much larger setting offered by contemporary biology and cosmology. This will mean a radical expansion of our view of the Creator, the work of the Holy Spirit, and the redemptive meaning of Christ: "The Love that rules the stars will now have to be seen as embracing two hundred billion galaxies, a cosmic epic of fourteen billion years' duration, and perhaps even a multiverse. Our thoughts about Christ and redemption will have to extend over the full breadth of cosmic time and space."[48]

TRAJECTORIES

There is need for ongoing discussion of human sin, and the terrible violence we encounter in our history, in relation to Teilhard's insights. His cosmic vision is also radically centered on the human, and may need further development to find a place for animals and plants if it is to be a resource for ecological theology. The same might be said of the centering of the whole trajectory of his thought on spirit. Is not there a future for matter and for biological life, in their own reality, in the fullness of resurrection? Nevertheless, Teilhard, leaves fundamental legacies for a twenty-first century theology of the natural world:

1. Teilhard's passionate love for matter, plants, animals, and the evolving and expanding universe.
2. His thorough embrace of evolutionary biology, and his vision of the evolutionary emergence of life on Earth and of human beings with their reflective consciousness.
3. Teilhard embraced early twentieth-century cosmology, and saw human beings as deeply interconnected with the universe.
4. While fully committed to biblical faith, he refused to be trapped in a literalist reading of the Genesis accounts, and embraced the cosmic Christology of Colossians and Ephesians.
5. The conviction that God speaks to us both in Jesus Christ and in what science reveals about the universe and life on Earth.
6. The vigorous and honest attempt to articulate a vision of Christian faith, a theology, and a spirituality, that thoroughly accept the insights of the sciences.
7. The insight of the convergence of human consciousness and of human love on our planet (the noosphere), which might be seen as partially confirmed in global communications of the twenty-first century, even as it is far from confirmed at the level of global relationships of love.

8. The transformation of a theology centred on the past, or the eternal present, to a theology centred on the future, on the God of an unfinished universe.
9. The powerful conviction that it is divine Love that moves the universe, and that it is this same Love that is the goal of matter and life in Omega; and that we are called to be participants in and agents of this Love in our planetary community of life.

Notes

1. On Teilhard's life, see Claude Cuenot, *Teilhard de Chardin: A Biographical Study* (London: Burns and Oates, 1958); Ursula King, *Spirit of Fire: The Life and Vision of Teilhard de Chardin* (Maryknoll: Orbis Books, 1996).
2. For an interesting account of Teilhard's participation in this discovery see Amir D. Aczel, *The Jesuit and the Skull: Teilhard de Chardin, Evolution and the Search for Peking Man* (New York: Riverhead Books, 2007).
3. King, *Spirit of Fire*, 42.
4. Ibid., 140.
5. Teilhard de Chardin, *The Heart of Matter* (San Diego: Harcourt, 1978), 15.
6. Ibid.
7. Ibid., 24.
8. Ibid., 25.
9. Ibid.
10. Ibid., 28.
11. The word is based on the Greek word for mind, *nous*. While the term *biosphere* had been used by geologist Edward Suess in 1875, it was taken up by the Russian-born geochemist Vladimir Vernadsky in the 1920s. He saw that living creatures are responsible for the oxygen, nitrogen, and carbon dioxide in the atmosphere, and

argued that not only physical forces but also living organisms shape the planet. Vernadsky would later speak not only of the *geosphere*, and the *biosphere*, but also of the *noosphere*. Teilhard and his friend and collaborator Édouard Le Roy both attended Vernadsky's lectures at the Sorbonne, and both used the term *noosphere*, as did Vernadsky in later writing. In a letter written two days after Le Roy's death in 1954, Teilhard spoke of Le Roy as a spokesman for his ideas at the Collège de France in 1920s, particularly the ideas of hominization and the noosphere. He goes on to say: "I believe, so far as one can ever tell, that the word 'noosphere' was my invention; but it was he who launched it." See Cuénot, *Teilhard de Chardin,* 59.

12. Pierre Teilhard de Chardin, *The Human Phenomenon*, trans. Sarah Appleton-Weber (Portland: Sussex Academic, 1999, 2003), 216.
13. Ibid., 217.
14. Ibid.
15. Ibid.
16. Teilhard, *The Heart of Matter*, 31.
17. See Teilhard de Chardin, "The Formation of the Noosphere: A Plausible Biological Explanation of Human History" in *The Future of Man* (New York: Doubleday, 1959), 149–78.
18. Teilhard, *The Heart of Matter*, 33.
19. Ibid., 35.
20. Ibid.
21. Ibid., 36.
22. Ibid.
23. Teilhard, *The Human Phenomenon*, 186.
24. Ibid., 187.
25. Teilhard, *The Heart of Matter*, 39.
26. Teilhard, *The Human Phenomenon*, 186.
27. Ibid., 187.
28. Ibid., 189.
29. Ibid., 188.

30. Ibid., 190.
31. Ibid., 192.
32. Ibid., 193.
33. Christopher F. Mooney, *Teilhard de Chardin and the Mystery of Christ* (London: Collins, 1964), 65–66.
34. Teilhard de Chardin, *Science and Christ* (London: Collins, 1968), 164–71.
35. Teilhard, *The Human Phenomenon*, 211.
36. Ibid., 213.
37. Teilhard, *The Heart of Matter*, 16.
38. Ibid., 40.
39. Ibid., 47.
40. Pierre Teilhard de Chardin, "The Christic," in *The Heart of Matter*, 93.
41. Ernan McMullin, "Natural Science and Belief in a Creator: Historical Notes," *Physics, Philosophy and Theology: A Common Quest for Understanding* eds. Robert John Russell, William R. Stoeger, and George V. Coyne (Vatican City State: Vatican Observatory, 1988), 49–79, 68–70. McMullin sees this as a neo-Lamarckian tendency in Teilhard's work. Teilhard himself writes of this as a neo-Lamarckian addition to Darwinism (*The Human Phenomenon*, 97–98).
42. Teilhard, *The Human Phenomenon*, 30–32, 36–37, 227–32.
43. Heather Eaton, "Pierre Teilhard de Chardin (1881–1955) – The Divine Milieu," in *Creation and Salvation, Volume 2: A Companion on Recent Theological Movements*, ed. Ernst M. Conradie (Berlin: LIT, 2015), 195–200.
44. Henri de Lubac, *Teilhard de Chardin* (New York: New American Library, 1965).
45. This is explored in Denis Edwards, "Teilhard's Vision as Agenda for Rahner's Christology," *From Teilhard to Omega: Co-creating an Unfinished Universe* ed. Ilia Delio (Maryknoll, NY: Orbis, 2014), 53–66.
46. See their contributions, along with that of others, in *From Teilhard to Omega*. ed. Delio. See also *Teilhard in the 21st Century: The*

Emerging Spirit of Earth, ed. Arthur Fabel and Donald St. John (Maryknoll, NY: Orbis, 2003).

47. John F. Haught, "Teilhard de Chardin: Theology for an Unfinished Universe," in *From Teilhard to Omega*, ed. Delio, 11.

48. Ibid., 13.

11.

Karl Rahner (1904–1984)

Life and Context: Rahner was born in the German university city of Freiburg. After secondary school he joined the Jesuits, and his life and his theology were profoundly influenced by the spirituality of Ignatius of Loyola. After becoming proficient in scholastic and patristic theology, he was sent for doctoral work in philosophy at the University of Freiburg. There he attended Martin Heidegger's seminars, and wrote his thesis on an interpretation of Aquinas's epistemology in the light of Kant, influenced in part by Joseph Maréchal. His dissertation was rejected by his doctoral supervisor, but later became an influential book, *Spirit in the World*. Rahner's second thesis on patristic theology was accepted by the University of Innsbruck and he taught theology in the Innsbruck faculty until the Nazis closed it in 1938. He served in the Pastoral Institute of Vienna and in parish ministry in Bavaria, and then took up teaching posts in the universities of Innsbruck (1948–1964), Munich (1964–1967), and Münster (1967–1971). Although there were difficulties with Roman authorities over some of his writings, in 1961, Pope John XXIII appointed him to a commission preparing for the Second Vatican Council, and Cardinal König of Vienna asked him to act as his theological advisor at the Council. Rahner engaged vigorously in the work of the Council and was influential in its outcomes. Much of Rahner's extensive work is in short articles, very often engaging with everyday topics alongside major theological issues. Many of his articles are found translated in the twenty three volumes of *Theological Investigations*, with others found in the reference work *Sacramentum Mundi*. In 1976, he published an overview of his theology, *Foundations of Christian Faith*.[1]

Karl Rahner is above all a theologian of grace. He insists that every human being, at every point in time, exists within a situation of God's self-offering love. This self-offering and self-giving of God is what Rahner means by grace.[2] This grace is always the grace of Jesus Christ, given in the Spirit. Rahner sees each person as free to accept or reject this divine offer. He also insists that not just great mystics and saints, but also ordinary people, experience grace. This occurs, he explains, in everyday acts of knowledge and love that are open to mystery and transcendence, as well as in more obviously religious experiences. However, we need revelation in Christ to interpret such experience, to know that the mystery we encounter at the heart of life is the presence of God offering God's self to us in love. Rahner calls the experiences of grace that occur in ordinary circumstances the mysticism of everyday life.

A fundamental structuring concept in Rahner's theology is his concept of God's self-giving, or self-bestowal. This is a Trinitarian concept: God (the Father) gives God's self to us in Jesus the Word made flesh, and in the Spirit poured out in grace. The great truths of Christian faith, the incarnation, the grace of the Spirit, and the Trinity, are summed up in the concept of God as bestowing God's self to us in the Word and Spirit. This divine self-giving begins in creation itself, and reaches its unthinkable depths in the incarnation. Creation and incarnation are linked together as distinct aspects of God's free decision to give God's self in love to a world of creatures.[3]

While for many theologians the reason for the incarnation is to bring salvation from sin, Rahner holds to the tradition, associated with Duns Scotus and others, that from the beginning God's creation is directed to the incarnation. Of course, Rahner believes that our sins are forgiven and we are saved in Christ. But he holds that irrespective of human sin, God's intention in creating a world of creatures was always freely to give God's self to these creatures in the incarnation, and so bring them to their fulfillment. Creation, then, is "a partial moment in the process in which God becomes world."[4] Harvey Egan says that the briefest summary of Rahner's theology is "his creative appropriation of Scotus's view that God creates in order to communicate *self* and that creation exists in order to be the recipient of God's free gift of self."[5]

In this chapter I will take up just four aspects of Rahner's theology of creation, his evolutionary theology of creation and salvation, his view that salvation in Christ involves not just humans but the whole universe, his understanding of incarnation as God's eternal commitment to matter and flesh, and his theological ideas on extra-terrestrial life.

AN EVOLUTIONARY THEOLOGY

From early in his career, it was clear to Rahner that the traditional theology of creation needed to be developed in response to the new picture of reality emerging from cosmology and evolutionary biology. While traditional theology assumed a static world, informed by the sciences, we now see massive transitions in the history of the universe and of life, particularly the transitions from matter to the first forms of life on Earth, and from these to modern humans, with their extremely complex brains.

In the traditional theology of creation, Rahner notes, we find the ideas of divine conservation and divine concurrence.[6] Divine conservation means that creatures do not exist of themselves, but only from God. They owe their actual existence to the ever-present, creative and conserving presence of the Creator. In a similar way divine concurrence points to the idea that God's ongoing creative act enables not only the existence of creatures, but also all their actions and interactions. In this traditional view, creatures are true agents and exercise a causality of their own. They have their own integrity. But at every point they are empowered to act by the creative presence and action of God.

As always it is important to note that God's creative act is not open to empirical investigation. It is of a completely different order to creaturely actions. For Aquinas, as I pointed out in an earlier chapter, and very much for Karl Rahner, the two orders are non-competitive. God is not a cause among other causes in the world. In the creation of a world of creatures, God is not a replacement for creaturely processes, and does not overturn the laws of nature, but acts creatively and providentially in and through the whole process. God's creative act enables creaturely acts to have their own integrity. Rahner insists, as a principle of the way God acts in both creation and grace, that the more creatures depend upon God, the more their own integrity and autonomy flourish.[7]

While Rahner recognizes that this traditional theology still has a great deal of meaning for a contemporary theology of creation, he finds that more is needed for an evolutionary view of the natural world. So he seeks to rethink God's creative act in terms that are suitable for an evolutionary age. In such an evolutionary theology, the relationship of creation needs to be understood not only as conferring on creatures their existence and their capacity to act, but also their capacity to evolve into something radically new. Whereas the theology of the past saw the immanent presence and power of God as "conserving and maintaining the abiding order of things," what is needed for an evolutionary time is a theology that shows "the immanence of the divine dynamism in the world as a becoming."[8] The divine presence needs to be understood as empowering the becoming of the world.

At the heart of Rahner's theology of "becoming" is his concept of the Creator as enabling the active "self-transcendence" of creatures.[9] Earlier, I pointed out that in Rahner's theology, God's creative act is understood as a divine act of self-giving love, which is always directed toward the incarnation. It is this divine self-bestowal that Rahner sees as enabling creatures to become something new, to transcend themselves. This self-transcendence, or becoming, occurs in and through all the empirical processes studied in sciences like cosmology and evolutionary biology. In Rahner's view, the creative and self-giving God, at a level far beyond the empirical, breathes life into the whole process. Rahner's insight transforms the classical theology of creation and enables it to function in a new, evolutionary era. The *self* in self-transcendence means that this capacity comes from within creaturely reality. In the relationship of creation, God gives to creatures themselves the capacity to cross thresholds into the new. God bestows on the world its own capacity for creativity and novelty. Rahner's view, then, is of a God like Mother Carey in Charles Kingsley's *The Water Babies*, who "can make things make themselves."[10] This insight offers new, deeper, insight into God, as one who creates in such a way that creatures participate in the process. A God who makes a world of creatures who evolve through processes of self-transcendence is a Creator who delights in participation, and in the emergence of creaturely reality through processes of increasing complexity.

Divine self-giving and creaturely self transcendence are deeply connected. The immanent presence of the self-giving God enables the self-transcendence of the creature. God's self-bestowal enables creatures to become something new. This view of God as delighting in the self-transcendence of creatures is operative in other related aspects of Rahner's theology. I will briefly mention three: his view of the human soul, his christology, and his eschatology.

In regard to the soul, Rahner seeks to hold together a fully evolutionary view of human emergence with the teaching of the Catholic Church that God immediately creates the hu-man soul.[11] Central to the emergence of modern humans is the evolution of the brain, with its capacity for language and intellectual and interpersonal life. The mind/soul emerges as profoundly connected to and dependent upon the brain in a social world. In Rahner's view, it is God's immediate creative presence that enables every level of self-transcendence in the whole evolutionary process, including that of the human mind and soul. He argues that the spiritual center of the human person can be understood as an emergent reality, as self-transcendence in the process of the evolution of the brain. At the same time this process can be understood as God's immediate creation of the soul, as long as one allows that God's creative act has this particular person's spiritual reality as a specific, directly-willed outcome. Each of us is called by name from our mother's womb.

Rahner also invokes the concept of self-transcendence in his Christology within an evolutionary context. Jesus, in his humanity, can be seen like all of us as a creature who is a product of biological evolution. But unlike us, Jesus can be seen as the unique and unforeseeable culmination of the process of self-transcendence, of matter to life, and of living creatures to self-conscious humans in a grace-filled world. Rahner sees the universe as borne from its very beginning by a thrust towards a dynamic and more conscious relationship with its Creator. The goal of the universe is God's communication with it. Jesus is the creature who responds to God with radical love, the love poured out in his life and ministry, which finds ultimate expression in the cross. From the perspective of his humanity, then, Jesus is the unique self-transcendence of creation to God. And, from the perspective of his divinity, Jesus is the unique, irreversible culmination of God's self-bestowal to a world of creatures. For Rahner, he is "absolute savior" because he is both God's irrevocable self-giving to creation, and in his human life and death, the radical response of creation to God.[12] He is both God's forgiving, healing, liberating embrace of creation in self-giving love and creation's unreserved "yes!" to God. In the resurrection and the ascension of the risen Christ, this creaturely reality of Jesus is fully taken into God, and irrevocably adopted as God's own reality, and is the beginning and the pledge of the transfiguration of the whole creation.

Self-transcendence is also important in Rahner's eschatology. He asks himself the question: what relation is there between our actions here and now and the promise of the new Earth?[13] How is the promised transformation, the kingdom of God, related to our work, to our science, and to our efforts to build a just and peaceful world? Rahner's response is to insist, on the one hand, that the coming kingdom will not be simply the outcome of human plans and actions. It will be God's transformative act that brings creation to its future. And this future remains utter mystery to us because this future is the incomprehensible God.[14] On the other hand, however, Rahner makes the claim that this transformative act of God can be understood as the self-transcendence of human history and of the wider natural world. What will endure in God's future, he says, is "the work of love expressed in the concrete in human history."[15] Our human history, our commitments, our action, our love and our prayer will endure, as taken up into God and as transfigured in God. In Rahner's theological vision, divine self-giving that enables creaturely self-transcendence characterizes God's creative and saving action at every level from the origin of the universe to its final fulfillment.

SALVATION IN CHRIST AS INVOLVING THE TRANSFORMATION OF THE WHOLE UNIVERSE

In an article written in the 1950s exploring the meaning of the resurrection, Rahner points out that Western theology has tended to concentrate its attention on Christ's death because of its juridical theology of the redemption, in which the cross is seen as offering satisfaction for human sin.[16] The resurrection, by contrast, is allocated only a marginal place. Compared to its New Testament origins, the theology of resurrection has suffered, he says, an "astonishing process of shrinkage."[17] In the theology of the East, by contrast, Rahner finds that the resurrection plays a far more fundamental role. The whole event of Jesus Christ, the life, death, and resurrection, is understood as being not only about the forgiveness of sin, but also about overcoming death, bringing life, and participation in God, to human beings and, with them, to the whole creation. Eastern theologians see our adoption as God's daughters and sons as a deification or divinization (*theosis*). For them, the incarnation of the Word that culminates in resurrection is about a transformation of reality for human beings and, with them, for the whole creation.

Rahner writes of this Eastern theology: "The redemption was felt to be a real ontological process which began in the incarnation and ends not so much in the forgiveness of sins as in the divinization of the world and first demonstrates its victorious might, not so much in the expiation of sin on the cross as in the resurrection of Christ."[18] Three of Rahner's themes find expression in this quotation: salvation as an ontological transformation of reality; this deifying transformation as involving not only humanity, but also the whole world of creatures; and the resurrection of the crucified Jesus as the beginning of this deifying transfiguration of all things.

Rahner sees the death of Jesus as the final act by which the whole of his life lived in love and obedience to God is gathered up in freedom. It is not simply one act among others, but the "totality of Christ in act, the definitive act of his freedom, the complete integration of his time on earth with his human eternity."[19] The resurrection can be seen then, not simply as an event that occurs after Jesus's death, but as the manifestation of what happens in the death, as Jesus hands his whole bodily existence into the mystery of a loving God. In the cross of Jesus, part of this world freely and radically gives itself to God in complete love and obedience and it fully taken up into God. Rahner sees this event as salvific and transformative for the whole of creation: "This is Easter, and the redemption of the world."[20]

In the resurrection of Jesus, God essentially and irrevocably adopts creaturely reality as God's own reality. This occurs by God's primordial act, which finds expression in the incarnation of the Word, and which culminates in the resurrection that transfigures the creaturely reality of Jesus. Because of the unity of the world that springs from God in the one divine economy, this transfiguration of the crucified Jesus is an event for the whole world. What occurs in Jesus, as part of a physical, biological, and human world, is ontologically and not just juridically "the embryonically final beginning of the glorification and divinization of the whole of reality."[21]

In a world in which creation and saving incarnation are radically united as aspects of the one divine act of self-bestowal, the resurrection can be understood as the irreversible beginning of the fulfillment of God's will in creating a universe of creatures. Rahner sees it as "the beginning of the transformation of the world as an ontologically interconnected occurrence"[22] He speaks of the risen Christ as the "pledge and beginning of the perfect fulfillment of the world" and as the "representative of the new cosmos."[23] The risen Christ is already at work in the whole universe as both the pledge and the reality of its future. As the risen one, Christ is freed from "the limiting individuality of the unglorified body" and in his glorified new state is already present to all of creation.[24] What we think of as his second coming in glory, then, will be the clear revelation of his transforming engagement with creatures that is already occurring: it will be "the disclosure of this relation to the world attained by Jesus in his resurrection."[25]

Rahner sees contemporary cosmology as a help to theologians in thinking about the final state of the universe. In earlier times, when the universe was thought of as a series of spheres, eternal life could be imagined as moving from the everyday sphere to a heavenly sphere. But with the current scientific picture of an evolving universe, we are better able to think about a God-given final state of the universe as a whole. Rahner recognizes, however, that there is no easy transition from the dismal scientific predictions of the end of Earth, and of the final state of the universe as a whole, to a Christian eschatology. The transition can happen only through a transformative act of God.

Rahner insists that the Second Coming of Christ will involve not only human beings, but also the whole world of creatures of which they are a part. It will not take place for humans in an unchanged world, but will involve a radical transformation of the whole of reality. The universe will reach its fulfillment by participating in the reality already possessed by the risen Christ: "the world as a whole flows into his Resurrection and into the transfiguration of his body," so that Christ "will be revealed to all reality and, within it, to every one of its parts in its own way, as the innermost secret of all the world and of all history."[26]

The bodily resurrection of humans and the transformation of the universe must be understood together, and Rahner insists that both are beyond our imagination, because our future, and that of the universe, is in God, who is always incomprehensible mystery. What we have is not a clear picture, but a promise of God in the risen Christ. In Christ, resurrection is revealed to be not the revival of a corpse, but radical transformation (1 Cor 15:44). In the God-given transformation of the universe, "it will then be equally correct to call the new reality a new heaven or a new earth."[27]

In a meditation on Holy Saturday, Rahner reflects on the relationship between the risen Christ and the creatures of our planet, and speaks of "all creatures" as striving, without knowing it, to participate in the glorification of Christ's body.[28] With this theology of all creatures striving in their own way to participate in Christ, Rahner is close to an ecological way of thinking.[29] But he was writing before theologians began to address the ecological crisis, and unfortunately he seldom speaks explicitly about insects, animals or plants, or the systems that support life on the planet.

If Rahner is not often very explicit about the theological status of biological life, he is fully explicit about matter. He makes it clear that he does not see the matter of the universe as disappearing, but as reaching its true fulfillment in Christ. Christians thus have, or should have, a very high regard for matter. Rahner insists that Christians are the true materialists: they are really "the most sublime of materialists . . . more crassly materialist than those who call themselves so."[30] It is true that the matter of the universe will also undergo a radical transformation, "the depths of which we can only sense with fear and trembling in that process which we experience as our death."[31] But because of their convictions about resurrection and ascension, Christians hold that matter will last forever, and be glorified forever in Christ. Rahner sees this transfiguration of the matter of the world as already begun in Christ, and as already "ripening and developing to that point where it will become manifest."[32]

FOREVER A GOD OF MATTER AND FLESH

I suggested earlier that Rahner is a theologian of grace. It is equally true to say that he is radically incarnational. He is a theologian convinced that God gives God's self to us both in the grace of the Spirit and in the incarnation of the Word. A consequence of his deeply incarnational theology is that he sees God as forever a God of matter and flesh. The Word is made flesh, and in the resurrection and ascension matter and flesh are irrevocably taken into God and forever embedded in the divine Trinity. The eternal Word of God is now forever an Earth creature.

In this section I will highlight what he says in a short article from 1950 that is entitled "A Faith that Loves the Earth."[33] He writes that we must not think of Jesus's death as an escape from Earth into a distant land of God's glory. He points out that the church teaches not only that Jesus died but that he descended to the dead and then rose. This suggests to Rahner that in his death, Jesus enters into the very heart of Earth in order to bring it to divine life:

> In his death, the Lord descended into the lowest and deepest regions of what is visible. It is no longer a place of impermanence and death, because there *he* now is. By his death, he has become the heart of this earthly world, God's heart in the center of the world, where the world even before its own unfolding in space and time taps into God's power and might.[34]

Christ dies, Rahner seems to be saying, into the heart of Earth, and also into God's creative act that is enabling and empowering the whole universe. He becomes "God's heart" at the very center of creation. And his resurrection is not to be seen as an abandonment of Earth and its creatures. Because he is raised precisely in the body, he remains profoundly connected to all that is bodily:

> No, he is risen in his body. That means: He has begun to transfigure this world into himself; he has accepted this world forever; he has been born anew as a child of this earth, but of an earth that is transfigured, freed, unlimited, an earth that in him will last forever and is delivered from death and impermanence for good."[35]

The risen Christ is still part of Earth, deeply connected to Earth's nature and destiny: "By rising he has not left the dwelling of the earth, since he still has his body, though in a final and transfigured way, and is part of the earth, a part that still belongs to the earth, and is connected with earth's nature and destiny."[36] In spite of the ongoing struggle and pain of life, at the very heart of Earth something radically new has begun. The forces of a transfigured world are already at work in the risen Christ, conquering impermanence, death, and sin at their core. While we continue to experience suffering and sin in the world, Christian faith holds that they have actually been defeated deep down at their very source. Here, too, Rahner sees the risen Christ as already at the heart of the nameless yearning of all creatures that are waiting to participate in the transfiguration of his body:

> Christ is already at the very heart of all the lowly things of the earth that we are unable to let go of and that belong to the earth as mother. He is at the heart of the nameless yearning of all creatures, waiting—though perhaps unaware that they are waiting—to be allowed to participate in the transfiguration of his body. He is at the heart of earth's history, whose blind progress amidst all victories and defeats is headed with uncanny precision toward the day that is his, where his glory will break forth from its own depths, thereby transforming everything.[37]

Earth is our mother, and we are children of Earth, and we are called to love her. Rahner insists that we do not need to think of ourselves as leaving her for God. Rather, Earth is, or will become, the body of the risen one. We are called to love

Earth and love God together, "for in the resurrection of the Lord, God has shown that he has adopted the earth forever."[38]

In one of his later articles, Rahner asks himself the question: What is specific to the Christian view of God? His answer is that while Christianity does not embrace any kind of pantheistic fusion, but maintains a clear distinction between God and the world of creatures, it maintains that "God himself is still the very core of the world's reality, and the world is truly the fate of God himself."[39] God so irrevocably commits God's self to creation in the free embrace of the incarnation that the human and wider natural world is now forever the fate of God.

Tertullian long ago spoke of the flesh as the connecting point, or hinge of salvation: *Caro cardo salutis*. In Jesus, God has come to us in the flesh, and Rahner says: "Since that time, Mother Earth has brought forth only creatures that will be transfigured, for his resurrection is the beginning of the resurrection of all flesh."[40] It is notable that Rahner explicitly includes all the creatures brought forth by Mother Earth in the promised transfiguration. These creatures would, then, embrace in some way all of biological life.

EXTRATERRESTRIALS

Rahner's thought about the natural world was not confined to our home planet. He reflects, for example on the experience he describes as "cosmic dizziness," the experience of being overwhelmed by what astronomy and cosmology tell us of the size of the Milky Way Galaxy and of the billions of galaxies in the observable universe. He speaks of cosmic dizziness as an element in the development of our theological and religious consciousness, because for believers it can bring to awareness what for Rahner is a primary theological datum, the radical incomprehensibility of God: the unthinkable size of the universe is "to a certain extent, nothing other than the spatial counterpart to the theological datum" of God's radically incomprehensible mystery.[41] Such experience of the universe can lead to a deeply religious sense of our human contingency and creatureliness.

Although astronomers had long believed that planets must exist around stars other than our sun, the first exoplanet was discovered only in 1992. Since then more and more have been found. Many of them are gas giants, like Jupiter, and only a few seem to resemble Earth in its hospitality to life, but it is natural in this context to ask about the meaning for theology of any extraterrestrial life that might be discovered. This is not a new question, but one that many philosophers and theologians of the past have addressed.[42] Several times Rahner comments on this issue beginning with an encyclopedia article on star-dwellers in 1964, followed later by an article in volume 21 of his *Theological Investigations* and a section in his *Foundations of Christian Faith*.[43]

A first question to be addressed is whether Christian theology has a view of its own on whether other intelligent creatures exist on exoplanets. Rahner's position on this, like that of most theologians, is that Christian faith, in itself, cannot answer this question. Its biblical sources are concerned only with the world we know and its relationship with God. Furthermore, Christians, who believe in the absolute transcendence and incomprehensible mystery of the Creator, cannot presume to claim knowledge of what God may or may not be doing in another part of the universe, or in any other possible universe. The existence or non-existence of extra-terrestrials cannot be predetermined by theology.

A further question arises: If such creatures do exist, might Christian theology see them as having their own history of God's grace. Rahner thinks we can answer this question positively. Christians believe that God's self-giving in their own history of creation and salvation is directed towards their free human response, and ultimately to the fulfillment of the whole universe. He argues that there is no reason to exclude the idea that God's free self-giving might well involve other histories of intelligent and free creatures. Such extraterrestrials might well experience their own economy of creation and grace:

> We would move towards the idea that the material cosmos as a whole, whose meaning and goal is the fulfillment of freedom, will one day be subsumed into fullness of God's self-communication to the material and spiritual cosmos, and that this will happen through many histories of freedom which do not only take place on our earth.[44]

Christians who see themselves as living in a world of grace, where God is present to them as self-offering love, would have to allow that God might well be offering God's self in love to intelligent and free creatures in another galaxy, or even in another universe. We can say nothing about the history such possible stories of grace and sin, except that we have every reason to trust that the God whom we know as radically faithful and generous would be so for others.

What of the incarnation? Can we think of an incarnation of the Word of God on another planet? Rahner says simply that multiple incarnations cannot be ruled out by us: "it cannot be proved that a multiple incarnation in different histories of salvation is absolutely unthinkable."[45] Theologians cannot say how God might freely act with regard to extraterrestrials. But if God's creation includes such creatures, we have good reason to trust that God also gives God's self to them in the Word and in the Spirit, with the same extravagant love we encounter in our own experiences of incarnation and grace.

TRAJECTORIES

There are times when Rahner's thought seems focused on the human. And while he is explicit about the fulfillment of Earth, and the universe in Christ, he seldom focuses attention on animal or plant life, and he does not anticipate the ecological crisis. But he is a theologian committed to an engagement with the sciences, and trajectories in his work are major contributions to a twenty-first theology of the natural world.

1. The vision of creation and incarnation as united in one divine act of self-giving love.
2. God's creative act as self-giving love that enables the evolutionary self-transcendence of creatures.
3. Jesus as the self-transcendence of creation to God.
4. And, at the same time, as God's radical self-bestowal to creatures.
5. The resurrection as a promise of transfiguration and fulfillment not only for humans but for the whole universe of creatures: "Mother Earth has brought forth only creatures that will be transfigured, for his resurrection is the beginning of the resurrection of all flesh."
6. The incarnation as meaning that God is forever a God of matter and flesh.
7. The risen Christ as at the heart of the yearning of all creatures.
8. The idea that creatures of intelligence and love may exist on other planets and they may well have their own economy of grace that may possibly include something like the grace of the Spirit and the incarnation of the Word.

Notes

1. Karl Rahner, *Theological Investigations*, 23 vols. (= *TI*), trans. various (Baltimore: Helicon Press, and New York: Crossroad, 1962–92); eds., Karl Rahner, et al., *Sacramentum Mundi: An Encyclopedia of Theology*, 6 vols. (New York: Herder and Herder, 1968); *Foundations of Christian Faith: An Introduction to the Idea of Christianity* (=*Foundations*), trans. William V. Dych (New York: Crossroad, 1978).
2. Rahner's emphasis, then, is very much on uncreated grace, on God present in self-giving love. Of course he also has a theology of created grace, which is the created effect of God's self-giving on the human person.
3. Rahner, *Foundations*, 197.
4. Ibid.
5. Harvey D. Egan, "Theology and Spirituality," in *The Cambridge Companion to Karl Rahner*, eds. Declan Marmion and Mary E. Hines (Cambridge: Cambridge University Press, 2005), 13–28, 16.
6. See, for example, Karl Rahner, "Evolution," in *Encyclopedia of Theology: A Concise Sacramentum Mundi*, ed. Karl Rahner (London: Burns and Oates, 1975), 478–84.
7. Karl Rahner, *Foundations*, 79.
8. Karl Rahner, "Christology in the Setting of Modern Man's Understanding of Himself and of his World," *TI 11*, 215–29, 219.
9. Karl Rahner, *Foundations*, 183–87.
10. Charles Kingsley, *The Water-Babies: A Fairy Tale for a Land-Baby* (New York: Hart Publishing Company, 1977), 255–56.
11. Karl Rahner, *Hominisation: The Evolutionary Origin of Man as a Theological Problem* (New York: Herder and Herder, 1968); "Evolution," in *Encyclopedia of Theology*, 478–88. See Rahner, *Foundations*, 178–203; "Christology within an Evolutionary View of the World," *TI* 5, 157–92.
12. Rahner, *Foundations*, 195.
13. See Rahner, "Immanent and Transcendent Consummation of the

World," *TI 10*, 273–292; "A Fragmentary Aspect of the Theological Evaluation of the Concept of the Future," *TI 10*, 235–241; "The Theological Problems Entailed in the Idea of the 'New Earth,'" *TI 10*, 260–272.

14. Rahner, "A Fragmentary Aspect," 237.
15. Rahner, "The Theological Problems," 270.
16. Rahner, "Dogmatic Questions on Easter," *TI* 4, 121–33.
17. Ibid., 122.
18. Ibid., 126.
19. Ibid., 128.
20. Ibid.
21. Ibid., 129.
22. Rahner, "Resurrection," in *Encyclopedia of Theology*, 1438–42.
23. Ibid., 1442.
24. Ibid.
25. Ibid.
26. Karl Rahner, "The Resurrection of the Body," *TI* 2, 203–16, 213.
27. Ibid., 215.
28. Rahner, "Hidden Victory," *TI* 7, 151–58, 157.
29. See Michael W. Petty, *A Faith that Loves the Earth: The Ecological Theology of Karl Rahner* (Lanham, MD: University Press of America, 1996).
30. Rahner, "The Festival of the Future of the World," *TI* 7, 181–85.
31. Ibid., 183.
32. Ibid., 184.
33. Karl Rahner, "A Faith that Loves the Earth," in *The Mystical Way in Everyday Life: Sermons: Essays and Prayers: Karl Rahner, S.J.*, ed. Annemarie S. Kidder (Maryknoll, NY: Orbis Books, 2010), 52–58.
34. Ibid., 55.
35. Ibid.
36. Ibid.
37. Ibid., 56–57.

38. Rahner, "The Resurrection of the Body," 58.
39. Rahner, "The Specific Character of the Christian Concept of God," *TI 21*, 185–95, 191.
40. Rahner, "A Faith that Loves the Earth," 58.
41. Karl Rahner, "Natural Science and Reasonable Faith," *TI 21*, 16–55, 50.
42. See Michael Crowe, *The Extraterrestrial Debate 1750–1900* (Cambridge: Cambridge University Press, 1986); *The Extraterrestrial Debate, Antiquity to 1915* (Notre Dame: Notre Dame University Press, 2008). See also Thomas O'Meara, *Vast Universe: Extraterrestrials and Christian Revelation* (Collegeville: Liturgical, 2012); David Wilkinson, *Science, Religion, and the Search for Extraterrestrial Intelligence* (Oxford: Oxford University Press, 2013); Steven Dick, ed., *Many Worlds: The New Universe, Extraterrestrial Life and the Theological Implications* (Philadelphia: Templeton Foundation, 2000).
43. Karl Rahner, "Sternenbewohner. Theologisch," *Lexikon für Theologie und Kirche* (Freiburg: Herder 1964) 9:1061–62; "Natural Science and Reasonable Faith," 51–52; *Foundations*, 445–46.
44. Rahner, *Foundations*, 445.
45. Rahner, "Natural Science and Reasonable Faith," 51.

12.

Jürgen Moltmann (1926-)

Life and Context: Jürgen Moltmann was born in Hamburg and brought up in a secularized family. In 1943, he was conscripted as an air force auxiliary and served on an anti-aircraft battery during "Operation Gomorrah," when allied forces fire-bombed Hamburg and forty thousand people were killed. He became a prisoner of war (1945–1947) and was held in camps in Belgium, Scotland, and England. In the camps he was confronted with what had been done in Auschwitz and Buchenwald, and experienced a weight of profound shame that never left him. In the Scottish camp of Kilmarnock, Moltmann read Mark's gospel, and was deeply moved by Jesus's dying words: "My God, why have you forsaken me?"[1] Eventually, in the darkness, he came to faith in Christ: "But right down to the present day, after almost 60 years, I am certain that then, in 1945, and there, in the Scottish prisoner of war camp, in the dark pit of my soul, Jesus sought me and found me."[2] At Norton camp in England he began a serious study of theology. Moltmann returned to Germany at the age of twenty-two and became a pastor in the Reform tradition, receiving his doctorate in theology from the University of Göttingen. He taught at Wuppertal (1958–63), Bonn (1963–67), and Tübingen (1967–94). Originally influenced by Karl Barth, Moltmann's theology soon embraced a strongly historical, eschatological, and political consciousness. This found expression in his

Theology of Hope (1964), a sustained argument for a thoroughly eschatological theology transformed by resurrection faith. This was followed by his theology of a God who suffers with suffering creatures in his *The Crucified God* (1972). The third book in this early trilogy was his *The Church in the Power of the Spirit* (1975). Moltmann's later works include his six major systematic contributions to theology, *The Trinity and the Kingdom* (1981), *God in Creation* (1985), *The Way of Jesus Christ* (1990), *The Spirit of Life* (1992), *The Coming of God* (1996), and *Experiences in Theology* (2000).

In this chapter, I will focus principally on two of Moltmann's books that are particularly concerned with creation, his *God in Creation* and *The Way of Jesus Christ*.[3] I will begin from his idea of the ecological community of creation, and then focus on the Trinitarian nature of his theology. In the third section I will discuss his view of evolution in relation to the creative action of the Spirit. The fourth section will be concerned with the redemption of creation in Christ, and the last with the Sabbath as the feast of creation.

AN ECOLOGICAL COMMUNITY OF CREATION

Moltmann stands out from major systematic theologians of the twentieth century, because he sees clearly that the ecological crisis is "deadly," and that it demands a response from theology.[4] His theology of creation published in 1985 is explicitly subtitled "An Ecological Doctrine of Creation." Moltmann does not engage directly with particular ecological issues in this book, nor does he direct it to specific ecological actions. He attempts, in the light of the devastation of the planet, to rethink the theology of God and creation from the ground up, seeking to transform the attitude of domination of nature into that of a participative community of all God's creatures.

Moltmann is critical of a great deal of modernity's scientific and technological way of knowing: "Modern thinking has developed by way of an objectifying, analytical, and reductionist approach."[5] But he also recognizes that the sciences themselves, particularly recent physics and biology, have shown that this approach does not do full justice to reality. What is needed, Moltmann proposes, is to see things as a whole, and to see them in all of their relationships. Moltmann, then, commits himself to a relational and participatory way of thinking.

He argues that integrating and holistic thinking and action are necessary at various levels for the regeneration of community between human beings and nature. At the legal and political level, it will involve a covenant with nature, in which the rights of nature will be respected. On the medical level, it will involve seeing the human as a psychosomatic totality. At the religious level, it will involve understanding nature in a theology of creation that is guided by the idea of humans and other creatures as a community of creation before God.

Moltmann sees it as theology's function to reawaken awareness of this community and to restore it. Moltmann consistently sees his theology as messianic, and he proposes a Christian ecological theology that understands creation in the light of Jesus the Messiah: "it will be determined by the points of view of the messianic time which had begun with him and which he defines. It is directed towards the liberation of men and women, peace with nature, and the redemption of the community of human beings and nature from negative powers, and from the forces of death."[6] As this statement makes clear, Moltmann's theology very closely unites creation and redemption in Christ; and it consistently involves both human beings and the wider creation, as one community of creation and salvation in Christ. He sees creation as involving both earth and heaven, and he understands heaven as the place of God's potentialities for the wider creation and of divine communication. His is a theology of hope for the transformation of both heaven and earth in the new creation.

TRINITY IN CREATION

Moltmann's concept of creation is profoundly relational, and deeply grounded in his view of God as a Trinitarian community of persons. At various points in his works, Moltmann enters into dialogue with Jewish thinkers, and with concepts such as the *Shekinah* and *zimzum*. Shekinah is a feminine word that refers to the dwelling, or presence, of God in the tabernacle and the temple. Following the Jewish theologian, Franz Rosenzweig, Moltmann sees God, in the Shekinah, as giving God's self away to be with God's people, being present with them on their journey, suffering with them in their sufferings, and going with them into the misery of the foreign land.[7]

Moltmann reflects about the Shekinah in terms of God's presence in creation, seeing the Creator as giving God's self away to creatures, as being with them in their creatureliness, and suffering with them in their sufferings. He interprets the Shekinah in Christian terms as the Spirit's presence to creatures in continuous creation and as the Word who is made flesh in the midst of creation. He says of the Spirit: "The God who in the Spirit dwells in his creation is present to every one of his creatures and remains bound to each of them, in joy and sorrow."[8] This is why, he says, that we hear in Romans 8 that the Spirit sighs with creation in its groaning. Moltmann sees the Word and Wisdom of God as the "pattern" through whom all creatures are made, who becomes flesh, embracing the suffering of the world in order to bring healing and redemption.[9] Both Spirit and Word, then, are forms of divine presence with creatures.

Moltmann takes up the idea of zimzum from the Jewish kabbalistic tradition, and specifically from Isaac Luria. The word zimzum refers to the divine self-contraction and self-limitation. In the Shekinah, God contracts God's universal presence so that God can dwell in the temple. But this same self-contraction occurs in creation. God withdraws into God's self in order to allow finite creation space for its own being. God's restricts God's presence and power to give finite creatures room to be: "God makes room for creation by withdrawing his presence. . . . The space which comes into being and is set free by God's self-limitation is literally God-forsaken space."[10] For Moltmann, then, God's creative act is grounded in God's "humble, self-humiliating love"; it is the beginning of the self-emptying of God which Philippians 2 attributes to the Messiah.[11] In creation, too, God takes the form of a servant.

While Moltmann insists that God is continually present to creation in the Spirit, creation is not yet what it will be, fully the dwelling place of God, imaged in the Sabbath. With regard to this present age, Moltmann is prepared to qualify Genesis's teaching of the goodness of creation:

> It is not possible for a biblically determined Christian theology to see the present condition of the world as pure divine "creation," and to join in the Creator's original verdict: "Behold it is very good" (Gen 1:31). Much more applicable to the present condition of the created world is Paul's recognition of the "anxious waiting" and the "longing" of creation, which is "subjected to futility, not of its own will, but by the will of him who subjected it, on the strength of hope" (Rom 8:19–21).[12]

For Moltmann, then, the natural world can only be understood theologically from the perspective of its messianic fulfillment, when creation will be, without reserve, the dwelling place of God.

Moltmann's view of the Trinity is original and controversial in two major respects. First, as he makes clear in his *The Trinity and the Kingdom of God*, he advocates for a strongly social model of the Trinity. His view of this social model is encapsulated in a later book, when he points to Jesus's prayer to the Father in Gethsemane, and argues that such a relationship between Jesus and the Father shows that we cannot hold that there is only a single will and a single consciousness in the three persons of the Trinity. He speaks of three distinct actors in the Trinity: "The biblical starting point for the doctrine of the Trinity is that there are three different actors in the divine history, Son – Father – Spirit; the question about their unity then follows."[13] Here, and elsewhere, Moltmann moves directly from what biblical texts say about Jesus and the Father to conclusions about the life of the Trinity.

With such emphasis on the distinction of persons, how does Moltmann safeguard the unity of God? He answers this question with his theology of *perichoresis*. This word, used long ago of the Trinity by John Damascene, has the meaning of embracing, surrounding, encompassing. It refers to the mutual indwelling of the divine persons in the Trinity. In Moltmann's usage it refers to a profound relational unity, which he sees as preferable to traditional ideas of the one divine substance of God, or the Enlightenment idea of the absolute subject. Perichoresis enables us to speak of the Trinity, he says, as a "non-hierarchical community."[14] Each person "ek-sists" outside themselves in the two others; each becomes the living space for the others; and each "prepares the wide space and dwelling for the two others."[15]

This relational life of the living God suggests that God's creation itself will also be radically relational. In fact Moltmann says of the universe of creatures that "relationships are just as primal as the things themselves."[16] Nothing in the world exists, lives and moves of itself: "Everything exists, lives and moves *in others*, in one another, with one another, for one another, in the cosmic interrelationship of the divine Spirit."[17] In the next section, I will return to Moltmann's idea of the Spirit as enabling the participation of all creatures in this interrelated community of creation.

The second distinctive aspect of Moltmann's Trinitarian theology of creation is his view that God is affected by the world, that God suffers with a suffering world. In *The Crucified God*, Moltmann argues that the suffering of the cross was suffered in the very life of the triune God. He speaks not only of a real abandonment of Jesus by the Father, and of suffering in the divine life, but also of division between Father and Son in the Trinity.[18] While not all theologians agree with Moltmann at this point, others have followed him in making their own attempts to acknowledge God's radical identification with, and suffering with, suffering creation.

Moltmann's theology of the Trinity is open to the created world. God's perichoretic life extends to God's relationships to creatures. The Trinitarian persons do not constitute a closed circle, but an open community in which creatures participate. Richard Bauckham says of Moltmann's theology of the open Trinity: "God has a *Trinitarian history* with the world, a history of mutual relationships, in which God not only acts on the world but is affected by the world and the Trinitarian relationships themselves change as human history is taken within them."[19] This Trinitarian history has as its goal the kingdom of God, which "Moltmann has long conceived as an eschatological panentheism, in which 'God will be all in all': creation will be glorified through its participation in the divine life and God will be glorified in his indwelling of his creation."[20]

The word *panentheism* refers to the idea that all things are in

God. It is to be distinguished from pantheism, which simply identifies God and the creation. For Moltmann it is always a Trinitarian concept. He distinguishes panentheism not only from pantheism, but also from what he calls monotheism, which in his unusual usage, refers to a non-Trinitarian or unitarian view of God. He sees Trinitarian panentheism as "binding together God's transcendence and God's immanence."[21] He writes: "In the panentheistic view, God, having created the world, also dwells in it, and conversely the world which he has created exists in him. This is a concept which can really only be thought and described in Trinitarian terms."[22]

EVOLUTION AND THE SPIRIT OF LIFE

Moltmann sees no need for a literalist or "biblicist" reading of the creation stories of the Bible. He points out that they originate in different historical eras, and that each narrative is a synthesis of belief in God as Creator and the understanding of nature at a particular time:

> It is a biblicist misunderstanding of the biblical testimonies to think that they are laying down once and for all particular findings about nature, and render all further research superfluous. The history of the biblical traditions themselves shows that the stories of creation belong within a hermeneutical process of revision and innovation, as the result of new experiences. Since they are testimonies to the history of God with the world, they themselves actually direct their readers to new experiences of the world in this divine history.[23]

For someone who is faithful to the Bible, then, it is not only possible to relate the biblical testimonies of God's creation to new scientific insights, it is essential to make this connection. In our time, biblical faith itself requires us to engage with contemporary cosmology and evolutionary biology. Openness to new syntheses is grounded in the openness to the future already found in the biblical testimonies themselves. Moltmann points out, however, that because of developments in science and other aspects of human experience, such openness to the future "turns every synthesis into a provisional draft, and permits no dogmatism."[24]

In Moltmann's theology, creation involves not only the original creation of a universe of creatures (*creatio originalis*), and their continuous creation (*creatio continua*), but also their redemptive new creation (*creatio nova*). He sees the theological phrase creation *out of nothing* (*creatio ex nihilo*) as referring to the sheer miracle of the world's existence, the contingency of the universe of creatures. He sees God, not as creating a static or fixed world, but one that is to become: "If God made creation to be the kingdom of his glory, then it was he who gave it movement and set it in motion, and the same time lending it an irreversible direction."[25] God creates a universe that is open to its own history. It is an open system, opening out to the God who brings it to its fulfillment in new creation.

Bara', the biblical word for creation, is used in the Bible not only for God's initial creation, but also of God's creative acts of liberation and salvation in history. This suggests to Moltmann that God's activity in history is not found only in continuous creation, but also in salvific events that anticipate the new creation. He sees God's creative activity as involving God's suffering with creatures in their suffering, and God's patient companionship with the whole evolving universe it its incompletion. God accompanies creation at every point. This accompaniment is directed towards the consummation of the whole creation. In Moltmann's view, such a God must transcend creation, and precisely as transcendent be profoundly immanent to creatures. So he insists that we must think of the world-transcendence of God simultaneously with God's "evolutive immanence."[26] And in his Trinitarian theology of creation, it is in the life-giving Spirit that God is immanent to the whole creation:

> Through his Spirit, God himself is present to his creation. The whole creation is a fabric woven and shot through by the efficacies of the Spirit. Through his Spirit God is also present in the very structures of creation.[27]

Moltmann sees the whole of matter as *informed* matter, as spirited matter, and he sees human beings as arriving at consciousness and spirit in a creaturely way through evolutionary processes. In participating in spirit, the whole cosmos corresponds to God "because it is effected through God the Spirit, and exists in God the Spirit, it also moves and is evolved in the energies and powers of the divine Spirit."[28] Moltmann proposes, then, a pneumatological interpretation of evolution, that encompasses both the emergence of the universe and the evolution of life on Earth: "The God who is present in the world and in every part of it, is the creative Spirit. It is not merely the spirit of God that is present in the evolving world; it is rather God the Spirit, with his uncreated and creative energies."[29]

The presence of the Spirit in the evolution of the universe is not yet the fullness of divine presence. It is the creative presence of God in the time when God has contracted God's self to make room for creation. Only in the fullness of time will God dwell fully in creation as God's dwelling. Ernst Conradie says of Moltmann's view of this fulfillment: "What comes into being through God's contraction is now gathered up again as God's own."[30] Creation will be completed through the fullness of divine indwelling: "then the new creation is indwelt by the unbounded fullness of the divine life, and glorified creation is wholly set free in its participation in the unbounded existence of God."[31] This will mean not a fullness of petrification, but "an openness *par excellence* of all life systems," a fullness and completion of "eternal livingness."[32]

According to Moltmann, God's accompaniment of creatures is not merely a relationship of causality, but a whole series of relationships: God acts in and through creatures; God acts with and out of creaturely actions; God provides the potentialities out of which creatures act; God creates the space for the free acts of creatures. Moltmann does not equate these relationships with divine intervention: "We do not have to expect the accompanying activity of God to take the form merely of supernatural interventions and spectacular interventions."[33] This accompanying activity is usually unobtrusive, but this does not exclude the idea that we may discern signs and wonders in our history.

CHRIST THE REDEEMER OF EVOLUTION

Moltmann takes up the role of Jesus Christ with regard to creation in his *The Way of Jesus Christ*. In this book he sets out to construct a messianic Christology, which is also a postmodern, ecological Christology. A key idea of the last section of the book, which deals with the "Cosmic Christ," is the need for a "differentiated" cosmic Christology, with three distinct but interrelated strands: 1. Christ as the ground of the creation of all things (original creation); 2. Christ as the moving power in the evolution of creation (continuous creation); 3. Christ as the redeemer of the whole process (new creation).[34] Moltmann sees the third of these as the neglected strand, a neglect he sets out to remedy.

While in *God and Creation* he stresses the close connec-tion between creation and salvation, in *The Way of Jesus Christ* he makes a very sharp distinction between them. The evolutionary processes by which creation takes effect in our world, he insists, are not themselves salvific. We do not evolve into the eschaton and we do not progress into the Kingdom of God. Evolutionary processes are characterized by transience and death, which are all part of the old creation, while resurrection and eternal life characterized the new creation in Christ.[35] Moltmann, at this point, expresses strong disagreement with Teilhard's view that the evolution of humanity and the universe towards Omega can be understood as a process of Christification, by which the universe is being brought to its eschatological fulfillment. In particular, Moltmann sees Teilhard as putting so much faith in progress that he fails to take account of the ambiguity of evolution and particularly of the costs to its victims:

> In his firm faith in progress Teilhard does seem to have overlooked the ambiguity of evolution itself, and therefore to have paid no attention to evolution's victims. Evolution always means selection. Many things are sacrificed in order that "the fittest"—which means the most effective and the most adaptable—may survive. In this way higher and increasingly complex life systems, which can react to changed environments, undoubtedly develop. But in the same process milliards of living things fall by the wayside and disappear into evolution's rubbish bin.[36]

Moltmann rejects all progressivist theologies that fail to focus on the victims, the victims of evolution as well as the human victims of catastrophic events such as the First World War and Hiroshima. He sees Teilhard's Christ-the-evolver as a story of winners. By contrast, he insists: "If Christ is to be thought of in conjunction with evolution, then he must become evolution's redeemer."[37] He accuses Rahner, along with Teilhard, of ignoring the victims of evolution. He thinks of Rahner as presupposing an evolutionary view, without adopting it in a *critical* way. And he criticizes Rahner for seeing Christ as the summit of evolutionary development, but not as the redeemer of evolution. Nevertheless, Moltmann accepts Rahner's concept of evolutionary self-transcendence when joined with the theology of Christ as the redeemer of evolution.[38]

For Moltmann, then, Christ the Evolver cannot be simply identified with Christ the Redeemer, and the evolutionary process cannot be simply identified with eschatology. Is it conceivable, he asks, that God's future for creation will be achieved by way of evolution or self-transcendence? Moltmann's answer is "no." Evolution takes place in time and does not lead to the immortality of individual creatures. God's salvation of creatures is conceivable only *eschatologically*.[39]

Moltmann sees the whole history of evolution, with every one of its victims, as being brought to its fulfillment and transformed in Christ. God's eschatological action involves the raising of the dead, the gathering of the victims and the seeking of the lost, a redemption no evolution can ever achieve. He understands this redemptive divine action as occurring *diachronically*: simultaneous to all things. It is a waking and a gathering of every creature of every time: "the parousia comes to all times simultaneously in a single instant."[40]

Moltmann's cosmic Christology leads to *ethical* conclusions. He insists that Christ's death for all creatures shows their meaning and value before God: "If Christ has died not merely for the reconciliation of human beings, but for the reconciliation of other creatures too, then every created being enjoys infinite value in God's sight, and has its own right to live."[41] The fact that Christ died for all creatures provides the basis "for an all-embracing ethic of life."[42] In Moltmann's ethical vision, God's love *toward* these creatures, Christ's giving himself *for* them, the indwelling of the Holy Spirit *in* them, leads to the conviction of their rights within the community of creation.[43] Moltmann, then, advocates for a community of human beings, plants and animals based upon *law*. He sees this position as grounded theologically in Christ's death and resurrection and in the Sabbath.

THE SABBATH: THE FEAST OF CREATION

Moltmann holds that the completion of every Jewish and Christian doctrine of creation must be the theology of the Sabbath.[44] In and through the Sabbath, God completes the creation, and in celebrating the Sabbath, humans recognize that the natural world of which they are a part is truly God's creation. The celebration of the Sabbath opens creation out to its true future. It is an anticipation of, and foretaste of the redeemed creation.

Much is lost, Moltmann suggests, when our thinking about creation is limited to the six days on which God works. Then the God who rests, the God who rejoices in creation and sanctifies it, disappears. The meaning of human life is then identified with work and busyness, and rest, joy in existence, and feasting are seen as insignificant. Creation and Sabbath go together, but the whole work of creation is performed "for the sake of the sabbath." Following Franz Rosenzweig, Moltmann sees the Sabbath as "the feast of creation."[45]

While the works of creation necessarily manifest God's transcendence over creation, the Sabbath points to the immanence of God to creation, to the God who will dwell fully in creation at its completion. The Sabbath is about stillness, about resting in the very being of God. It is a foretaste of the fullness of divine presence and of divine glory. God's blessing of the Sabbath gives to creatures themselves the capacity to rest in God. We are told that God "hallowed" the Sabbath (Gen 2:3). A time is sanctified, a time for human beings, and for the whole creation.

Moltmann writes: "The celebration of the Sabbath leads to an intensified capacity for perceiving the loveliness of everything—food, clothing, the body and the soul—because existence itself is glorious."[46] The Sabbath is about freedom from striving, performance, and achievement, and about being wholly present in the presence of God. Moltmann sees Israel as giving the nations two archetypal images of liberation, exodus and sabbath. The exodus is about liberation from external slavery. The sabbath is the symbol of inner freedom. For Moltmann, exodus and sabbath are indivisible.

Moltmann suggests that Christians today need to recover the Sabbath, not seeing Sunday as replacing the Sabbath, but more as continuing it. They celebrate the beginning of new creation with the resurrection of Jesus from the dead, but this will have more meaning if they genuinely celebrate the Sabbath on the evening before their Sunday celebration. The ecological day of rest should be one without pollution of the environment, so that nature too can celebrate its Sabbath.[47] Ernst Conradie sums up Moltmann's view of the fullness of divine indwelling to which the Sabbath points:

> God not only comes to dwell in creation (*adventus* and *Shekinah*); the whole creation is called to participate (*perichoresis*) in the life of the triune God. For Moltmann, creaturely reality is opened up for God's indwelling. Through this perichoretic indwelling of God in the world every wrong in history is redressed, every form of suffering is healed. This allows for the participation of God and creation in the celebration of an eternal Sabbath—characterized by festivities, joy, laughter, dancing and play.[48]

TRAJECTORIES

On some issues I differ from Moltmann: I am committed to the unity of the one, undivided, divine being, or substance (*ousia*), of God the Trinity; I do not follow him when he speaks of division between Father and Son at the cross. But I agree with Celia Deane-Drummond when she concludes that Moltmann's "imaginative brilliance" is an important corrective to sterile theologies of creation.[49] Although she raises critical questions, she sees his theology as an important step in the direction of a truly green theology: "Like most great theologians, his thought should serve to stimulate further dialogue. . . . If a green theology is to have a message for this ecologically damaged fragile earth, it has to include Moltmann's concept of hope in God, who through Christ makes all things new."[50] Some important trajectories from Moltmann's theology of creation include the following:

1. Moltmann's theology is one of hope in God, who through Christ, and in the Spirit makes all things new.
2. His is a theology that seeks to be fully ecological, and which accepts and engages with evolutionary science.
3. It is a creation theology that is fully Trinitarian, and where creation is understood always in relation to salvation in Christ.
4. Moltmann has a fully explicit theology of the salvation of the rest of the natural world.
5. He has a theology of the Spirit as the energy enabling the evolution of a universe of creatures.
6. He sees God as suffering with suffering creatures.
7. In his theology, the risen Christ is the redeemer of the victims of evolution and violence.
8. His theology has practical ecological consequences in commitment to ecological action and social justice.
9. He proposes a Christian recovery of the meaning of the

Sabbath, and brings out its ecological meaning for the present time.

Notes

1. Jürgen Moltmann, *A Broad Place: An Autobiography* (Minneapolis: Fortress Press, 2008), 30.
2. Ibid.
3. Jürgen Moltmann, *God in Creation: An Ecological Doctrine of Creation: The Gifford Lectures 1984–1985* (London: SCM, 1985); *The Way of Jesus Christ: Christology in messianic dimensions* (London: SCM, 1990).
4. Moltmann, *God in Creation*, 20. On Moltmann's theology of creation, see Celia Deane-Drummond, *Ecology in Jürgen Moltmann's Theology* (Lewiston, NY: Edwin Mellin Press, 1997); Richard Bauckham, *The Theology of Jürgen Moltmann* (Edinburgh: T&T Clark, 1995); Geiko Müller-Fahrenholz, *The Kingdom and the Power: The Theology of Jürgen Moltmann* (London: SCM, 2000).
5. Moltmann, *God in Creation*, 2.
6. Ibid., 5.
7. Ibid., 15.
8. Ibid.
9. Ibid., 16.
10. Ibid., 87.
11. Ibid., 88.
12. Ibid., 39.
13. Jürgen Moltmann, *Experiences in Theology: Ways and Forms of Christian Theology* (London: SCM, 2000), 321–22.
14. Ibid., 317.
15. Ibid., 318–19.
16. Moltmann, *God in Creation*, 11.
17. Ibid.

18. Jürgen Moltmann, *The Crucified God* (London: SCM, 1984), 151–52; 241–46.
19. Bauckham, *The Theology of Jürgen Moltmann*, 185.
20. Ibid., 185–86.
21. Moltmann, *God in Creation*, 98.
22. Ibid.
23. Ibid., 192.
24. Ibid., 193.
25. Ibid., 207.
26. Ibid., 206.
27. Ibid., 212.
28. Ibid.
29. Ibid.
30. Ernst Conradie, "Jürgen Molmann (1926-) – The Justification of God," in *Creation and Salvation: Volume 2: A Companion on Recent Theological Movements*, ed. Ernst M. Conradie (Zurich: LIT, 2012), 139.
31. Moltmann, *God in Creation*, 213.
32. Ibid.
33. Ibid., 211.
34. Moltmann, *The Way of Jesus Christ: Christ*, 286.
35. Bauckham, *The Theology of Jürgen Moltmann*, 194.
36. Moltmann, *The Way of Jesus Christ*, 294.
37. Ibid., 297.
38. Ibid., 299–300.
39. Ibid.
40. Ibid., 317.
41. Ibid., 307.
42. Ibid., 308.
43. Ibid., 307.
44. Moltmann, *God in Creation*, 276.

45. Ibid., 257.
46. Ibid., 286.
47. Ibid., 296.
48. Conradie, "Jürgen Moltmann," 139.
49. Deane-Drummond, *Ecology in Jürgen Moltmann's Theology*, 295–305.
50. Ibid., 305.

13.

Sallie McFague (1933-)

Life and Context: Sallie McFague was born in Quincy, Massachusetts, and studied English literature and theology at Yale University. Originally influenced by the theology of Karl Barth, she soon developed her own distinctive approach, eventually becoming a leading eco-feminist theologian. She taught for thirty years at the Vanderbilt University Divinity School in Nashville. More recently she has been Distinguished Theologian in Residence at the Vancouver School of Theology in British Columbia. She is a member of the Anglican Church of Canada. A key idea in McFague's work is that theological language has a metaphorical character, something she explores fully in her *Metaphorical Theology* (1982). McFague proposed her own feminist and ecological metaphors for God, and for the God-world relationship, in her *Models of God: Theology for an Ecological, Nuclear Age* (1987). In response to the ecological crisis, she proposed a theology of creation as God's body in *The Body of God: An Ecological Theology* (1993), and further explored a theological response to the natural world with her *Super, Natural Christians: How We Should Love Nature* (1997). She turned to an ecological economics, lifestyle, and ethics, in her *Life Abundant: Rethinking Theology and Economy for a Planet in Peril* (2000). McFague summoned her theological resources to respond directly to the climate change crisis of the twenty-first century in *A New Climate for Theology: God, the World* *and Global Warming* (2008) and has taken up the concept of restraint, grounded in the Christian notion of *kenosis* (self-emptying), in her *Blessed Are the Consumers* (2013).

For much of her academic life, Sallie McFague has been engaged in the development of a Christian ecological theology and, particularly in more recent work, has been responding directly to the global climate crisis. I will begin this chapter by exploring her concept of metaphor and then take up her models of God. In the third section I will consider her model of creation as the body of God. Then I will focus on her theological response to the issue of climate, and in the last section point to two Christian ecological practices she proposes, the practice of the loving eye and the practice of restraint.

MODELS OF GOD

In her *Models of God*, McFague begins from the assumption that what can be said with confidence about Christian faith is very little, and that even this little is highly contested. She suggests that at the heart of what can be said are two Christian convictions. The first is the claim that the universe is not indifferent and not malevolent, and that there is a personal power that is on the side of life and its fulfillment. The second conviction is that there are clues for fleshing out this claim in the life, death, and the appearances of Jesus of Nazareth.[1] In McFague's view, it the task of each new generation of Christian theologians to find appropriate ways to express these convictions.

Each theological interpretation will involve images, or metaphors, that support a particular theological system. In spite of the efforts of contemporary theologians to reinterpret Christian faith, McFague thinks that the basic metaphors for

God remain unchanged. They remain triumphalistic, monarchical, and patriarchal. The task of theology, in her view, is not only to deconstruct metaphors such as God the king, but also to construct new metaphors.

Metaphor, she says, is a word or phrase that is used *in*appropriately: what belongs in one context is used in another, as when we speak of the arm of a chair, or of God as father.[2] Although metaphor has often been understood simply as an illustration or decoration, McFague agrees with those who insist that metaphor is a necessity. There are many instances where a metaphor cannot be replaced by more direct speech because it is the only way we have to express something. In such instances we have no choice but to use metaphor if we want to communicate: "Here, metaphor is a strategy of desperation, not decoration."[3] When we use a metaphor we express the unfamiliar in terms of the familiar, and the unknown in terms of the known. This leads McFague to one of the key insights in her theological approach: metaphor always implies not only an *is*, but also an *is not*:

> Metaphor always has the character of "is" and "is not": an assertion is made but as a likely account rather than a definition. That is, to say, "God is mother,' is not to define God as mother, not to assert identity between the terms "God" and "mother," but to suggest that we consider what we do not know how to talk about—relating to God—through the metaphor of mother. The assumption here is that all talk of God is indirect: no words or phrases refer directly to God, for God-language can refer only through the detour of a description that properly lies elsewhere. To speak of God as mother is to invite us to consider some qualities associated with mothering as one partial but perhaps illuminating way of speaking about certain aspects of God's relationship to us.[4]

McFague's understanding of metaphor thus has some parallels to the tradition of analogy in theology, as found, for example, in Karl Rahner's statement, made at the end of his life: "theologians are worthy of the title only when they do not seek to reassure themselves that they are providing clear and lucid discourse, but rather when they are experiencing and witnessing, with both terror and bliss, to the analogical back and forth between affirmation and negation before the abyss of God's incomprehensibility."[5] But McFague's choice of metaphor rather than analogy reflects her interest in engaging in a post-modern, creative, and partial approach to God-talk that does not involve metaphysical claims. She speaks often of her theological works as experimental, sometimes as a thought experiment. She says that she prefers metaphor, in part, because it remains fragmentary and, unlike analogy, does not result in organic, systematic works.[6] How are metaphors related to models? McFague sees a model as a metaphor with staying power, one that has gained sufficient stability to provide a level of coherence. An example of a metaphor that has become such a model is the image of God as a father.

In exploring her own models of God, the first model she takes up is that of God as mother. She points out that the biblical and Christian God is beyond male and female, and language for God that is exclusively male can promote an idolatrous limitation of God. It can carry the implication, as well, that women are not in the image of God. If, as Christians believe, both men and women are made in the image of God, then both male and female metaphors should be used of God. Because God is not simply mother, but far more, McFague insists that female metaphors should not be limited to maternal ones. And in using the image of God as mother, she understands it in an inclusive way, not as ruling out paternal images, but as directed towards offering a richer view of the divine love as parental.

McFague sees the model of God as mother as representing

the creative, birthing love associated with the Greek word *agape*: "All of us, female and male, have the womb as our first home, all of us are born from the bodies of our mothers, all of us are fed by our mothers."[7] The activity she associates with God as mother, then, is that of creating and bringing to life the universe of creatures: "the universe is bodied forth from God."[8] The basic ethic that arises from this image, McFague suggests, is justice: if God is mother, we humans are called to be caretakers of what she has brought forth: "our positive role in creation is as preservers, those who pass along and who care for all forms of life so that they may prosper."[9]

The second model McFague takes up is that of God as lover. McFague sees the frequent use of this image in the Christian mystical tradition, based on the *Song of Solomon*, as remaining subject to the dangers of dualism, individualism, and otherworldliness. In her own usage, the model of God as lover is not to be understood simply as an individual relationship with God, in a world apart from the one we know. Rather it expresses the divine love for "all creatures, body and spirit, here and now."[10] The kind of love suggested by this image, according to McFague, can be seen as related to the Greek word *eros*, the love associated with passion, desire, and sex. It expresses God's passionate love for creatures:

> God as lover finds all species of flora and fauna valuable and attractive, she finds the entire, intricate, evolutionary complex infinitely precious and wondrous; God as lover finds himself needing the help of those very ones among the beloved—of us human beings—who have been largely responsible for much of the estrangement that has occurred. We are needed lest the lover lose her beloved; we are needed so that the lover may be reunited with his beloved. The model of God as lover, then, implies that God needs us to help save the world![11]

The activity of God as lover, McFague suggests, is that of saving. God as lover embraces a suffering world, participating in the pain of the beloved. God as lover becomes incarnate in the flesh, in the body of the world as a whole, and in the bodies of creatures who have a special capacity to respond to God as lover and hence to manifest this love. McFague sees Jesus is uniquely paradigmatic of this love, but not as ontologically different to other paradigmatic figures.[12] The content of salvation in this model involves conversion from individualism to commitment to the well-being and restoration of the whole global community of life. The ethic is that of healing the creation, participating with others in the salvation of the world.[13]

McFague's third model is of God as friend, expressed in Greek by the word *philia*. This love is characterized by freedom, mutuality, and reciprocity. God is the friend of the whole creation, and we too are called to love what God loves: "If God is the friend of the world, the one committed to it, who can be trusted never to betray it, who not only likes the world but has a vision for its well-being, then we as the special part of the body—the *imago dei*—are invited as friends of the Friend of the world to join in that vision and work for its fulfillment."[14]

McFague sees the activity of God as friend as sustaining the creation, and she notes that this role of the immanent God is usually associated with the Holy Spirit. At this point in *Models of God*, she is critical of the image of God as spirit,[15] but in later work she tells us that her own thinking has changed and she has come to embrace the language of God as spirit.[16] The ethic involved in the image of God as friend is to act as loving companions to the wider creation so as to enable its flourishing: "To participate in the ongoing, sustaining work of God as friend of the world means, as the word 'sustain' suggests, to support the world, to be its companion, both as advocate for its needs and as partner in its joys and sufferings."[17]

In her conclusion to *Models of God*, McFague reflects on

the three images of God as mother, lover, and friend in relation to the Christian doctrine of the Trinity. She says that in the kind of theology she is developing, "a trinity is not a necessity, nor should the divine nature be circumscribed by it."[18] But she sees a trinity as fitting well with the models with which she has been experimenting. She emphasizes the experimental and heuristic nature of her own work by saying that "it is mostly fiction," which fleshes out some basic metaphors in as deep and comprehensible way as possible, in order to see what their implications might be, and perhaps to provide "a habitable house in which to live for a while."[19]

CREATION AS THE BODY OF GOD

How might we think of the relationship between God and the creation? McFague's preferred model for this relationship is that of the universe as the body of God. Her reflections begin with the biblical account of Moses asking to see God's glory. The divine response is that no one can see God and live. But God does allow Moses a glimpse of the divine body, not of the face, but of the back: "And you shall see my back; but my face shall not be seen" (Exod 32:33).[20] In her reflection on this text, McFague finds an indication that in the creatures around us we can see the body of God, even if is not full sight of God's face, but only like a glimpse of God's back.

McFague takes up the language of sacrament from the Christian tradition in order to explore the model of creation as God's body. She writes of the universe of creatures as the sacrament of God, as a sacramental embodiment of the living God. The creatures around us are the symbolic expression of the God who is profoundly present to and in the whole creation. In encountering this sacramental embodiment of God, we can be lead to a this-worldly contemplation of the divine glory and transcendence. We can discover the God who is immanent in the natural world. But we are also led to a contemplative stance before a God far beyond any creaturely limits. For McFague, then, the model of the creation as the body of God involves radical transcendence as well as immanence. In her approach, we do not have direct sight of God, but only a glimpse of God as embodied in the creatures around us. We do not have a clear description of God, but simply a metaphorical model.

In *The Body of God*, McFague sees *spirit* language as playing an important role in the model of the created universe as the body of God. She writes: "Spirit, as wind, breath, life is the most basic and inclusive way to express centered embodiment. All living creatures, not just human ones, depend upon breath."[21] Spirit is the breath, the life, of the universe, and thus of the body of God. McFague points out that *spirit*, like *body*, is used as a metaphor. Both words refer properly to creatures: "Neither describes God, for both are back, not face, terms."[22] But the metaphor *spirit* can point to the life-giving creative action of God. The spirit of God is the breath of God that sustains and energizes the fecundity, abundance, and diversity of all that is bodied forth from God. For McFague, this action of the spirit of God is not an alternative to scientific accounts of evolutionary emergence, but speaks of the creative God present and acting in and through all that is described in the sciences.

For a Christian theology, McFague points out, the spirit of God at work in creation is also the Holy Spirit that transforms human lives. With the emergence of the human, she says, evolution has entered a new historical and cultural phase and, in this phase, the Holy Spirit is both the guide and the one who works through human beings: "we become the mind and heart as well as the hands and feet of the body of God on our planet."[23] The action of God as the spirit of the body is, then, twofold: "The spirit is the source of life, the breath of creation; at the same time, the Holy Spirit is the source of the renewal of life, the direction or purpose for all the bodies of the world—a goal characterized by inclusive love."[24]

This model of God, in McFague's view, is not pantheist but panentheist: "Everything that is is *in* God and God is *in* all things and yet God is not identical with the universe, for the universe is dependent on God in a way that God is not dependent on the universe."[25] She does not see God as necessarily embodied, nor as totally embodied: "God is sacramentally embodied: God is mediated, expressed, in and through embodiment, but not necessarily or totally."[26] McFague sees this model of the universe as God's body as compatible with both viable interpretations of Christian faith and modern science. And, of course, she sees it as underscoring our bodiliness, the physicality that we share with other creatures of the universe. It is a model "on the side of the well-being of the planet, for it raises the issue of ethical regard towards all bodies as all are interrelated and interdependent."[27]

In order to give shape to the theology of the body of God, McFague turns to Christology, and to what she calls the Christic paradigm. She makes two moves here.[28] The first is to relativize the incarnation in relationship to Jesus, so that he is not seen as the only one in whom God is incarnate. The second is to extend the incarnation to the whole universe:

> In other words, the proposal is to consider Jesus as paradigmatic of what we find everywhere: everything that is is the sacrament of God (the universe as God's body), but here and there we find that presence erupting in special ways. Jesus is one such place for Christians, but there are other paradigmatic persons and events—and the natural world, in a way different from the self-conscious openness to God that persons display, is also a marvelous sacrament in its diversity and richness.[29]

She finds hints and clues for an embodied theology in the story of Jesus. His destabilizing parables, his healing ministry, and his inclusive meals suggest that all are invited to the banquet of life. On the basis of this story of Jesus she makes a direct proposal: the shape of the body of God, informed by the Christic paradigm, includes all. It means "the inclusion of the neglected oppressed—the planet itself and its many distinctive creatures, including outcast human ones."[30] Because of human actions, nature is the new poor. This does not mean that poor human beings should be replaced as the center of concern, nor that every microorganism is included in the same way as humans. But it does mean that nature is also among the poor of Earth, and that microorganisms have their place in God's creation.

Each creature, McFague insists, has its own intrinsic value as valued and loved by God.[31] This Christic paradigm thus leads to an understanding of reality that differs from the evolutionary principle of natural selection, because it involves solidarity with the outsider and the vulnerable. McFague sees God as suffering with creatures who suffer the cost of evolution:

> God cannnot set aside the laws of nature to benefit a chosen few. Life, diversity, complexity, novelty—and even our free will—all rest on the randomness of natural selection as well as the diminishment, waste and death of its processes. And yet, while accepting the inevitability of this pattern, we still grieve for and suffer with—as God does also in the cosmic Christ—those who are diminished and wasted.[32]

Nothing happens in the world that does not happen to God. McFague sees Christ now as the cosmic Christ, the presence of the liberating, healing, and suffering love of God to all creatures.[33] In the Christic paradigm, she says, the body of God can be understood as the cosmic Christ. She explains that this metaphor indicates that creation is moving towards salvation, and that salvation takes place in the whole creation. In the cosmic Christ, Christians find a direction and a basis for hope that is not evident from science, and are led to commit themselves to Earth's healing.

CLIMATE CHANGE

McFague begins her 2008 book on climate change with a review of the scientific evidence that leads her to conclude: "Climate change, quite simply, is the issue of the twenty-first century. It is not one issue among many, but, like the canary in the mine it is warning us that the way we are living on our planet is causing us to head for disaster."[34] We have entered a time when, whatever we do, the world will be different from the one we know. There are signs that we are approaching a tipping point of radical change with unforeseeable consequences.

In McFague's analysis, the way we treat creation is related to our most basic assumptions about reality, particularly about the nature of God, and the human. In her response to climate change, then, she seeks to offer an ecologically responsible theology of the human and of God. She points to the extremely individualistic anthropology many of us Western Christians inherit from post-Reformation Christianity, market capitalism, and the founding documents of the USA government. Religion, economics, and government have joined forces, supporting the internalization of radical individualism that results in unthinking damage to Earth's climate.

Theology, then, must contribute to the internalization of a different anthropology if the planet is to survive and flourish. As a step in this direction, McFague proposes that we need to see the scientific story of the universe and of life on Earth as our common story. We share this common story with other creatures of our planet, and with them have Earth as our common home. And in our common home, there are house rules, the most important of which is that "everything is related to everything else."[35] Internalizing this house rule is the task for a lifetime. It requires that we see ourselves as part of the web of life, "an incredibly vast, complex, subtle, beautiful web that would both amaze and call forth our concern."[36] In so doing, we experience awe before the rest of creation, and are also drawn to commitment to care for our planet. McFague sees the anthropology we need as that of a participatory community of creatures sharing a common, God-given home.

The view of God that McFague brings to the urgent issue of climate change is her theology of the universe, and Earth, as God's body. Such a theology focuses on God's loving presence to Earth's creatures, and on the bodily nature of Christian commitment:

> It focuses attention on the near, on the neighbor, on the earth, on meeting God not later in heaven but here and now. We meet God in the world and especially in the flesh of the world: in feeding the hungry, healing the sick—and in reducing greenhouse gases. An incarnational understanding of creation says nothing is too lowly, too physical, too mean a labor if it helps creation to flourish. We find God in caring for the garden, in loving the earth well: this becomes our vocation, our central task. Climate change, then, becomes a major religious, a major Christian, issue. To be a Christian in our time, one must respond to the consequences of global warming.[37]

In the light of suffering built into nature, and of horrific human events like the Holocaust and Hiroshima, McFague does not see God as controlling all events. But ultimately, she says, the resurrection gives Christians the assurance that God is "in charge."[38] We are human partners with God in helping the world to flourish, but "*we* are not *finally* in charge: God is, so says the Yes of the resurrection."

McFague says that a Christian response to the climate change crisis demands not only a transformation of our anthropology and our view of God, but also a radical change in our economics. McFague describes this as a move from neoclassical economics to ecological economics. The crucial assumption of neoclassical economics is that "human beings are self-interested individuals, who, acting on this basis, will create a syndicate, even a global one, capable of benefitting all eventually."[39] The view of human nature is individualistic, and the goal is growth.

Ecological economics, by contrast, embraces the values of distributive justice and sustainability. Its goal is "the well-being and sustainability of the whole household, planet Earth."[40] Climate change shows clearly that neoclassical economics is a failure. We need a new vision of the good life, one consistent with an ecological economics, where what are valued are "the bare necessities for all, universal medical care and education, opportunities for creativity and meaningful work, time for family and friends, green spaces in cities and wilderness for other creatures."[41]

ECOLOGICAL PRACTICES: THE LOVING EYE AND RESTRAINT

In her book *Super, Natural Christians*, McFague highlights the importance of the way we see others, human others, but also animals, birds, trees, rivers, and mountains. She does this by contrasting the arrogant eye and the loving eye, building on insights or feminist philosopher Marilyn Frye.[42] The arrogant eye is characteristic of much of the typical Western attitude to the natural world. It objectifies, manipulates, uses, and exploits. The loving eye enables us to see the other rightly. It attends to the other, allowing it to be truly other, seeing the other in the detail and specificity of its own reality, respecting its integrity.

Learning to see the creatures around us with a loving eye requires conversion in our way of seeing. McFague points out that it is a practice that requires detachment if we are to see the difference, distinctiveness, and the uniqueness of the other:

> This is the eye trained in detachment in order that its attachment will be objective, based on the reality of the other and not on its own wishes or fantasies. This is the eye bound to the other as is an apprentice to a skilled worker, listening to the other as does a foreigner in a new country. This is the eye that pays attention to the other so that the connections between knower and known, like the bond of friendship, will be on the real subject in its real world.[43]

The loving eye recognizes the limits of what we know of the other, and accepts the mystery of the other in humility. The loving eye requires that we learn to see and love others, human and non-human, with a love that can involve both otherness and intimacy. It involves the practice of loving attention to the specificity of this bird, this tree, this human being.

In a more recent book, *Blessed are the Consumers*,[44] McFague proposes the practice of restraint, in order that others, human and non-human, might live. She explores the practice of self-emptying love in the lives of key Christian witnesses, John Woolman, Simone Weil, and Dorothy Day. She proposes that this kind of love is the gospel way of life that is required in a time of climate crisis and terrible human inequality. We are called, she says, to enter the "wild space" of voluntary poverty.[45] For Christians, this is grounded in the kenotic (self-emptying) love of God in Christ (Phil 2:7), a love McFague sees as characterizing not only the incarnation, but also the divine act of creation, and the life of the Trinity:

> A deeply incarnational understanding of Christianity claims that at every stage—who God is, what creation is, who we are, and how we should live—the focus is on *embodiment*. Jesus gives himself in his life and message of empathetic love to others, gives his body on the cross in solidarity with all who suffer, and thus points to God as the divine giver par excellence, whose being is composed of persons, as movements of interweaving love. Likewise, creation is the pulling in of the divine self to allow space for others to live fully embodied, physical lives.[46]

Christian discipleship, then, involves following the pattern found in the life of Jesus, and in the Trinity, a pattern of "limitation, restraint, self-sacrifice of one's own body that others might flourish."[47] It means learning a truly universal other-centered love that reaches out to all life on Earth. It involves kenosis that is personal as well as public and political. Ultimately it is a spirituality of radical trust in God: "We are cupped within the divine hands, warmed in the divine breast, held close through our greatest fears, comforted when things go wildly wrong."[48]

TRAJECTORIES

In reading McFague, I am conscious of someone doing a different kind of theology to myself. While she puts a strong emphasis on the constructive and experimental nature of theological claims, my own approach to theology, and to science, is more that of critical realism. I am committed to the uniqueness of the incarnation and its meaning for ecological theology in a way that she is not. Her commitment to both feminist and ecological theology represents a major new trajectory in Christian theology. Her long-standing and faithful theological advocacy for our common home is thought-provoking, challenging, and often inspiring.

Some further trajectories from her thought are these:

1. The whole creation as the self-expression, the sacramental embodiment of God.
2. Her images of God as mother, lover, and friend to the whole community of creation are wonderfully fruitful.
3. She offers a bodily, physical, this-worldly theology.
4. She develops a theology of the Spirit of God as the source of life for the whole creation, at work in and through the evolutionary processes described in the sciences.
5. She sees all creatures as loved passionately by God and as having their own intrinsic value.
6. She sees the incarnation as defining all aspects of God's dealing with creation, and the whole creation as participating in salvation in Christ.
7. She sees the Christic paradigm as differing radically from the evolutionary principle of natural selection, because it involves solidarity with the outsider and the vulnerable, including not only vulnerable humans but also the wider creation in its vulnerability.
8. In the vision of the cosmic Christ, Christians find a direction and a basis for hope in creation that is not evident from science, and are called to participate in the healing of the planet.
9. In response to the climate crisis, she offers a vision of humans as part of the one community of life, sharing a common story of the universe and life on Earth, where everything is related to everything else.
10. She advocates for an ecological economics rather than a neo-classical economics, one that embraces the values of distributive justice and sustainability.
11. She encourages the ecological practice of learning to see

other creatures with a loving eye rather than an arrogant eye, and the practice of Christ-like kenotic restraint that others might flourish.

Notes

1. Sallie McFague, *Models of God: Theology for an Ecological Nuclear Age* (Philadelphia: Fortress Press, 1987), x.
2. Ibid., 33.
3. Ibid.
4. Ibid., 33–34.
5. Karl Rahner, "Experiences of a Catholic Theologian," in *The Cambridge Companion to Karl Rahner*, ed. Declan Marmion and Mary E. Hines (New York: Cambridge University Press, 2005), 297–310, 301.
6. Sallie McFague, *A New Climate for Theology: God, the World, and Global Warming* (Minneapolis: Fortress Press, 2008), 108–9.
7. McFague, *Models of God*, 106.
8. Ibid., 110.
9. Ibid., 122.
10. Ibid., 128–29.
11. Ibid., 135.
12. Ibid., 136.
13. Ibid., 150.
14. Ibid., 165.
15. Ibid., 170–71.
16. McFague, *A New Climate for Theology*, 160.
17. McFague, *Models of God*, 178.
18. Ibid., 184.
19. Ibid., 182.
20. Sallie McFague, *The Body of God: An Ecological Theology* (Min-

neapolis: Fortress Press, 1993), 131.

21. Ibid., 143.
22. Ibid., 144.
23. Ibid., 148.
24. Ibid., 149.
25. Ibid.
26. Ibid., 150.
27. Ibid.
28. Ibid., 162.
29. Ibid.
30. Ibid., 164.
31. Ibid., 165.
32. Ibid., 176.
33. Ibid., 179.
34. McFague, *A New Climate for Theology*, 15.
35. Ibid., 50.
36. Ibid., 53.
37. Ibid., 73.
38. Ibid., 78.
39. Ibid., 88.
40. Ibid., 88–89.
41. Ibid., 95. For a fuller development of her view of an ecological economics, and of what might constitute a genuinely good life, see Sallie McFague, *Life Abundant: Rethinking Theology and Economy for a Planet in Peril* (Minneapolis: Fortress Press, 2000).
42. Sallie McFague, *Super, Natural Christians: How We Should Love Nature* (London: SCM, 1997), 67–117.
43. Ibid., 116.
44. Sallie McFague, *Blessed are the Consumers: Climate Change and the Practice of Restraint* (Minneapolis: Fortress Press, 2013).
45. On her view of "wild space," see McFague, *Life Abundant*, 48–51, 188–95.

46. Ibid., 201–2.

47. Ibid.

48. McFague, *A New Climate for Theology*, 172.

14.

Elizabeth Johnson (1941-)

Life and Context: Elizabeth Johnson grew up in an Irish Catholic family in Brooklyn, New York, and as a young adult joined the Sisters of Saint Joseph of Brentwood.[1] She studied at Brentwood College, Manhattan College, and at The Catholic University of America, where in 1981 she became one of the first two women to graduate with a doctorate in theology. She was invited to join the faculty at The Catholic University of America, teaching there until she moved to Fordham in 1981, where she is Distinguished Professor of Theology. In 1991, she published *Consider Jesus*, a widely-read book on Christology. In 1992, she produced a ground-breaking work, *She Who Is*, a feminist theology of God the Trinity, which builds on the biblical theology of *Sophia* and the resources of the theological tradition, particularly Thomas Aquinas. In 1993, she responded to ecological destruction and the marginalization of women with a theology of the Creator Spirit, in her *Women, Earth, and Creator Spirit.* Two major books followed, a feminist reading of the Communion of Saints, *Friends of God and Prophets* (1998), and a theology of Mary, *Truly Our Sister* (2003), focusing on Mary in her historicity and openness to the Spirit. In 2007, she published a book which surveyed and mapped the various theologies of God appearing in different contexts in her *Quest for the Living God.* To the surprise of many, this book was criticized by the Committee on Doctrine of the US bishops. Johnson responded to the criticisms clearly and fully. Her own work then centered once more on creation theology, as she engaged with both evolutionary science and the ecological crisis, with the book that is the focus of the chapter, *Ask the Beasts: Darwin and the God of Love* (2014).

In her presidential address to the Catholic Theological Society of America (1995), Elizabeth Johnson called for a new turn in theology, a turn to Earth, a turn to "the entire interconnected community of life and the network of life-systems in which the human race is embedded, all of which has its own intrinsic value."[2] She points out that while early Christian and medieval theologians took it for granted that theology deals with three major areas, God, humanity, and the world, Western theologians, particularly since the Reformation, have focused on God and the human, and left out the natural world. Johnson insists that two factors make it imperative that theology now embrace the natural world. One is the extraordinary developments in the sciences, above all in evolutionary biology and in cosmology. Intellectual integrity demands that theology responds to the scientifically informed worldviews that many of today's people take for granted. The second factor is the devastating damage that humans are inflicting on the planet, which results in the extinction of species, brings trauma and suffering to the poorest humans, and adds greatly to the burdens of oppressed women. Moral integrity demands that theology embrace the planet under threat. The vision that can motivate such theology, Johnson proposes, is that of "a flourishing humanity on a thriving earth, both together a sacrament of the glory of God."[3]

Johnson had already begun to respond to this challenge in, among other places, her *She Who Is* from 1992,[4] and her *Women, Earth, and Creator Spirit.*[5] Various articles and book chapters followed, including the penultimate chapter of her *Quest for the Living God*, entitled "Creator Spirit in an evolving world."[6]All of this prepared the way for a full articulation of a theology of the natural world in *Ask the Beasts*, a book, Johnson says, which addresses one much neglected question: "what is the theological meaning of the natural world of life?"[7] In the light of evolutionary science and the crisis of life on our planet, she focuses on the natural world in its own right as a central theological project. Her way of approach to this project is "by conducting a dialogue between Charles Darwin's account of the origin of species and the Christian story of the ineffable God of mercy and love recounted in the Nicene Creed."[8]

I will trace her work in six steps, beginning with her reading of Darwin, and then exploring in turn her theology of creation as the dwelling place of God, the Spirit as empowering evolution, the groaning of creation and deep incarnation, cosmic redemption, and ecological conversion and the community of creation.

DARWIN'S *ON THE ORIGIN OF SPECIES* (1859)

Johnson's reading of Darwin is detailed and empathetic. She brings the reader to an appreciation of his intellectual achievement, the rigor of his work, and the sheer beauty of his discovery. Darwin's *Origin* begins with something well-known to his readers, that domestic breeding has the capacity to change characteristics of plants, birds, and animals. Individual creatures are born with slightly different characteristics, and over generations breeders can deliberately select for such characteristics. Good breeders succeed by the cumulative power of such selection, producing better fruit, hardier grain crops, faster horses or dogs, and new varieties of pigeons.

By invoking the analogy of human selection in the breeding process, Darwin sets the stage for his proposal that there is a far more powerful selection process going on in nature. He points first to the variations between organisms, inherited variations. He then analyses what he calls the struggle for existence. This struggle involves all the relationships between creatures, including cooperation as well as competition for resources. Variations which, in the context, provide an advantage in surviving and reproducing will tend to be passed on to offspring. Nature, thus, over great lengths of time, acts powerfully in "selecting" some characteristics, while others disappear. In this way natural selection brings about what Darwin at first calls "descent with modification," the process of the evolution of species.

Johnson points out that Darwin's theory completely undercuts the concept of special divine creation of species, a dominant paradigm of his time not only in religious, but also very much in scientific circles: "Time and again in the *Origin* Darwin contests the prevailing scientific view that species originate by separate divine acts of creation, reasoning against it with the vigor one uses in trying to reshape the governing paradigm of a whole field of study."[9] Darwin's view consistently opposes the idea of God directly intervening to create each new species. This, of course, does not rule out the Creator working through natural processes, in what Darwin speaks of as secondary causes.[10] Johnson summarizes Darwin's explanation:

> Over incredibly long ages and diverse conditions organic beings have produced variations; some of these are useful in the struggle for existence; nature selects for these advantages; selected organisms diverge into new species while others go extinct. Everything alive today has come forth from this synthesis of birth, change and death. . . . All organic beings, living and dead, are related to one another, historically and biologically. All take their place in a single narrative of creative struggle, divergence, thriving, death, extinction, and further breakthrough. Common descent with modification by nat-

> ural selection is the explanatory principle which interprets how species originate from one another, naturally.[11]

Johnson discusses a great deal more of Darwin's careful argument, as well as recent developments in evolutionary biology and cosmology. But it is Darwin's fundamental breakthrough in *Origins*, his explanatory theory of natural selection, with which she seeks to engage as a theologian. She sees this engagement as required because Darwin's *Origin* still remains "a groundbreaking treatise for the contemporary discipline of biology."[12] And, equally, it remains "a watershed for human awareness, profoundly altering our understanding of the natural world and, just as profoundly, of our own membership in this evolving community of life."[13] It involves a radical transformation of human consciousness, so that we can no longer think of ourselves apart from our evolutionary and ecological interrelationships with the other creatures of our planet. Darwin's breakthrough continues to set a fundamental agenda for Christian theology in the twenty-first century.

THE DWELLING PLACE OF GOD

The starting point that Johnson chooses for her theological engagement with Darwin is the third article of the Nicene- Constantinopolitan Creed that confesses belief in the Holy Spirit as "Lord and Giver of life." Building on this creedal statement, Johnson sees the Creator Spirit as always and everywhere at work in continuous creation, as the one who "quickens, animates, stirs, enlivens, gives life even now while engendering the life of the world to come."[14] In the biblical and theological tradition, the Spirit is the divine presence that breathes life into creatures. The creedal expression of a fully Trinitarian theology of the Spirit makes it clear that the Giver of Life is not a lesser form of God, or some kind of intermediary being, but the incomprehensible holy mystery of God drawing near to creatures, love in person, the vivifying God "who actually arrives in every moment."[15] In the Spirit, the triune God of love dwells in the creation.

Johnson enriches this theological conviction of divine indwelling by tracing the way beautiful biblical images for the Spirit express the Creator's active presence and enlivening of the natural world. She focuses on the images of wind, water, fire, and bird, and traces the interrelationship between Spirit and Wisdom. This range of biblical images gives expression to the "ineffable presence" that is innermost in creatures, the "vital power that enlivens, nurtures, sparks, and fructifies them in every instant."[16]

Johnson turns to Thomas Aquinas in order to further articulate this enlivening creative presence of God in the Spirit to the whole creation.[17] She points out that, for Aquinas, God's very nature is to-be. He uses the Latin verbal form *esse* (to be). God is the absolute fullness of being, sheer being, without beginning, without limitation, without end. God, then, is never one being among others, not even the greatest of beings. God is not a being at all in the sense of the various beings of creatures. Rather, God is the "infinite divine aliveness," the active force of being, the source of the existence of all creatures.[18] Creatures exist, in this theology of Aquinas, through participation. God gives to creatures a participation in being that is proper to their own natures. Creation is a relationship of participation: "all beings apart from God are not their own being, but are beings by participation."[19] Johnson points out that theologians like Walter Kasper and Catherine LaCugna have insisted that God's to-be is always to-be-in-relationship. God's being is Communion—"God is love" (1 John 4:16).

God's relationship with creatures, in creation and salvation, always springs from this divine self-giving love. Creatures exist, and creatures are saved, by participation in the divine Communion of love. Aquinas says that God is in all things, enabling them to be, like fire igniting wood. It is only this action of God that enables a creature to exist. Since the being of each thing is what is innermost to it, Aquinas concludes "it must be that God is in all things, and innermostly."[20] But Aquinas not only holds that God is in all things, but also insists that "all things are in God."[21] All things are contained in God, embraced in the divine creative presence. Johnson sees Aquinas's view, then, as a form of what contemporary theology calls panentheism. God is in all things and all things are in God in a kind of mutual indwelling. It is not a symmetry of two equal partners, but an asymmetrical indwelling "of the infinite God who dwells in all things sparking them into being and finite creatures who dwell within the embrace of divine love."[22]

The universe of creatures is thus the dwelling place of God. And God dwells in creatures as that which continuously enables their existence and their becoming. This continuous creation of each entity is, then, an absolutely unique relationship. For each creature it is "a certain relation to the Creator as to the principle of its being."[23] Creatures participate not only in the divine being but in the divine goodness, and they represent this goodness in their wonderful diversity: "the whole universe together participates in the divine goodness more perfectly, and represents it better than any single creature could."[24] The biodiversity of our planet, then, manifests the goodness of God that is beyond imagining.

The whole universe of creatures, all the plants, birds, and animals of Earth, exist because God is present to them in the Creator Spirit. In their turn, they are the self-expression of the Creator. The creation, then, is a primordial sacrament and, as Augustine teaches, a "book of God."[25] In the Spirit, God dwells in creation, enabling its existence and flourishing, enabling it in all its abundance and diversity to express something of the wonder and mystery of the divine goodness and love.

CREATOR SPIRIT IN THE EVOLUTION OF A FREE UNIVERSE OF CREATURES

Johnson's view of Creation as the dwelling place of God, fundamental as it is for an ecological theology, is not yet an explicit response to Darwin. So she asks herself the question: how are we to think of God's creative action in an evolutionary world? Before Darwin, she points out, a dominant model of God as Creator was that of the divine monarch, and this was accompanied by another image of God as the grand designer. Johnson chooses the model of divine lover rather than divine monarch, with the Creator Spirit understood as divine love in person. Like a lover wanting the beloved to flourish in his or her own right, the Spirit creates in ways that respect the proper independence and participation of creatures.

God's creative activity brings into being a universe endowed with the innate capacity to evolve by the operation of its own natural powers, making it a free partner in its own creation. This position differs from deism, where the Creator creates and then leaves the world to its own devices like a clock wound up and left to tick away undisturbed. The difference lies in the presence of the indwelling Spirit of God who continually empowers and accompanies the evolving world through its history of shaping and breaking apart, birthing and perishing, hitting dead ends and finding new avenues into the future. . . . The Giver of life freely and generously invests nature with the power to organize itself and emerge into ever-new and more complex forms, and to do so according to its own manner of operating.[26]

Rather than a theology of a divine designer, or a blue-print theology of creation, Johnson proposes a theology of the Spirit as enabling a universe to participate freely in its own unpredictable becoming: "Far from compelling the world to develop according to a prescribed plan, the Spirit continually calls it forth to a fresh and unexpected future."[27] We humans know how God respects our human freedom. Johnson proposes extending something of what we know of God's ways of being with human beings to the rest of the natural world. She refers to Rahner's intuition that "nearness to God and genuine human autonomy grow in direct and not inverse proportion."[28] In a neat summary, Johnson sums up her theological view of the way God works with evolving creation: "Its relationship to the living God is marked simultaneously by ontological dependence and operational autonomy."[29]

Johnson deepens the idea of an ontological dependence that enables operational autonomy by appealing to Aquinas's view of primary and secondary causality, discussed earlier in this book. She reviews various recent approaches to divine action discussed in the science-theology literature, but opts for the approach of Aquinas. In his theology, she says God is not ever a cause among causes, but the utterly transcendent "wellspring of Being itself, the Cause of all causes," who enables creatures themselves to be truly causes.[30] Johnson finds in Aquinas's theology of respect for secondary causes the basis for a strong view of the natural world's autonomy and integrity. She sees this autonomy as at work in biological evolution in the creative interwork of randomness and lawfulness that enable the evolution of species. In her view, the chance and lawfulness at work in biological evolution are secondary causes through which the Creator Spirit acts.

Chance is involved in the mutations that give rise to natural selection, and in all the variations of the external environment. But in its interrelationship with an environment, natural selection also acts in a lawlike way, screening out mutations maladapted to the environment, and preserving those that are beneficial. Chance acting within a lawlike framework enables novelty to emerge, and ultimately produces the community of life as we know it: "Propensities given to creation by the Creator in the beginning are gradually realized by the operation of chance working within lawlike regularities over deep time."[31] It is through the reciprocal operations of chance and lawfulness, that the Spirit's creative purposes are being realized. Johnson writes: "The interaction of chance and law becomes a creative means, over time, for testing out, tweaking, and finally evolving every new structure and organism of which the physical cosmos is capable."[32] Several times she notes the comment of scientist and theologian Arthur Peacocke, that the interaction of chance and lawfulness is what one would *expect* if God wanted a universe like our own, above all one that participates in its own emergence.[33]

Johnson sees the world as given innate propensities from the beginning, and thinks of God as immanent in the world as its final cause, but she also understands the history of the evolution of the universe as a free and "unscripted adventure."[34] The universe tends towards its richness and diversity "through the outworking of its own creative self-organization." But it is the Spirit as immanent divine Love that empowers this whole movement, and it is thanks "to this gracious Love that the natural world freely participates in its own creation."[35]

GROANING OF CREATION, DEEP INCARNATION, AND THE CROSS

In a post-Darwinian view of the world, pain that functions as a stimulus to action, the suffering of sentient animals, predation by creatures on other creatures, the death of organisms, and the extinction of species, are all seen as built-in to the natural world. How can theology respond to this picture? Johnson argues that this pattern, which existed long before humans came on the scene and would continue if humans all disappeared, cannot be explained theologically as simply due to human sin. She seeks a further theological way of responding to suffering and death. If realities like suffering and death are intrinsic to evolutionary process, she asks, how can theology interpret them coherently in relation to its view of the world as God's beloved creation, a creation that God declares is "very good" (Gen 1:31)?[36]

Her response is governed by two convictions. The first is that the realities of pain, death and extinction are not to be attributed directly to the divine will, but are the result of the autonomous operation of creation. In its free working, acting within its finite limits, evolutionary process brings forth a wonderful world of creatures, but it does this in a way that also involves suffering and death. Johnson's second conviction is of "the compassionate presence of God in the midst of the shocking enormity of pain and death."[37] She sees the whole Bible as witnessing to God's feeling for God's suffering creatures. Above all, God identifies with suffering creatures in the incarnation of the Word, in the life, ministry, death and resurrection of Jesus. Johnson here takes up the concept of "deep incarnation," introduced by Niels Gregersen, which seeks to show that, when the Word of God is "made flesh" (John 1:14), this is an event not just for human beings, but for the whole interconnected reality of matter and life. While the incarnation of the Word is often thought of as encompassing the human, deep incarnation takes this much further:

> Deep incarnation extends this view to include all flesh. In the incarnation Jesus, the self-expressing Wisdom of God, conjoined the material conditions of all biological life forms (grasses and trees) and experienced the pain common to all sensitive creatures (sparrows and seals). The flesh assumed in Jesus Christ connects with all humanity, all biological life, all soil, the whole matrix of the material universe down to its very roots.[38]

Johnson notes that it can be argued that this extension is faithful to the whole intent of the prologue of John's Gospel, in which it is declared that "the Word became flesh" (John 1:14), and to that of its wider biblical context. But it can also be argued on the basis of contemporary science, because there can be no scientific understanding of humans apart from the interconnections of their evolutionary history, and their ecological relationships of interdependence. In joining humanity, the God who creates and empowers the world now joins the whole world of flesh of which they are part, and the cosmic dust from which they are formed. Johnson writes: "The one transcendent God who creates and empowers the world freely chooses to join this world in the flesh, so that it becomes a part of God's own divine story forever."[39]

Johnson joins Sallie McFague in seeing the ministry of Jesus as constituting a "Christic paradigm," characterized by "liberating, healing and inclusive love." Jesus's fidelity to his mission leads to the extreme suffering of the cross. In this event, Johnson sees God as participating in pain and death "from *within* the world of all flesh."[40] She insists that the suffering of the human nature of Jesus on the cross is the suffering of the Word of God. It is the Word who suffers. God suffers. Along with Walter Kasper, Johnson sees the self-emptying, weakness, and suffering of the cross as the true revelation of divine love, and the true revelation of God. The logic of deep incarnation suggests that the suffering solidarity of God in the cross of Jesus is not limited to human beings, but extends to the whole community of life: "Calvary graphically illuminates the insight that the God of love whose presence continually sustains and empowers the origin of species is a God of suffering love in solidarity with all creatures' living and dying through endless millennia of evolution, from the extinction of species to every sparrow that falls to the ground."[41] The God of love is present to every creature holding it in love in its life and its death.

Jesus did not die into nothingness, but "into the embracing arms of the ineffable God who gives life." What awaited him, Johnson says, "was not annihilation, but a homecoming into God's mystery."[42] Christ's resurrection is a promise of God, one that involves not only humanity, but also the whole creation: Christ is not only "firstborn of the dead," but also "firstborn of all creation" (Col 1:15).[43] Johnson proposes, then, that a theology of deep incarnation also involves a theology of "deep resurrection," a promise that the groaning community of life will participate in the coming transformation of all things in Christ.

THE PROMISE OF COSMIC REDEMPTION

Biblical texts such as Romans 8:18–25, Colossians 1:15–20, and Ephesians 1:10, among others, speak of the redemption, reconciliation, or gathering up, of "all things" in Christ. In the book of Revelation, the One who sits on the throne declares: "See, I make all things new" (21:50). This biblical promise of cosmic redemption, Johnson points out, continued to find expression in the great patristic writers, and continues still in the Orthodox Christian tradition. But since the time of Anselm, Western theology has been so focused on the overcoming of human sin that there has been little room for a cosmic theology of salvation in Christ.

Within cosmic theology there is a further important question: Will other living creatures, animals and plants, participate in final salvation? Johnson points to Paul Santmire's analysis of the way theologians have answered this question. Some theologians, a minority, including Irenaeus and the later Augustine, hold that *all* creatures will participate in the promised transformation. In this view, then, there is a symmetry between God creating all things and God saving all things. But others hold an asymmetrical view: while God creates all creatures, not all will participate in final salvation. Those representing this asymmetrical view include the great medieval theologians, Aquinas and Bonaventure, and Reformers Luther and Calvin.[44]

Johnson takes the symmetrical position, arguing that based on what we know of the character of God, as love poured out on creation, there is reason to believe that God not only sustains and cares about every sparrow (Matt 10:29; Luke 12:6), but that God will also bring each to redemptive fullness. This position, she says, is based on the following core truths of faith and is coherent with their dynamism:

- The living God creates and cares for all creatures.
- This love encompasses all creatures even in their suffering and dying.
- These creatures are part of the flesh of the World which the Word of God joined via incarnation.
- The death and resurrection of Jesus offers hope of redemption for all flesh.
- The life-giving power of the Spirit who empowers all creation is also the power of resurrected life for all beings.[45]

At the same time, Johnson insists that we have no clear advance knowledge of life after death, even for humans. We have no good imaginative picture of how God might accomplish the salvation of other creatures. What we can assume is that the redemptive fulfillment of each creature will be appropriate to each creature's capacities. Johnson recognizes that science offers no support for the position she takes. It is grounded simply in faith. And at the heart of this is the revelation of the nature of the divine love found in Jesus Christ: "Given the personal presence of divine love to every creature in every moment, and the further revelation of the character of this love in the suffering and hope-filled story of Jesus Christ, there is warrant for holding that species and even individual creatures are not abandoned in death but taken into communion with the living God."[46] Nothing, then, is lost. All is transfigured in the life of God.

ECOLOGICAL CONVERSION AND THE COMMUNITY OF CREATION

Towards the end of *Ask the Beasts*, Johnson explores in some detail the presence of human creatures on our planet and their destructive ecological impact. I will highlight two of the theological responses she develops, the call to ecological conversion, and the vision of a community of creation before God. In her treatment of ecological conversion, Johnson builds on statements made by Pope John Paul II and Ecumenical Patriarch Bartholomew of the Orthodox Church.[47] Ecological conversion means recognizing and repenting of our sins against creation, and it means a change, a turning, in our way of being in the world. Johnson highlights three aspects of this conversion to Earth. *Intellectually*, it means moving away from an anthropocentric view of the world to a theocentric one that finds religious meaning and value in other species. *Emotionally*, it involves a turning from the delusion of the separated human to a felt interconnection with creatures of other species as kin. *Ethically*, it widens our moral universe to the community of life, and to the protection of other species, our kin, that possess their own intrinsic value.[48]

Johnson encapsulates her view of ecological conversion: "In sum, ecological conversion means falling in love with the Earth as an inherently valuable, living community in which we participate, and bending every effort to be creatively faithful to its well-being, in tune with the living God who brought it into being and cherishes it with unconditional love."[49] She insists that being converted to Earth and its inhabitants in this time of enormous distress is a moral imperative, one that transforms us towards greatheartedness, in union with the Love that creates and empowers our planetary community of life.

Johnson's thought on ecological conversion is very closely connected to the theme of the community of creation. She explores this theme as a biblically-based paradigm that in today's world can serve us better than the dominion paradigm of Genesis 1:28. The dominion paradigm, she shows, can be interpreted in various ways. It is ambiguous, and "wide open to readings that promote human self-interest at nature's expense."[50] She notes that the dominion paradigm has been used both explicitly and implicitly "as an ideological justification for exploitative practices."[51]

The paradigm of the community of creation, by contrast, is based on the belief that we, with other species, and the rest of the natural world, have a great deal in common as fellow creatures of God. She finds this paradigm wonderfully developed in God's answer to Job from the whirlwind (Job 38–42), in the Psalms, particularly Psalms 104 and 96, and in the Prophets, in texts such as Hosea 4:1–3; and Isaiah

35:1–2.[52] When we rediscover ourselves as part of a community of creation we begin to be transformed: "Inspired by the Spirit who pervades and sustains the community of creation, the human imagination grows to encompass 'the other' and the human heart widens to love the neighbors who are uniquely themselves, not human."[53] We begin to think, feel and act differently.

If we are all "kin in the evolving community of life now under siege," then our vision will be one of "flourishing for all."[54] Johnson finishes *Ask the Beasts* by further specifying this vision: "A flourishing humanity on a thriving planet rich in species in an evolving universe, all together filled with the glory of God: such is the vision that must guide us at this critical time of Earth's distress, to practical and critical effect."[55] Living the ecological vocation that is ours in the power of the Spirit, Johnson says, sets us off on a "great adventure of mind and heart, expanding the repertoire of our love."[56] This, she says, is what the beasts ask of us.

TRAJECTORIES

Johnson engages with evolutionary science and the ecological crisis from the perspective of the faith and theological resources of the Christian tradition to create a twenty-first century theology of the natural world. Where in her earlier work, *She Who Is*, Johnson seeks to speak rightly of the mystery of God who is beyond male and female and inclusive of both, in this book she explores more fully what it means to speak rightly of God as the God of all creatures. Some important insights:

1. Johnson offers a full theological engagement with Darwin and his theory of natural selection.

2. *Ask the Beasts* constitutes a fully ecological theology for the twenty-first century.
3. It engages deeply and convincingly with the Christian theological tradition, in a Trinitarian theology of the Creative Spirit and the redeeming Word.
4. It offers a development of the theological resource of deep incarnation.
5. It is a theology that embraces the proper autonomy of creaturely reality, of evolutionary processes, and of the sciences.
6. It is a theology that embraces both chance and lawfulness in evolutionary processes.
7. Johnson advocates a view of God as one who suffers with suffering creation, and a theology of hope for the whole creation, including plants and animals.
8. It is a practical theology that involves the call to ecological conversion.
9. It offers a theological paradigm of human beings as interrelated to all other creatures within the one community of creation in God.

Notes

1. For Johnson's life, see Heidi Schlumpf, *Elizabeth Johnson: Questing for God* (Collegeville, MN: Liturgical, 2016).
2. Elizabeth A. Johnson, "Turn to the Heavens and the Earth: Retrieval of the Cosmos in Theology," in *Turning to the Heavens and the Earth: Theological Reflections on a Cosmological Conversion: Essays in Honor of Elizabeth A. Johnson*, eds. Julia Brumbaugh and Natalia Imperator-Lee (Collegeville, MN: Liturgical, 2016), xxix-xlvi, xxx. This essay is also found in *CTSA Proceedings* 51 (1996),

1–14.

3. Ibid., xliii.
4. Elizabeth A. Johnson, *She Who Is; The Mystery of God in Feminist Theological Discourse* (New York: Crossroad, 1992), 133–39.
5. Elizabeth A. Johnson, *Women, Earth, Creator Spirit* (New York: Paulist, 1983).
6. Elizabeth A, Johnson, *Quest for the Living God: Mapping Frontiers in the Theology of God* (New York: Continuum, 2007), 181–201.
7. Elizabeth A. Johnson, *Ask the Beasts: Darwin and the God of Love* (New York: Bloomsbury, 2014), xiv.
8. Ibid., xv.
9. Ibid., 33.
10. Ibid., 34.
11. Ibid., 65.
12. Ibid., 99.
13. Ibid.
14. Ibid., 128–29.
15. Ibid., 133.
16. Ibid., 143.
17. There is necessarily some overlap between what is said in this section on Johnson's work with Aquinas and the material discussed in chapter 7 of this book on Aquinas's theology of creation.
18. Johnson, *Ask the Beasts*, 144.
19. Ibid., 148. See Aquinas, *Summa theologiae*, 1.45.3.
20. Ibid., 146. See Thomas Aquinas, *Summa theologiae*, 1.8.1.
21. Ibid., 147. See Aquinas, *Summa theologiae*, 1.8.1 at 2.
22. Johnson, *Ask the Beasts*, 147.
23. Ibid. See Aquinas, *Summa Theologiae*, 1.45.3.
24. Johnson, *Ask the Beasts*, 149. Aquinas, *Summa theologiae*, 1.47.1.
25. Johnson, *Ask the Beasts*, 152. Augustine, "Sermon 68:6," *Sermons* III/3, trans. Edmund Hill (Brooklyn: New City Press, 1991), 225–26.

26. Johnson, *Ask the Beasts*, 155–56.
27. Ibid., 156.
28. Ibid., 157.
29. Ibid., 160.
30. Ibid., 163.
31. Ibid., 172.
32. Ibid.
33. Ibid.
34. Ibid., 173.
35. Ibid., 174.
36. Ibid., 191.
37. Ibid.
38. Ibid., 196.
39. Ibid., 197.
40. Ibid., 203.
41. Ibid., 205.
42. Ibid., 206.
43. Ibid., 209.
44. Ibid., 228–29. Paul Santmire, *The Travail of Nature: The Ambiguous Ecological Promise of Christian Theology* (Minneapolis: Fortress Press, 1985).
45. Johnson, *Ask the Beasts*, 230.
46. Ibid., 231.
47. This is, of course, also a theme in the work of Pope Francis, above all in his *Laudato Si'*, published after *Ask the Beasts*.
48. Johnson, *Ask the Beasts*, 258–59.
49. Ibid., 259.
50. Ibid., 265.
51. Ibid.
52. Johnson develops her thought on the community of creation in dialogue with Richard Bauckham in his *The Bible and Ecology: Rediscovering the Community of* Creation (Waco, TX: Baylor Uni-

versity Press, 2010).

53. Johnson, *Ask the Beasts*, 284.
54. Ibid., 285.
55. Ibid., 286.
56. Ibid.

Trajectories

In the introduction I described the approach of this book as a hermeneutics of critical retrieval, an attempt to reclaim trajectories from the history of theology that can assist in the envisioning of a renewed theology of the natural world. Such a renewed theology is required by two important factors of contemporary experience: the explosion in scientific knowledge that presents us with a worldview radically different to that presupposed in earlier theologies, and the crisis of life on our planet. In the context of these two realities, this search into the history of the theology of creation attempts to receive what is offered by the various theologies of the past in a stance of critical appreciation. In this conclusion to the book I will take a broader look at the trajectories identified in the individual chapters.

The critical element in this work is formed particularly from the awareness of how Christian theology itself has contributed to a damaging view of the natural world. In the introduction and in the later chapters I have mentioned the principal ways in which this has happened: in spite of Christianity's incarnational grounding, particularly in its engagement with Greek philosophical thought there have been tendencies to other-worldly expressions of Christian faith; in the second millennium, particularly since the Reformation, there has been a focus in Western Christianity on human salvation, on the human before God, while the wider natural world has been almost completely omitted from theology and preaching; there have been instances where the dominion text (Gen 1:28) has been read, or misread, in a way that provides the basis for an exploitative stance to the rest of the natural world; the great theologian Aquinas at times presented other living creatures as directed towards human use, and neither he nor Bonaventure saw them as participating in the transformation of new creation. The proposal has been that, alongside these negative trajectories, there are positive trajectories that can offer much to a renewed theology of the natural world.

Biblical Theologies of Creation: A major intention of the chapter on biblical trajectories was to show that there are multiple creation texts, multiple creation theologies, and multiple trajectories on creation in the Bible. The opening chapter of Genesis provides a brilliant picture of the one God who creates absolutely everything, who finds the whole creation good, and who creates human beings in the image of God. But we find also in the First Testament that God puts humans in their place before the wonders of creation and before the incomprehensible mystery of its Creator (Job 38:1–41:34); that humans form with other creatures one community of creation before God (Psalms 104; 148); that God creates through Wisdom (Prov 8:22–9:6); and that the Creator promises a wonderful new heavens and a new earth (Isa 65:17–25). In the New Testament, we are told that the Word of creation is the Word made flesh (John 1:1–18); that the whole creation awaits its participation in redemption (Rom 8:18–25); and that the risen Jesus is now the Cosmic Christ (Col 1:15–20). The trajectories of these texts are all significant for the theologians studied in subsequent chapters, particularly what is said of the Word of God in the first chapter of John: "All things came into being through him . . . And the Word became flesh" (John 1:3, 14).

Irenaeus: In Irenaeus's work, trajectories are established that have a foundational role in the history of the theology of creation. Even when they have been lost from sight in certain periods, they have always been there to recover. These trajectories can be foundational again, I believe, for a renewed theology of the natural world in the twenty-first century: creation is one undivided act of the Three, from the Father, through the Word, and in the Spirit; creation and salvation in Christ are inseparable in the one divine economy of God; God creates *ex nihilo*, bridging the ontological gap between God and humanity out of love; disembodied theologies are absolutely rejected in favor of a theology that is earthy, physical, and fleshly, centering on the bodily reality of the incarnation and the cross; the eschatological promise of resurrection involves the whole creation, with not only humanity but also the wider creation recapitulated in Christ.

Athanasius: Trajectories that spring from Athanasius have echoes throughout the whole Christian tradition. They are consistent with, and at times build on, those of Irenaeus: the Word of Creation is the Word of incarnation; creatures exist because they participate in the Word of God; God is immediately present through the Word and in the Spirit to all creatures enabling their existence and flourishing; "The Father creates and renews all things through the Word in the Holy Spirit"; the actions of the Trinity spring from the eternal dynamic generativity of divine Trinitarian life; each creature bears the imprint of the image of the Wisdom of God; the Word became flesh for the deification of human beings and, with them, of the wider creation; the whole creation will share with human beings in their transformation in Christ.

Augustine: An important trajectory from Augustine for the later tradition is his view that each creature represents the beauty of its maker and exemplar, the Wisdom of God. The focus in the chapter on Augustine was largely on his approach to biblical interpretation, which offers trajectories for reading Scripture in the light of science today: he offers a model for contemporary discussions between science and theology with his commitment both to the truth of Scripture and to the truth established by reason and experiment, and his conviction that both Scripture and reason spring ultimately from divine truth; he exemplifies a theological method which, while committed to the truth of faith, nevertheless sees the theologian's interpretations as revisable in the light of new information from reason or the sciences, or from another's interpretations of the texts; his commitment to engage with secular fields of knowledge and his development a theology of seminal reasons offer a great deal of encouragement to contemporary theologians to be equally creative, brave, and humble, in engaging with contemporary science, particularly with evolutionary biology.

Hildegard: Hildegard's theology carries forward major trajectories found in Irenaeus, Athanasius, and Augustine, in a rich Trinitarian theology of Word and Spirit, with creation and incarnation understood as profoundly interconnected in the eternal will of God. She offers fruitful and beautiful trajectories of her own: God is life that gives life; Divine Love empowers the whole universe of creatures; creatures declare the Word in whom they are created; greenness (*viriditas*) unites all forms of life, biological, spiritual and divine, in the work of the "green finger of God," the Holy Spirit; her active empirical engagement with the natural world of animals, plants, fish, rivers and rocks suggests active theological engagement today with sciences like biology and neuroscience; her theology of music invites new thinking about music in twenty-first century theology; her holistic vision inspires a theology that sees all aspects of creation as integral to the journey of life in God.

Bonventure: Bonaventure stands very much in the tradition of Augustine, and his theology of creation is in agreement with Irenaeus and Athanasius in the fully Trinitarian structure of his thought and in the way he links creation and incarnation in a theology of the Word. Some key trajectories of this thought: like Athanasius, but building on Pseudo-Dionysius, Bonaventure sees the Trinity as radically dynamic, fruitful, and self-communicating by nature; the Father is the Fountain Fullness, the Source of all fecundity for the triune life, and for the whole creation; the Word is the self-expression of the Fountain Fullness in creation, revelation and in incarnation, and the Exemplar for all creatures, so that each creature is the expression of this eternal Art; creation is the free overflow of this inner-Trinitarian fruitfulness and divine self-communication; all creatures reflect the Trinity, witnessing to the power, wisdom and goodness of their Creator; echoing Augustine, Bonaventure sees creation as a book of God that we can read in the light of the Christ.

Aquinas: In many ways Aquinas encapsulates the tradition before him, but does so in a fully integrated and systematic way: in his metaphysical view of creation, it is God's nature to exist, and God is interiorly and intimately present in all creatures, constantly enabling their existence; creatures possess existence by participation, with each expressing something of the fullness of God; the dynamic, eternal, coming forth of the Word and Spirit in the divine life is the model, source, and cause of the production of the world of creatures; the Father, as principle of the Word and the Spirit, is the ultimate principle and source for all creation; the Word comes from the Father and receives creative power from the Father, so that it is through the Word that the Father creates; the Spirit, as the Love that comes from both the Father and the Word, has creative power from both, and brings life and completion to the creation; as in Augustine and Bonaventure, each creature, each star in our galaxy, each bird, is an expression of an idea in the mind of God, the divine artist, the Word; each is the product of the divine will, the fruit of divine Love, the Holy Spirit; the variety and diversity of creatures express the divine goodness better than any single creature could ever do; Aquinas offers an important trajectory in his view that God acts through created secondary causes that have their own integrity, with the consequence that God's creative act and the laws of nature operate in non-exclusive and non-competitive ways—a trajectory that opens the way for a respect for the integrity of the laws of nature, and respect for the integrity of the sciences.

Luther: For Luther, as for Augustine and many others in the tradition, the Word of God who is made flesh for our salvation is the Word of Creation. Some trajectories that Luther brings to the tradition of creation theology: he represents a lively, personal, existential sense of being a creature among the other creatures of our world; his stance is that of radical receptivity and thankfulness to the Creator for the gifts given in every life; Luther advocates a revolutionary view of vocation in ordinary life, where marriage, family, home, work, meals, the body, sexuality, and nature are understood as the place of God; God can be so small as to be in a single grain of wheat and yet God's majesty is so large that neither this world nor a thousand worlds could ever encompass it; his conviction that God is hidden in the creation can be meaningful today in facing up to the violence, suffering, and loss built into the natural world; Luther insists that being justified by the grace of God leads to a new, far more developed appreciation of the natural world; he is convinced that the risen Christ who is now at the right hand of God is also mysteriously present and at work in the whole creation.

Calvin: Calvin also sees creation and salvation as deeply interconnected in a fully Trinitarian theology, and like Athanasius and Augustine, he sees the knowledge of God as shining forth in the universe that God creates, sustains, and governs. Calvin brings his own insights and images to this tradition: he sees the creation as the first revelation of God, and presents it as the theater of God's glory, the image of God, and the beautiful garment of God; like Bonaventure, but in his own way, he says that because of sin, we need the "spectacles" of the Word of God to see creation rightly; he has a strong sense of providence at work in nature, and also as directed intentionally to humans: "Kindness is uttered again in everything that nourishes" (Marilynne Robinson); he finds delight in birds and animals, in the sight and the smell of trees and flowers, and expresses amazement and delight in the glorious starry heaven above, a trajectory that can have new meaning today in a world informed by contemporary astronomy and cosmology; he sees humans as custodians and stewards, as exercising moderation, frugality, and freedom from possessiveness, and insists that we must not damage or destroy what God requires us to preserve.

Teilhard de Chardin: Teilhard draws on the biblical tradition, particularly on what Colossians and Ephesians say on the cosmic role of the risen Christ. Like Augustine and

Aquinas he is convinced that God speaks to us both in revelation in Christ and in what science reveals. His passion for matter, plants, animals, and the universe itself echoes something of Hildegard. However his work represents original trajectories in the Christian theology of creation: Teilhard embraces fully twentieth century cosmology and evolutionary biology; he articulates a vision of Christian faith that thoroughly accepts the insights of the sciences; he envisions a convergence of human consciousness and of human love on our planet (the noosphere), which can be seen as partially confirmed in global communications of the twenty-first century, even if it is certainly not confirmed at the level of relationships of love; his theology is not centered on the past, nor the eternal present, but on the future, on the God of an unfinished universe; Teilhard sees the risen Christ as the Omega of evolution; in his view it is divine Love that moves the universe, and the human community is called to be agents of this Love.

Rahner: Karl Rahner builds on Aquinas, draws on Eastern theologians like Athanasius, and is influenced by the issues raised by Teilhard. Trajectories of his thought on creation include these: creation and saving incarnation are united in God's one act of self-giving love; God's creative act can be seen as enabling the evolutionary self-transcendence of creatures; Jesus is absolute Saviour because he is both God's radical self-bestowal to creatures, and creation's self-transcendence to God; the resurrection is a promise of transfiguration and fulfillment not only for humans but for the whole universe of creatures; the incarnation means that God is forever a God of matter and flesh; the risen Christ is already at work in the whole creation as the promise and the beginning of final transfiguration; creatures of intelligence and love may exist on other planets and they may well have their own divine economy, including something like our experience of the grace of the Spirit and the incarnation of the Word.

Moltmann: Moltmann embraces the trajectory that goes back to Irenaeus of a creation theology that is fully Trinitarian, where creation is always understood in relation to the incarnation and salvation in Christ. Some of his contributions include the following: he proposes a theology of hope in God, who through Christ, and in the Spirit will make all things new; God is a God who suffers with suffering creatures; his theology is fully and explicitly ecological, and he accepts and engages with evolutionary science; it is also a fully explicit theology of the salvation of the rest of the natural world; he sees the Spirit as the energy enabling and empowering the evolution of a universe of creatures; the risen Christ is the redeemer of the victims of evolution and violence; this theology has practical ecological consequences in commitment to ecological action and social justice; he proposes a Christian recovery of the meaning of the Sabbath, and brings out its ecological meaning for the present time.

McFague: Sallie McFague's ecofeminist theological work engages with the trajectories of the theological tradition, in an experimental and creative way. Her view of God beyond male and female, and her commitment to both feminist and ecological theology represents a new and, I believe, irreversible moment in Christian theology, including the theology of creation. Some other trajectories of her theology are these: the whole creation can be seen as the self-expression, the sacramental embodiment of God; God can be imaged as mother, lover and friend to the whole community of creation; creatures are loved passionately by God and have their own intrinsic value; the incarnation defines all aspects of God's dealing with creation, and the whole creation participates in salvation in Christ; the Christic paradigm involves solidarity with the outsider and the vulnerable, including the vulnerable creation; in response to the climate crisis, she offers a vision of humans as part of the one community of life, sharing a common story of the universe and life on Earth, where everything is related to everything else; she advocates for an ecological economics rather than a neo-classical economics, which embraces the values of distributive justice and sustainability; she encourages the ecological practice of learning to see other creatures with a loving eye rather than an arrogant eye, and the practice of Christ-like kenotic restraint so that others might flourish.

Johnson: Johnson, with McFague, takes theology decisively beyond male images and language for God, to a bigger view of the God who is not only beyond male and female, but also beyond the human, and who is a God for all creatures. She engages both critically and appreciatively with the trajectories that have emerged in the history of Christian theology. She embraces the Trinitarian theology of the Nicene Creed and brings it into creative dialogue with evolutionary science, in the context of today's ecological crisis. Some of her own contributions: she offers a thorough theological engagement with Darwin and his theory of natural selection; she develops a theology of creation as the dwelling place of God, engaging with a biblical trajectory on the indwelling Creator Spirit, and with a trajectory from Aquinas on creation as a participatory relationship; taking up another trajectory from Aquinas's theology of God acting through secondary causes, she sees the Creator Spirit as enabling evolutionary emergence in a way that respects the proper autonomy of natural processes, and as working through the chance and lawfulness that are intrinsic to the evolution of life; she advocates a view of God not only as incomprehensible mystery, but also as one who suffers with suffering creation; she explores the redemptive meaning of Christ for suffering creatures; she explores the meaning of incarnation for the whole creation in a theology of deep incarnation; her theology is one of explicit hope for the whole creation, including plants and animals; it is a practical theology that involves the call to ecological conversion, and promotes the theological paradigm of human beings interrelated to all other creatures within the community of creation.

Is there *one* overarching trajectory that emerges from the many trajectories of this study? Perhaps such a trajectory might be expressed in the following three points:

1. *Creation is a Trinitarian Act*: God, the Source of All, creates all things through the Wisdom/Word of God and in the Spirit. In the indwelling Spirit, God is intimately present to each creature, enabling it to participate in existence, and setting it free to be itself within a community of creation.
2. *Creation is always directed towards the radical self-giving love expressed in the incarnation*: God creates each creature out of love, and then embraces human beings, and with them the whole creation, in the unbreakable bond of love expressed in the life, death and resurrection of Jesus.
3. *The incarnation is a dynamic and inclusive act of transformation*: The incarnation, involving the life, death and resurrection of Jesus, is for the sake of salvation and deification, the liberation and adoption of humans and the healing and final fulfillment of all creation in Christ.

The ethical outcome of this trajectory, which has not always been understood, is that humans are to see other creatures as kin, within a community of creation before God, where each creature has its own intrinsic value. They are to see themselves as called by God to love and respect other creatures, and their habitats, and to see Earth as our common home. They are called to act to protect the planetary community of life, and and to support the well-being and flourishing of other species.

Index